ENGLISH MONASTERIES

IN THE MIDDLE AGES

Mediaeval Chantries and Chantry Chapels
The English Mediaeval Parish Church
Old S. Paul's Cathedral
The English Cathedral Through the Centuries
English Collegiate Churches

The Round Nave, Temple Church, London.

ENGLISH MONASTERIES

IN THE MIDDLE AGES

G. H. COOK

WITH FRONTISPIECE, 45 PHOTOGRAPHS,
AND 41 PLANS

PHOENIX HOUSE LTD
LONDON

© G. H. Cook   1961
All rights reserved
printed by The Bowering Press of Plymouth
in 11 point Monotype Baskerville
Plates printed by The Aldine Press · Letchworth · Herts
for Phoenix House Ltd, 10–13 Bedford Street,
Strand, London, W.C.2
First published 1961

Contents

Illustrations

PLATES

The Round Nave, Temple Church, London   *Frontispiece*

7

PLANS

Acknowledgments

THE AUTHOR and Publisher are indebted to *The Sphere* for permission to reproduce Figure 28; and to The Architectural Press and Walter H. Godfrey for Figures 36 and 37. Our thanks are also due to the undermentioned for providing photographs for reproduction in this book:

B. T. Batsford, Ltd., XVIII
Mrs. P. Bicknell, IV, XXV, XXIX, XXX
British Railways, Western Region, XII
Fred. H. Crossley, X, XX, XXXII, XXXVI, XLI, XLV
H. E. Illingworth, XVII, XXXVII
Jarrold and Sons Ltd., XV, XXVII
A. F. Kersting, XXIV, XXXVIII
National Buildings Record, Frontispiece, I, II, VI, VIII, XI, XVI,
    XXIII, XXVI, XXVIII, XXXI, XXXIII, XXXIV, XL,
    XLII, XLIII
C. H. Noble, III
Photochrom Co. Ltd., XIX, XXXV
Rigden and Hodge, XLIV
Walter Scott Ltd., XXXIX
J. H. Stone, XXII
F. R. P. Sumner, V, VII, XIII
Valentine, Dundee, XIV
Veale and Co., IX

Foreword

IN THE FOLLOWING pages an attempt has been made to give some account in general of the monastic establishments of this country from the seventh to the sixteenth century. There are chapters dealing with the origin and ideals of the various Orders of monks; the personnel and the internal organisation of their abbeys and priories; the activities and daily observances of the brethren, and their relations with the world outside the precincts. Necessarily, the planning of monastic churches and of the conventual buildings attached to them is of outstanding importance in a book of this kind, and emphasis is laid on the variations occasioned by the requirements peculiar to the respective Orders.

More than four centuries have passed since the monastic system came to an end and the order went forth that the religious houses were to be demolished. Henry VIII's agents of destruction, the royal commissioners, were given instructions to 'pull down to the ground all the walls of the [monastic] churches, stepulls, cloysters, fraterys, dorters, and chapter howsys', and similar injunctions were issued to those who purchased monastic properties. So within a few years after the Suppression a wealth of mediaeval architecture, the loss of which is incalculable, was rased to the ground. In countless instances no vestige of a monastery has survived in the locality, except the name 'abbey' or 'priory' applied to a mansion that now occupies the site. Fortunately a great number of monastic churches wholly or in part are still in use for Christian worship, but cloisters and conventual buildings are comparatively scanty.

Even in their ruined state, the remains of many abbeys and priories are extensive enough to enable us to determine the plan of the church and conventual buildings and the character of the architecture; and excavations undertaken in the present century have brought to light valuable information concerning monastic planning. Further, research by many eminent scholars amongst mediaeval documents and records preserved in State and private collections have added considerably to our knowledge of monastic life and history.

Within recent times much has been done to stimulate the interest of the general public in the ancient monuments of this land, and the ruined abbeys are visited by increasing numbers every year. It is hoped that this book will lead such 'pilgrims' to a more complete understanding and appreciation of monastic architecture and of the religious ideals underlying it.

I. Introduction

The Purpose of Monastic Life—Vows taken by the Religious—Their Communal Existence—Obligations of Monks—Apostasy—The Probation and Admission of Novices—Number of Monasteries—Abbeys and priories —The Cathedral-Priories—Dependent Houses—Alien Priories—The Number of Monks in Various Monasteries—Distribution of Alms to the Poor and Needy—The Burden of Hospitality—Entertainment of Royalty, Travellers and Pilgrims—Provision for Visitors at Christ Church, Canterbury—Monastic Hostels—Non-paying Guests in Religious Houses— Royal Personages planted in Abbeys by the King—Corrodians as Residents and Annuitants—The Privilege of Sanctuary—The Procedure at Durham —Crimes in the Registers of Chartered Sanctuaries—Violation of Sanctuary at Waverley and Westminster—Abuses arising from the Privilege— Beaulieu Abbey in the Fifteenth Century—Monasteries as Safe-Deposits in the Middle Ages—The Banking Business of the Knights Templars— Papal Denunciation of Usury—The Robbery of the Royal Treasury at Westminster in 1303—Richard de Podelicote and his Booty—Monastic Tenure of Land under the Feudal System—Abbots as Tenants-in-Chief— Their Obligation to raise Feudal Musters—The Position of Nunneries —Payment of Scutage—Monastic Liability for Subsidies and Loans in Time of War—Use of Lands and Estates by the Monks—Farming—The Granting of Leases—Types of Tenants—Monk-Agents in Distant Granges—Treatment of the Tenantry—The Cathedral-Priory of Durham and its Tenants—The Rentalia of Glastonbury Abbey—Lay Officials for Administration of Conventual Estates—The Office of Steward—Forest Rights—The Appropriation of Parish Churches to Monasteries—The Offerings of Pilgrims at Shrines of the Saints—The Growth of Towns about Abbeys—Disputes between Monks and Burgesses—Disturbances at S. Albans, Norwich and Bury S. Edmunds—Monastic Historians and their Work from Saxon Days—Durham, S. Albans and Canterbury— Matthew Paris—The Colchester Family of Artists at S. Albans—Chartularies compiled by Monk-Scribes—Glastonbury.

A MEDIAEVAL MONASTERY was a community of men or women who gave up their possessions and retired from the world to devote themselves to a life of prayer and praise of the Almighty, and of intercession on behalf of departed benefactors. The English

13

monastery was 'a great chantry foundation in which intercession for the dead never relaxed, coupled with prayers for the good estate of the living whose names were inscribed in the books of the church.[1] Monks and nuns, the religious (*religiosi*) as they were called, lived under obedience to a superior in accordance with a fixed Rule or code of life (*regula*), to which they were bound by vows of poverty, chastity, and obedience. Corporate worship in the church, the chief building in every monastery, was of paramount importance; day and night were consecrated to the recitation of the religious offices at regular intervals. The distinctive habit worn by a monk was an outward sign that he had abandoned the world, abjured his family ties, subjected himself to the will of his superior, abbot or prior, and had merged his individuality into the common life of the convent.[2] After being professed, a monk was to possess no property. All things were to be in common; he was to live with the brethren, to feed with them in the refectory or frater, to sleep in the common dormitory, and worship with them in the choir. The vows taken at his initiation were irrevocable; once a monk, always a monk. Apostasy was a crime in the eyes of the world as well as of the Church, for the religious were under the legal obligation of offering up prayers for the founders and benefactors of their houses. If a monk deserted his house a warrant was issued for his arrest, and when apprehended he was delivered to the head of his convent for punishment. In 1351 Edward III gave instructions to his serjeant-at-arms to arrest certain runaway monks of Castle Acre priory who had 'spurned the habit of their Order', and were wandering about the country in secular dress; and in 1364 a mandate was issued for the arrest of Richard de Hexton, a canon, and John Kayso, a lay-brother, of S. Bartholomew's priory, Smithfield, who were then vagabonds in secular habit and rebels to the prior. They were to be delivered for punishment according to the discipline of the Order. Similarly, in 1385 Richard II ordered his serjeant-at-arms to arrest Mary de Felton, an apostate nun of the Poor Clares without Aldgate, and then hand her over to the abbess for correction.

A postulant served a year's probation before he was professed. On his arrival he was housed in a lodging near the gate of the monastery for four or five days, after which he presented himself to the chapter on three consecutive days and petitioned to be admitted to the convent as a novice. If he was deemed worthy, the would-be monk was committed to the care of the master of

---

[1] A. H. Thompson, *The Cathedral Churches of England*, 1928.
[2] The term 'convent' was used to designate any house of monks or nuns in the Middle Ages, its exclusive use for a nunnery being comparatively modern.

the novices, who trained him in the Rule and observances of religious life, and in the customs of the house. At the end of a year's probation, after minute inquiries had been made as to his parentage, character, and health, he was formally admitted by the abbot in chapter as one of the brethren, and he then received the tonsure and was clothed in the monastic habit. Henceforward his waking hours were occupied with worship in the church, study and meditation in the cloister, literary work or clerking in the scriptorium (p. 60), or manual labour in one of the many departments or the workshops of the monastery.

At the Dissolution in Henry VIII's reign there were about 650 religious houses of various Orders in England and Wales, excluding the Mendicant establishments, of which there were about 200. At one time and another there were 245 abbeys, priories, and nunneries observing the Benedictine Rule, 108 of the Cistercian Order, and 212 houses of Augustinian canons and canonesses; but many of these had ceased to exist before the general Suppression, as also had a great number of alien priories (p. 51).

The greater monasteries were usually known as abbeys, but other houses were classed as priories and were as self-contained, and in many instances as wealthy and as large, as the greater abbeys. Foremost were the cathedral-priories, i.e. the monastic establishments that were attached to the seat of a bishop, such as Durham and Winchester, the head of the house being the prior (*praelatus*), for though the bishop was the titular abbot he was not a member of the convent. The name priory was also given to daughter houses that were colonised by monks from an abbey, and to monasteries that were dependants of larger houses in England or on the Continent.[1] Most of the houses of regular canons (p. 177) and all the Carthusian establishments were denominated priories, and the term was often applied to distant manors and estates owned by a convent and occupied by two or three monks as agents. Normally the prior of a dependent or daughter house was chosen from the senior brethren of the parent abbey, an arrangement that sometimes led to disputes. In 1217 the abbot of Westminster signed an agreement empowering the monks of Great Malvern priory to elect their own superior, their choice being subject to confirmation by the abbot, and in 1282 there arose a bitter quarrel between him and Bishop Giffard of Worcester, who had taken upon himself to depose the prior of Great Malvern and put another in his place.

---

[1] At one time there were a hundred or more alien priories subject to foreign abbeys, as for instance Boxgrove, a dependant of Lessay, and Blyth priory, a daughter house of Mont-Ste-Catherine, Rouen.

When a monastery was founded the minimum number of brethren prescribed was twelve, with a thirteenth as abbot or prior. The Conqueror's abbey at Battle, founded in 1070, was intended to house sixty monks, but it is doubtful if there were ever more than fifty, and when the Suppression came the convent consisted of the abbot and only eighteen monks. The cathedral-priory of Christ Church, Canterbury, was planned by Archbishop Lanfranc to accommodate a hundred and fifty brethren, though it is unlikely that there were ever a hundred, and after the twelfth century the number rarely exceeded seventy or eighty. When the Norman abbot Serlo was installed at S. Peter's abbey, Gloucester, in 1072 he found only two monks and eight novices in residence; in 1076, when the Norman Ingulph was made abbot of Crowland, there were fifty-eight in the house. According to the charter, Beaulieu abbey, founded by King John in 1204, was to have thirty monks; at Peterborough in 1240 the inmates numbered a hundred and ten and two centuries later there were sixty-four. At a Visitation of Romsey in 1501, the abbess stated that the statutory number of nuns was forty; in 1333 there were ninety and an abbess, but that number had fallen to twenty-six in 1502 and was not exceeded between then and the Dissolution. Within twenty years of the founding of Fountains abbey in 1132 the thirteen brethren multiplied to such an extent that colonies were sent forth to found no fewer than twenty daughter houses, one of which was at Lysa in Norway. The royal abbey of Westminster was intended to accommodate about fifty monks; during the fourteenth century the average was forty-four; the lowest number was thirty-two in 1362, when the convent had not recovered from the effects of the Black Death (p. 50). Early in the fifteenth century the number rose to forty-nine, after which there was a gradual decline to forty-four for the years preceding the Suppression. The deed of surrender was signed by the abbot and twenty-four monks. At the end of the twelfth century John de Cella, abbot of S. Albans, limited the number of brethren in his house to a hundred, and at the Dissolution there were thirty-eight in residence. The cathedral-priory of Ely was planned for seventy monks, though there were seldom more than forty, many of whom held some office as obedientiaries; and after the Black Death there were twenty-eight. Including the prior there were thirty-seven at Ely in 1533. In the early years of the thirteenth century the priory of Bath housed forty-one religious, and the average after the Black Death was little more than half that number.

Every religious house was under the obligation of distributing alms to the poor and needy in the form of food, clothing, or money, definite sums being charged for this purpose on the revenue or real property of the house. Although no needy person was ever sent empty away from the gate of any abbey, every monastery had certain days in the week when a dole of broken meat was distributed to the hungry. At S. Augustine's abbey, Canterbury, there were two days in every week throughout the year when food and meat from the monk's refectory, the abbot's table, and the misericord were given at noon to the poor at the gate; and when there was a shortage of bread the almoner was entitled to draw extra grain from the granary for making additional loaves. To the almoner was assigned the duty of doling out food and alms (p. 99). One mediaeval writer says that the almoner 'must have his heart aglow with charity . . . and be ever ready to cheer the lot of the poor'. In the Benedictine priory of S. Nicholas, Exeter, was a chamber called 'poor men's parlour' to which 'there repaired daily seven poor men before dinner-time, and to every one of them was delivered on the flesh-days a two-penny loaf, a pottle of ale and a piece of flesh; and on the Fridays likewise at afternoon, as soon as dinner was done, all such poor men as were tenants came, and every one of them should have also a two-penny loaf, a pottle of ale, a piece of fish and a penny in money . . . and likewise at the after dinner, there came to the said parlour all other poor folk which were either tenants to the said monastery or dwelling within their fee, and they should have meat and drink sufficient; and upon every day called S. Nicholas Day, there was . . . delivered to every poor body one loaf, and likewise upon every Good Friday there was used a general alms, which was one penny in money to every poor body coming.'[1]

At the time of the *Valor Ecclesiasticus*, 1534, the convent of Glastonbury were spending £140 16s. 8d. a year, equal to £10,000 today, on charitable distribution, and the Carthusians of Norwich £77 6s. 9d. Such large sums must have been exceptional. In the Account Roll of Romsey nunnery for 1412 appears an entry of '£8 19s. 4d., alms for the poor'.

Several religious houses, chiefly of the Benedictine Order, either founded or held as dependencies hospitals for the sick, the blind and lepers. The term hospital, of much broader significance in the Middle Ages than at present, also included almshouses, infirmaries for the aged, and hostels for poor pilgrims and travellers. These establishments, staffed by a master or warden and chaplains, were not necessarily situated within the precinct or in the neighbourhood of the parent monastery. The hospital for the sick at Smithfield was attached to the priory of S. Bartholomew

---

[1] *Monastican diocesis Exoniensis.* Oliver.

B

(p. 179); an infirmary for the destitute stood within the walls of Waltham abbey. In the town of Cirencester were a hospital for lepers and one for the aged, both dependencies of the great abbey near by. The nunnery of Barking had a lazar-house for thirteen men at Great Ilford; at Bridgnorth were two hospitals for lepers, in the patronage of Lilleshall abbey; and the monks of Reading founded two hospitals in the town, one for the local poor and the other for lepers. The Premonstratensian canons of Shap had a small lazar-house at Appleby; and in Abingdon were three hospitals of the almshouse type, under the control of the abbey. It is difficult to say to what extent the monastics exercised their authority over dependent hospitals.

An obligation imposed on all mediaeval convents was hospitality, often a very heavy charge on monastic revenue. The term may be interpreted in various ways. In its simplest form it implied the provision of bed and board for the belated traveller, who preferred to put up at a religious house rather than endure the discomforts of the mediaeval inn. Usually the period during which a visitor was afforded free accommodation was limited to two days and nights, after which he was expected to take his departure. If he wished to remain longer, the guest-master had to obtain permission from the abbot or the head of the house. Travellers who were constantly on the road knew well the good or bad reputation of the convents whose hospitality they might seek. Crowland abbey in the Fens was not held in high esteem by travellers. An ancient rhyme speaks of

'Crowland, the courteous of their meat and drink,
    The beds are like stones, they break a man's bones'.

The entertaining of royalty or noblemen with a numerous retinue for periods of unlimited duration placed a heavy burden upon houses so honoured. When the Court was on the move from one part of the country to another, the religious houses in many cases offered the only accommodation fit for a king; they were in fact the 'Hotels Royaux' of the Middle Ages, where kings and nobles were entertained at the expense of the abbot and convent. In 1314 Edward II's queen, Isabella, stayed at Christ Church priory, Canterbury, and apparently enjoyed herself so much that on her departure she left her pack of hounds in the care of the prior for two years. When a seven weeks' Parliament was held at Gloucester in 1378, Richard II accepted the hospitality of the abbeys of Gloucester and Tewkesbury in turn, and so great were the crowds of his followers that S. Peter's abbey 'seemed more like a fair', and the cloister garth was so trodden down by the visitors playing games, that not a vestige of green was to be seen when the session of Parliament was at an end. At Christmas 1423 Henry IV's son, Humphrey, Duke of Gloucester, and his family were entertained at S. Albans abbey for a fortnight, and in their train were three hundred or more persons of all ranks. Hospitality on such a scale was a very broad interpretation of the Benedictine Rule. Apart from the enormous cost it entailed, the presence of boisterous and unruly retainers within the abbey precinct undoubtedly proved a disturbing element in the life of the convent. On All Saints' day 1453 Henry VI announced his intention of spending Christmas at Bury S. Edmund's abbey, preparations for which were immediately begun by the abbot. Eighty workmen were engaged in building a lodging, or 'palace' as it was termed, for the King. The abbot arranged for a hundred officers of every rank to attend on Henry during his stay, and he organised a reception by the civic dignitaries and townsfolk to the number of five hundred. The abbot's hospitality left nothing to be desired, for it was not until Easter 1454 that the King took his departure. A few months before Thornton abbey, Lincolnshire, was suppressed, Henry VIII and his queen, Jane Seymour, on their progress southwards honoured the convent with a ceremonious visit. There they were lavishly entertained for several days, and the great banqueting hall on the first floor of the great gatehouse was put to good purpose.

Religious houses were often hard put to it to provide hospitality for all and sundry. The resources of the convent of Birkenhead priory were strained to the utmost by the stream of travellers who awaited the ferry across the Mersey; the prior complained to Edward II that the house was 'often burdened with so many sojourners that it can no longer endure; the house has not sufficient for all the multitude of those passing and coming'.

In the convent of a pilgrimage church, to which crowds flocked to pay homage at a saint's shrine, hospitality took on a special significance. Archbishop Winchelsea, 1292-1313, complained in his *Statutes de Hospitalitate* that at the priory of Christ Church, Canterbury, 'the hospitality of the house had declined to such a pitch that religious men . . . receiving only food are compelled to lodge in the city', and he therefore enjoined 'that all such guests with their horses and servants shall be cheerfully received and lodged for one day and one night, and be provided with all such things necessary; and the same with respect to secular guests who shall be admitted with their horses and servants'. Under the rule of prior Chillenden, 1391-1411, the convent of Christ Church made ample provision within and without the precinct for accommodating all visitors. A great inn known as the Cheker of the Hope was built by Chillenden at the corner of Mercery Lane, Canterbury, at a cost of £876 14s. 4d. At S. Albans and Glastonbury, both of which were the resort of pilgrims, inns were erected by the monks outside the precincts.

In the later Middle Ages it became the practice for royalty and patrons to foist upon monasteries retainers who had grown old in their service, there to end their days as non-paying guests. Edward I planted John of Windsor, an aged servant of his who was supposed to be nearing his end, upon the abbot and convent of Bath. Evidently John was well looked after for he dwelt within the precinct for thirty-four years after his admission in 1302. By the order of Edward II, a cook of the royal household was received as a permanent guest at Great Malvern priory where he was housed and fed for the rest of his life. Another of Edward II's retainers, Robert le Orfevre, was sent to Reading abbey, but the convent being already burdened with several ex-servants, Robert was summarily packed off to the daughter house of Leominster.

Occasionally a monastery served as an honourable place of detention for royal personages. When King John of France was brought to England by the Black Prince after his capture at Poitiers in 1356, he was committed to the care of abbot De la Mare of S. Albans for a time, and was there entertained in a manner befitting his state; and Elizabeth Woodville, widow of Edward IV, was virtually imprisoned in Bermondsey abbey by Henry VII shortly after his marriage with her daughter, Elizabeth of York, and there she ended her days in 1492. Further, an abbot might have thrust upon him for safe keeping an ecclesiastic who was guilty of an offence against the Church. In 1457 Archbishop Bourchier of Canterbury consigned Reginald Pecock, formerly Bishop of Chichester, who had been degraded for his heretical doctrines, to the care of the abbot of Thorney, Cambridge. Until his death in 1462 the ex-bishop was kept in confinement, half prisoner, half guest, at the abbey, £40 a year being granted for his maintenance there. The Archbishop sent detailed instructions to the abbot respecting the treatment of the deposed prelate. He was to have a secret closed chamber with a chimney, and was allowed 'one servant, serious and well disposed, to make his bed and fire'. No one else was to speak to him without leave of the abbot. For the first quarter after his arrival, he was to have the same fare as the monks of the house, but 'somewhat better afterwards as his disposition etc. shall require. For all which and for fitting up the closed apartment for the bishop' the Archbishop was to pay the convent £11. A century and a half earlier a canon of S. Osyth's, convicted of serious charges which 'tended to the scandal of the

Order', was sent by the Bishop of London to S. Bartholomew's priory, Smithfield, for a period of penance, his superior being ordered to pay 12*d*. a week for his maintenance.

From the fourteenth century onwards it became the practice for monasteries to receive paying guests, or *corrodians*, persons who by the payment of a capital sum were granted lodging, food and clothing, and fuel by the convent as a provision against old age. Many houses in financial straits resorted to the sale of *corrodies* as a means of obtaining ready money.[1] Between the years 1418 and 1423 the treasurer of Westminster abbey granted five corrodies, one of which, worth £5 6*s*. 8*d*. a year, had been sold to a Thomas Stone for £150; as he died five years later the convent was much to the good by the transaction. In the sixteenth century a number of corrodies were purchased by the Crown for ex-officers of the royal household such as ushers of the wardrobe, secretaries, and clerks of the kitchen; and shortly before the Suppression a corrody was sold by the convent of Ford abbey, Dorset, to a Mr Mitchell and his wife, who were given a house and garden, bread and ale, flesh and fish, and an annuity of 8 marks.

Of a different nature was the limited hospitality that was extended to less desirable persons, men who were guilty of a serious crime and sought refuge in a monastery to escape the consequences. From Saxon days a number of religious houses possessed the privilege of sanctuary, by virtue of which 'all manner of men who had committed any great offence such as killing a man in his own defence' remained outside the law by entering the sacred precincts. The law of sanctuary was more clearly defined in 1070 by William the Conqueror and its privileges were in some instances remarkable. The abbot of Battle for instance was vested with authority to save any malefactor from the gallows if he happened to be present at the place of execution, and the abbey church was a place of safety for any felon or murderer.

On the door of the north-west portal at Durham cathedral is the curious sanctuary-knocker of bronze (*Pl. XXXV*) that brought the protection of the Church to any fugitive, by rousing 'serten men that dyd lie alwaies in two chambers over the church dore . . . that when any such offenders dyd come and knocke, straight waie they were letten in at any our of the nyght'. On being admitted, a sanctuary man was required to confess his crime, to take

---

[1] Sometimes the corrody was merely a pension payable on the revenue of the house in return for a gift or loan made by some benefactor. Of this type were the sixteen corrodies sold by the canons of Kirkham priory, Yorkshire, who had landed themselves deeply in debt by the rebuilding of the choir in the thirteenth century. At the time of the Dissolution, the priory of Great Malvern was liable for the payment of twenty-five corrodies, most of which were annuities.

an oath of obedience to the abbot, and to wear a badge of cognisance on his apparel. At Durham he was dressed in a black gown with a yellow cross on the shoulder; he was forbidden to leave the precinct, nor was he to carry a sword or any other weapon. Within forty days after a fugitive had taken refuge, he was to appear before a coroner, and unless pardoned in the meantime he was to abjure the realm. Bearing in his hand a wooden cross he was conducted to the nearest port, and crossed the sea into exile. The crimes entered in the registers of the chartered sanctuaries included manslaughter, horse-stealing, coining and being in debt, but the Church offered no protection to persons guilty of treason. During the sixty years, 1464–1524, the number of sanctuary men at Durham reached nearly three hundred, all but sixteen of whom were guilty of homicide.

Heavy penalties were imposed on people who violated sanctuary by pursuing a fugitive within the prescribed bounds and removing him by violence. The *Annales Waverliensis* record an instance of retribution that followed such misdeed. In August 1240 officers of the law arrived at Waverley abbey with the king's warrant to arrest on a charge of murder a man who had sought refuge there and was being employed by the convent as a shoemaker. Despite the protests of the abbot the man was taken off. An appeal was made to the Papal legate who was then in England, but obtaining no satisfaction the abbot put his case before Henry III, and produced the charter conferring the privilege of sanctuary on the house. As a result the shoemaker was returned to his protectors, and the officers guilty of the violation were condemned to crave pardon at the gate of the monastery, to be publicly whipped, and to do appropriate penance. A more tragic scene was enacted in the royal abbey of Westminster in 1378. On the morning of 11th August, when the monks were assembled in the choir for High Mass, Sir Alan Boxhull, the Constable of the Tower, and fifty armed men forced their way into the church in pursuit of two prisoners, who had broken from the Tower and taken sanctuary in the choir. One of the fugitives was seized, but the other, a Robert Haule, put up a fight and was pursued round the ambulatory with his enemies hacking at him as he ran. Eventually he was surrounded between the choir stalls in front of the prior's seat. Pierced with twelve wounds he sank dead, and one of the brethren who had come to his aid was slain at his side. The tragedy stirred the whole country, and the abbey church was closed for four months. The case was brought before Richard II, who pronounced that the chief assailants should be excommunicated and should pay a fine of £200. They were only saved from a more dire penalty by the intervention of John of Gaunt.

A famous personage who sought sanctuary at Westminster was Elizabeth Woodville, queen of Edward IV, and there in 1470 she gave birth to a son, afterwards Edward V. Probably she was given apartments in the abbot's house, Cheyney Gates. She claimed sanctuary there a second time in 1483, when Richard III was a very real menace to her personal safety. The right of sanctuary was much abused at Westminster. Long before the Suppression the privilege had rendered the whole precinct of the abbey 'a vast cave of Adullam' for all the distressed and discontented in the metropolis. 'What a rabble', men said, 'of thieves, murderers and heinous traitors were to be found there! Thieves bring hither their stolen goods and live thereon. Nightly they steal out to rob and kill and then come in again.' The vice and iniquity that gathered round the abbey sanctuary brought about its abolition, for the privilege was finally surrendered in 1566.

Amongst the twenty or more chartered sanctuaries of the Middle Ages was the Cistercian abbey of Beaulieu, Hampshire, to which Margaret of Anjou, queen of Henry VI, resorted in 1471; and the pretender Perkin Warbeck, after his unsuccessful attempt to seize the city of Exeter by force of arms, was harboured within the precinct of the abbey in 1497. During his stay three hundred horsemen encamped outside the walls by day and night, and ultimately Warbeck surrendered to Lord Daubigny. When Beaulieu was suppressed thirty-two fugitives were safely ensconced in the abbey, but the King's Commissioners made short work of them all.[1]

In other ways the religious houses of mediaeval England rendered service to the world outside their walls. Owners of land and properties were well aware that title deeds and documents could be in no safer place than in the strong-room of a monastery, which also provided a safe-deposit for plate, specie, jewellery, and valuables of any kind. Within the treasury of the cathedral-priory of Durham, a chamber beneath the monks' dormitory, were deposited 'the evidences [title-deeds] of several gentlemen's lands in the country, who thought them safer there than in their own custody', (*Rites*). In 1307 the widow of Bartholomew de Badlesmere claimed the deeds of her late husband's estate that were in the keeping of the prior of Holy Trinity, Aldgate. In the twelfth century much of the banking business of Western Christendom

---

[1] The right of sanctuary was curtailed in Henry VIII's reign and was finally abolished in 1624.

was in the hands of the monasteries.[1] The establishments of the Knights Templars were the banking houses of the twelfth and thirteenth centuries, the Temple in London being used as such by the nobility and the wealthy. In 1212 King John ordered the Master of the Temple to deliver 20,000 marks that were on deposit in his house. Twenty years later it came to the ears of Henry III that a considerable sum of money, the property of Hubert de Burgh who was then confined to the Tower, was in the custody of the London Templars, whereupon the King's Justiciar was sent to the Master to demand the keys of the treasury. The Master protested that the money being in trust 'could not be delivered without the licence of him that committed it to ecclesiastical protection'. Eventually the treasure was surrendered to the King; in addition to ready money, it consisted of 'vessels of gold and silver unpriceable, and many precious stones that would make all men wonder if they knew the worth of them' (Stow's *Survey of London*).

The tables were, however, turned on the Crown in 1303, when the sensational robbery of the royal treasury in Westminster abbey took place whilst Edward I was campaigning in Scotland. The scene of the robbery was the chapel of the Pyx beneath the monks' dormitory, and many of the brethren were implicated. The actual thief was a Richard de Podelicote, who the previous year had helped himself to plate from the monks' refectory, apparently with ease, and his success encouraged him to a much more hazardous exploit, the robbery of the King's treasure. He obtained an entry to the chapel of the Pyx by cutting an opening in the wall below the dormitory, and it was revealed at the inquiries that the monks' cemetery at the east end had been sown with hemp to conceal his operations, that took the enterprising Podelicote four months to complete. Suspicions were first aroused by the appearance in a London goldsmith's shop of pieces of royal plate. Five of the monks had been seen carrying heavy baskets of the booty to the Thames by night. When the treasury was examined, money and goods to the value of £100,000 intended for the Scotch wars were found to be missing. Podelicote and his accomplices, probably embarrassed by the richness of the spoil, left the crown and the crown jewels on the floor of the chapel. When the theft was discovered abbot Wenlock and forty of the monks were arrested and committed to the Tower of London, where a number of them

---

[1] As early as 1163 the monastic practice of usury was condemned by Pope Alexander III, for it brought into disrepute houses 'who lent money to others who were in need, and take their possessions in pledge and receive the fruits therefrom beyond the principal lent'. In 1421 the General Chapter of the Franciscans issued decrees forbidding friars of the Order to indulge in usury.

remained for two years. Eventually Podelicote was hanged and his skin was nailed to a door in the abbey precinct as a warning to others.

The *Calendar of Close Rolls* for 1384 records the use of the priory church of S. Bartholomew, Smithfield, as a place of custody for public records. In that year the justices of the Common Bench were informed by the Keeper of the Rolls that certain writs that were in the care of the prior were damaged by rain, which 'because of the disrepare of the church roof . . . fell by night upon a chest wherein they were kept'.

For three centuries following the Norman Conquest every monastery possessing large estates was under the obligation in time of war of raising and maintaining a body of armed men for service with the king. The landed properties, that provided the revenue for the support of the convent, were subject to tenure under the feudal system, and abbots as tenants-in-chief were required when occasion arose to furnish their quota of men for military service. No sooner was Symeon the Norman installed as abbot of Ely than he was called upon to maintain forty soldiers completely equipped and ready to fight in the king's wars. To secure exemption from the obligation Symeon offered to pay a fine, but without success, and the men, either dependants of the abbey or mercenaries, were quartered on the abbey. Their upkeep must have proved a drain on the resources of the house, and the presence of forty idle if not unruly men-at-arms within the precinct was subversive to monastic discipline. However, the abbot discharged his responsibilities by imposing upon each of the tenants of the monastic estates the burden of providing a certain number of recruits for military service.

A number of nunneries as well as houses of monks were under the liability of raising feudal musters. The abbess of Barking, holding lands as a tenant-in-chief, possessed thirteen knights' fees[1] and in the reigns of Henry III and Edward I was required to provide men-at-arms. Likewise early in Edward II's reign, the abbess of Romsey was compelled to send a contingent of armed men to Newcastle against the Scots, and again in 1322 as many as she

[1] The obligation of the knight's service was to equip a fully armed horseman to serve at his own expense (i.e. the convent's) for forty days. Occasionally an abbot would take up arms when invasion or the threat of invasion imperilled the safety of the realm. In 1320 the abbot of Selby was in personal combat against the Scots, and in 1386 when rumours of a French invasion were rife, abbot Litlington of Westminster at the age of 70 decided to join up in defence of his country. Equipped for battle, he and two of his monks made their way to the coast, only to find that adverse winds had kept the French away. Amongst the abbey muniments is an inventory of Litlington's effects at his death, which includes various accoutrements such as six hauberks, helmets with visors, a pair of steel gloves, some leg-harneys and lance-heads.

could mobilise to Coventry, for action against the adherents of the Earl of Lancaster.

In course of time monasteries rid themselves of their feudal obligations in this respect by the payment of *scutage*, a sum of money in commutation of military service.

Further, in times of war, in addition to the money granted by Parliament, the king often demanded a subsidy of the religious houses, usually a tenth of their revenue, and many of them were also called upon to aid the king by loans. Not infrequently an abbot or prior of some standing was appointed as collector of such exactions, and was required at short notice to deliver the money to the king's receiver. In 1347 Edward III borrowed money from 141 religious houses to meet the expenses of the war with France, the amounts varying from 9 marks from Dorchester abbey to £60 from Glastonbury.

Before the middle of the fourteenth century the greater part of the lands owned by the religious were retained by the monks for farming, for rearing cattle and for breeding sheep. The Cistercian monks and the Gilbertine canons specialised in sheep farming and found a ready sale for their wool in the Flemish market, particularly in the thirteenth century. But after the Black Death of 1349, when labour became scarce and costly, the brethren took to letting out their lands, the rent-roll of which furnished them with a revenue that was not subject to fluctuation. A home-farm would be retained, the produce being needed for consumption by the community, though other manors and estates were either leased to tenants or were put in the hands of lay-stewards who managed the estates and handed over the profits derived from the farming. Even so, when monasteries farmed their own lands, bad harvests, droughts and floods, a shortage of food-stuffs for the cattle, and murrain amongst the sheep reduced some convents to such straits that they were compelled to resort to Jewish money-lenders to furnish the means to live. By leasing their manors to tenants at a fixed rent they were freed from such anxieties. The tenants of monastic lands were of all classes, from those who held property under military obligation and so many knights' fees to the humble cottier with an acre or two. Where the estates were far distant from a monastery, two or three of the brethren were sent to reside in a cell or grange on the property, to act as agents or receivers of the rents and dues. Llanthony priory, Gloucestershire, had two of the canons living on a grange at Dulek in East Meath that belonged to the convent, and in one year late in the thirteenth century the sum of £81 was sent by the receivers. At Appletreewick, a few miles from Bolton priory, Yorkshire, is a well-preserved stone mansion known as Monks' Hall, that was a grange tenanted by two or more of the canons who attended to affairs on the manor belonging to the priory. Appletreewick had been acquired in 1300, and as the place developed the canons mined lead there and established a cloth trade.

Records go to show that the tenants of monastic lands and the villeins tied to the soil were as a rule justly treated by the religious landlords. The terms on which the clearings made by the monks or their lay-brothers were leased, the commuting of labour for merely nominal payment in some cases, and the opportunity for manumission or freedom, are indications of the easy relations that often existed between the conventual landlord and his tenants. In the *Chartulary* of the Benedictine abbey of Burton-on-Trent appear accounts of the tenantry on their manors in Staffordshire and Derbyshire, in the early twelfth century. In several cases a cottage was leased the rent for which consisted of a day's work once every week during harvest time on the conventual farmland. Two bovates of land were held by a villein in return for two days' labour a week; other *ad opus* leases consisted of ploughing the monks' land once in the winter and twice in the spring. In the reign of Richard I, tenants who laboured at harvest time on the farms of Titchfield abbey, Hampshire, were provided with ample meals twice a day; those who worked one day a week were given a meal of bread, potage, flesh or fish, and beer in the early afternoon, and for supper they had a wheaten loaf weighing forty ounces, and a mackerel or two herrings.

The *Halmote Court Rolls* of the cathedral-priory of Durham from 1296 to 1384[1] present a picture of the life of the various types of tenant on the thirty-five vills controlled by the convent. 'We see them in their tofts, surrounded by their crofts, with their gardens of pot-herbs. We see how they ordered the affairs of the village when summoned by the bailiff to consider matters affecting the commonweal of the community. We hear of their trespasses and wrong-doings, and how they were remedied or punished; of their strifes and contentions; of their relations with the prior, who appears always to have dealt with his tenants either in person or through his officers, with much consideration; and in the imposition of fines, we find them invariably tempering justice with mercy.'

The *Rentalia* of Glastonbury abbey also affords evidence of the consideration shown to tenants of monastic property, some of whom were required to pay their rent partly in labour or in kind. There were payments of salmon, eels, and honey; small cottagers

[1] Printed by the Surtees Society in 1889; edited by W. Booth.

performed light labours in lieu of rent, as for instance a woman named Alice, who occupied a cottage and half an acre of land, by the service of sharpening reapers' sickles at harvest time and bringing them water.

To each of the abbot's officers or obedientiaries (p. 96) was assigned a portion of the property, a manor or part of an estate, the profits of which went to the maintenance of his department, an arrangement that brought the monks into close contact with their tenants from time to time to their mutual advantage.

Attached to every religious house in the later Middle Ages were a number of paid officials who administered the conventual estates. There were the receiver, the bailiff, and most important of all the steward, who acted for the convent in all civil matters and exercised the authority of the abbot or prior in the manorial courts. The office of steward in a wealthy house was much coveted and was generally conferred upon a member of the nobility. In Henry VIII's reign the Earl of Shrewsbury was the steward of eleven abbeys, and the Earl of Derby of seven.[1] In the lesser houses the stewards were drawn from the local gentry, many of whom were lessees of monastic lands.

The religious houses were intimately associated with the forests that covered extensive tracts of England in the Middle Ages, in all of which several monasteries possessed certain privileges conferred upon them by royal charter, though not necessarily situated within the forest bounds. Thus, the abbeys of Roche, Welbeck, Merivale, and S. Mary, Leicester, amongst others, held rights in the wide stretch of forest-land in the Peak District; as also had Chertsey abbey in Windsor Forest, Newstead priory in Sherwood, and Beaulieu abbey in the New Forest. In the main these rights pertained to the felling of timber for use in the conventual buildings and farmsteads, and the gathering of dead wood and undergrowth for fuel. Cattle grazing and pannage (the right to turn swine into the forest for food) were often granted to a convent in the locality, and occasionally an abbot was given limited rights over the game and deer in a chase bordering on a forest. Venison grants generally took the form of a tithe of the hunt. S. Mary's abbey, York, had a tithe of the deer stalked in Pickering Lythe, and S. Peter's, Gloucester, of all the wild boars killed in the Forest of Dean. Only occasionally was the superior of a religious house haled before the verderer of a forest court on a charge of venison-trespass.

A profitable source of revenue was derived from parish churches that were appropriated to a monastery. When lands were bestowed upon a convent by the king or a lay patron, the parish churches

---

[1] P. Hughes, *The Reformation in England*, Vol. I, Hollis & Carter, 1954.

situated thereon, together with the first-fruits, tithes, fees for bap-
tism, marriage, churching, and burial became the property of the
house. The episcopal registers of the fourteenth century abound in
petitions from monasteries poorly endowed and unable to make
ends meet, requesting a bishop's sanction to appropriate parish
churches, the main reason given being insufficient revenue to meet
the needs of hospitality, particularly by houses situated on a high-
way of busy traffic. Legal appropriation was subject to the consent of the bishop of the diocese, and to confirmation by the Pope.
Then the monastery became the rector and patron of the benefice,
and as such had to appoint the priest or vicar for the cure of souls
in the parish, and to pay him a fixed stipend out of the fruits. At
the same time the convent was responsible for maintaining the
chancel of the parish church in a state of repair, the nave being
the property of the parishioners. On account of this, the greater
tithes of a large number of parish churches passed into the hands
of the new owners of monastic lands after the Suppression.

In pilgrimage churches a considerable income was derived from
the offerings made by the devout and others at the shrine of a
saint. Oblations at the shrine of Edward the Confessor at Westminster abbey amounted to £74 in 1358, after which there was a
progressive decline; in 1460 the receipts had fallen to £8, and by
the end of that century the cultus of S. Edward had lost its popular
appeal and the offerings were negligible. At Christ Church, Canterbury, where the shrine of the murdered Becket was the great
attraction, the offerings in 1350, the year after the Black Death,
enriched the priory by £800, a sum equal to £30,000 in modern
value, and in 1420 the receipts amounted to £570. The shrines of
the martyred saints were always the greatest purse-openers; even
a worthless king who had met with a violent death brought prosperity to a religious house. When Edward II was foully done to
death at Berkeley castle in 1327, the abbot and convent of S.
Peter's, Gloucester, accepted the body for burial in their church.
Popular sympathy for the murdered monarch exalted him to the
rank of a saint and martyr, and a wondrous tomb was erected on
the north side of the choir. Before long multitudes of pilgrims
flocked thither, and their oblations enabled the monks to remodel
the choir and transepts, and were eventually sufficient to rebuild
the whole of the abbey church.

In the vicinity of many great abbeys, notably those of the Benedictine Order such as Abingdon, Bury S. Edmunds, Canterbury,
Reading, and S. Albans, there grew up settlements of lay-folk that
developed into populous towns, over which the abbots exercised
almost complete jurisdiction. They maintained the roadways and

bridges, appointed the civic officers, controlled the trade, the markets and fairs, and set up courts for the administration of justice. The time came when the townsfolk sought to free themselves from abbatial domination, to manage their own affairs and establish their own courts. In many places the burgesses lived on good terms with the religious, but in some towns the abbot and convent were continually at feud with the people, and disputes respecting their rights culminated in open hostility and outbreaks of violence. At Canterbury the citizens and the prior of Christ Church fought over meadows, mills and markets, sometimes before the courts and sometimes with bows and arrows.[1] For more than a century the monks of S. Albans and the townspeople were at daggers drawn. In 1274 a dispute arose about the grinding of corn, the people claiming the right to have their own handmills, the abbot insisting upon their using the abbey mills. In the year 1327 the rejection of the town's demands for a charter of freedom led to open revolt, during which the abbey was attacked and its food supplies cut off. Royal intervention and the findings of a court of arbitration favoured the malcontents, and the abbot was obliged to grant them a charter of liberties, though the right to possess their own mills was denied them. A few years later the attempted arrest of a townsman on the abbot's warrant provoked a riot, in the course of which the man was slain. At the inquiry that followed, the justices pronounced in favour of the abbot, and the townspeople were made to surrender their charters and their handmill. There was further trouble during the Wat Tyler rising of 1381. The men of S. Albans threw in their lot with the rebels; they stormed the abbey and set free the prisoners who were in the great gatehouse. Eventually the arrival of King Richard II, the trial of the ringleaders by the chief justice and their execution at S. Albans put an end to the outbreak.

More serious were the disturbances that arose at Norwich in 1272 between the citizens and the cathedral-priory, engendered by the imposition of tolls and dues on merchandise at the annual fair held in Tombland to the west of the cathedral. The outbreak of hostilities occurred on Trinity Sunday, when the citizens drove the monks back into the priory precinct. In retaliation the prior sent to Yarmouth for a band of armed men, some of whom ascended the belfry and fired with bows and catapults on the riotous populace: others sallied forth and pillaged the town. Roused to a pitch of madness the townsmen assembled in force and compelled the mercenaries to take refuge in the priory, to which they laid siege. Flaming brands were hurled on to the conventual buildings,

[1] H. Maynard Smith, *Pre-Reformation England*, 1938.

and before long the monks' dormitory, the refectory, the infirmary, the guest-house and other buildings were gutted and part of the cathedral damaged. As a result of this violence, the city of Norwich was excommunicated, the ringleaders were brought to justice before Henry III and were hanged, and the citizens were fined 3,000 marks, the money being used for the restoration of the priory buildings and for the purchase of a golden pyx weighing ten pounds.

No monastery suffered so severely from the lawlessness of towns-people as did Bury S. Edmunds. Determined to extort from the abbey their right to administer the affairs of the town, the discontented burgesses took forcible possession of the abbey. On 13th January 1327 some three thousand of the rioters broke through the gatehouse, and made their way to the cellarium, where they drained the beer-casks; they entered the cloisters and carried off the books and muniments; they ransacked the prior's lodging of plate, vessels and jewels, and took the prior and twenty of the monks to the chapter house where they forced them to sign documents subversive of the privileges of the convent, and bonds for large sums of money that would free the town from debt. Meanwhile the chests of the sacristan were broken open and everything of value was seized; the treasury of the abbey church was despoiled of a vast amount of money, of gold and silver vessels, jewels and charters, and the vestry was plundered of its rich collection of vestments and copes. In the summer the malcontents looted the abbot's lodging, carrying off the wardrobe and arras hangings; they destroyed the conduit, cut off the water supply, and damaged the doors and windows of the church. For ten months they remained in possession, a reign of terror for the monks, who were powerless to resist. The looting and destruction were followed in October 1327 by the burning of the buildings in the outer court of the abbey, including the almonry, the guest-house, the brewery, bakehouse and granary, the stables and mill, and various buildings occupied by the officers or obedientiaries. For several days these buildings were given up to the flames; the insurgents carried off the molten lead that poured from the roofs. When the sheriff arrived on the scene to put an end to the orgy of destruction, he had to shelter his horses in the monks' parlour, so complete had been the devastation. After prolonged litigation to recover damages of the townspeople, the convent was awarded the enormous sum of £140,000, but at the instance of Edward III the whole was remitted except a fine of 2,000 marks.

To the monks we owe much of our knowledge of the mediaeval history of this country, a priceless heritage bequeathed by scribes and historiographers who lived the sheltered life. In addition to the gospels, missals, and psalters, copies of the classics and countless charters, deeds, and agreements that were copied in the scriptoria, chronicles dealing with national, ecclesiastical, and local history, and biographies of the saints and fathers were compiled by the religious, particularly by those of the Benedictine Order. An early work of inestimable value was the *Ecclesiastical History of the English People* by the Venerable Bede (673–735), whose early years were passed in the monastery of Jarrow. To his writings we are indebted for almost all that is known of the introduction of the Christian faith into Great Britain, of the early history of the Church and of the Saxon kingdoms. A century and a half after it was written, portions of Bede's History were translated into English by King Alfred for the benefit of his countrymen.

It was under the inspiration of Alfred that the *Saxon Chronicle* was commenced at S. Swithin's priory, Winchester. It consists of a collection of manuscripts, now in the British Museum, that comprise the earliest systematic history of this country, compiled from earlier annals then available; and it furnishes a contemporary narrative of the Danish wars of Alfred's reign. Copies were sent by the King's order to some of the greater monasteries such as Canterbury, Abingdon, Evesham, and Peterborough, where monk-scribes of the succeeding centuries added the history of their own time and place to the Chronicle. Thus, the *Chronicon Petroburgense* (Peterborough) enriched English history by an account of the reigns of Henry II and Richard I. The Life of King Alfred by John Asser (*d.* 909), reader to the king and formerly a monk of S. David's, was the first biography of an English monarch.

In the century following the Conquest the Benedictine monks were extremely prolific in the production of chronicles both national and domestic, embellishing the history of their own houses with accounts of wondrous events that may or may not have figured in their annals, and of ancient privileges they claimed to possess, in order to enhance the prestige of their houses; and in later times the monks were prone to fabricate chronicles and spurious charters to make good defective titles and claims.[1]

The Benedictine monks made a point of writing lives of the saints associated with their houses. In the Life of Edward the Confessor compiled by a monk of Westminster about the time of the

---

[1] In the fifteenth century the monks of Crowland compiled the *Chronicle of Ingulf*, that was purported to be the work of the Norman abbot installed by the Conqueror in 1076. The narrative is largely 'a patchwork of piracies' interspersed with imaginary episodes.

Conquest is a description of the abbey church built by the Confessor; and between 1072 and 1081 Sulcard, a monk of the same house, wrote an account of the legendary foundation of the abbey, which was elaborated by William of Malmesbury c. by 1125, Osbert de Clare, prior of Westminster, in 1141, and again by Flete c. 1445. In his story of the founding of the abbey by S. Dunstan c. 958, Flete quoted a forged charter now preserved in the abbey muniments.

Foremost amongst the post-Conquest 'schools' of historical writing was S. Albans abbey, that owed so much to the first Norman abbot, Paul of Caen, and reached its climax in the thirteenth century. Second in importance was the cathedral-priory of Durham, where the Norman abbot Simeon and his successors fostered the tradition that dated from the time of the Venerable Bede; and another monkish historian was Florence of Worcester, whose *Chronicon ex Chronicis*, commencing with the Creation and ending c. 1117, was largely supplementary to an earlier English work, although from 1106 Florence wrote independently. His History was continued up to the year 1141 by another monk, John of Worcester.

The monasteries of Malmesbury, Winchester, and Canterbury were flourishing as seats of letters and culture in the first half of the twelfth century, the most famous monk-historians being William of Malmesbury, precentor and librarian, and Ordericus Vitalis. Amongst the works of Malmesbury were the *Gesta Regum Anglorum* and *Historia Novella*, embracing English history from early times to 1142, and the *Gesta Pontificum Anglorum*, a treatise on ecclesiastical history. He also wrote lives of S. Dunstan and S. Wulfstan. The monk Ordericus Vitalis compiled the voluminous *Historia Ecclesiastica* in thirteen books which he completed in 1141. Both Christ Church priory and the abbey of S. Augustine, Canterbury, were productive of histories and biographies. Late in the eleventh century a monk of S. Augustine's, who had previously written a life of S. Etheldreda of Ely, was engaged in preparing biographies of S. Augustine and his successors, and Sprott, a monk of the same house, was the author of a history from the Creation to 1232. A later monk-historian named Thorne compiled a chronicle of all the abbots of S. Augustine's from its foundation to 1397, in which were transcribed original documents, royal charters, and Papal bulls. The monk Eadmer of Christ Church wrote a life of S. Anselm, and S. Thomas the Martyr (Becket) was the subject of several biographies. *The Account of the Burning and Repair of the Church of Canterbury in 1174*, written by the monk Gervase, is a precious record of the rebuilding of the cathedral

c

choir, of the master-masons employed by the convent, and of the progress of the work year by year.

The famous Jocelyn of Brakelond, who became a monk of Bury S. Edmunds in 1173, compiled a narrative of the fortunes of the abbey during the rule of abbots Hugh and Samson. He relates in detail the affairs and administration of the convent between 1173 and 1203, and presents a kindly portrait of abbot Samson whom he served as chaplain.

It became the common practice for monastic houses to send copies of the works produced in their scriptoria to other houses.[1]

In the thirteenth century the abbey of S. Albans, pre-eminent as a school of learning and the arts, was unrivalled for its historical writing. The chief sources of the early history of the abbey are the Chronicles of Roger Wendover, c. 1236, and his more famous successor, Matthew Paris, 1200–59, the greatest historian of the Middle Ages. Paris continued the *Chronica Majora* of Wendover up to the year 1259, the first two volumes of which are now at Corpus Christi College, Cambridge. Amongst other of his works is the *Gesta Abbatum*, incorporating the lives of twenty-three abbots of S. Albans. When Henry III visited the abbey on the Feast of Edward the Confessor 1257, Paris sat at meat and conversed with the King, who enjoined him to write 'a special and full account of the proceedings, in a fair writing, indelibly in a book, so that the memory of them be not lost by any length of time'. After Paris's death the *Chronica Majora* was continued in the *Flores Historiarium* by a succession of brethren of the abbey.

Whilst the historians of S. Albans were poring over their manuscripts, there arose within the abbey precinct a school of painters, illuminators, goldsmiths, and metal-workers that flourished for more than a century. The artists and craftsmen, the most distinguished of whom were members of the Colchester family, came to S. Albans at the invitation of the monks, and here they settled, executing any work required for the adornment or furnishing of the abbey church—a figure of the Virgin Mary, a painting for a reredos, a rood, a lectern, tablets of silver-gilt, or mural paintings. The founder of the school of painting, Master Walter of Colches-

---

[1] It is not generally known that the law of copyright is of monastic origin. The principle was first established in the ancient kingdom of Tara in Ireland. There were two monasteries in Tara, rivals for the tourist trade of the day, one of which acquired a very beautiful psalter that was hung near the High Altar and attracted large numbers of visitors. The brethren of the other house wondered at the decline in the number of their pilgrims, and on discovering the cause, the abbot ordered an exact copy of the psalter to be made for his church. The abbot of the first monastery appealed to the king, whose judgment was 'to every cow her calf', and ordered that the infringing copy should be destroyed. Thus was early established the principle of copyright now recognised throughout the world.

ter, came to the abbey in the year 1200 accompanied by his brothers William and Simon, and his nephew Richard. They were then lay artists but after a time Walter and Richard embraced the religious life, and in 1213 'the incomparable Walter' was made the sacrist of the convent. His fame spread far and wide, so much so that, as Matthew Paris records, he was employed by the monks of Christ Church, Canterbury, to make the shrine of S. Thomas the Martyr.[1]

Before the end of the thirteenth century the standard of historical writing in religious houses was on the decline, probably because monks with a flair and aptitude for literary work were sent to one or other of the monastic halls at Oxford to study at the University (p. 48). Immediately after the Black Death abbot de la Mare of S. Albans, in an attempt to revive the fame of the house as a school of letters and the arts, ordained that the brethren and those of dependent priories should devote themselves to study, writing, illumination, and book-binding rather than to outdoor occupations.[2]

Of no less importance than the writing of chronicles was the transcription of the literary treasures of the great ages of Greece and Rome, for it was the unwearied industry of monk-scribes that preserved for us the masterpieces of classic literature. In one of his letters S. Anselm specially recommended the study of Virgil and other classical writers to his brethren, and so popular became pagan literature in the cloister that eminent monastic teachers warned the religious of the danger of an all-absorbing passion for the classics to the exclusion of Christian literature and theological works.[3] However, the sayings and writings of the illustrious fathers and doctors of the Early Church would have been irretrievably lost had not generation after generation of monkish scholars laboured in the scriptoria.

In every monastery two or more of the brethren were engaged in copying and preserving the innumerable documents and records of the house; legal agreements, leases·and rentals, accounts and customaries, Papal bulls and letters, episcopal injunctions, and

---

[1] In December 1959 a superb illuminated manuscript of the *Apocalyspe*, dating c. 1250 and attributed to the school of S. Albans, was sold at Sotheby's for the record price of £65,000. It measures about 12 in. by 8 in. and is remarkable for the eighty-two illuminations.

[2] A printing press was set up in the great gatehouse of S. Albans in 1480, the earliest book produced being *Rhetorica Nova Fratris Laurencii Gulielmi de Soana*. Other books followed notably *Aristotle's Physics*, the *Chronicles of England*, and in 1486 a treatise entitled *The Gentleman's Recreation*, written by the prioress of Sopwell nunnery and, strangely enough, dealing with hawking, hunting, and brass armour.

[3] During the rule of abbot Benedict, 1179–92, the monks of Peterborough translated classics such as Seneca, Martial, Terence, and Justinian's *Institutes*.

most important of all charters and deeds that the convent would need should they be involved in litigation. In houses of any size one of the monks was appointed keeper of the archives. The *Chartulary of Glastonbury abbey*, compiled between 1338 and 1340,[1] comprising more than 1,300 legal documents, presents a fascinating picture of this famous house a few years before the Black Death. Figuring largely in the archives are the rents and leases of properties owned in several counties, the relations between the convent and the tenants, as well as the internal affairs of the abbey. In the first volume is an account of the visit of Edward I and Queen Eleanor to Glastonbury in 1278, during which the tomb of the legendary King Arthur was opened and his remains and those of queen Guinevere were found in two painted chests. On the completion of the *Chartulary*, a keeper of the archives was appointed, and he was 'to have one of the junior monks by his side, whom he shall carefully train in the method of keeping the records'.

In the later Middle Ages professional scribes and illuminators were employed by the religious houses, especially for copying books and making missals and service manuals. Before the end of the thirteenth century lay craftsmen were plying for custom at the gates of various abbeys. Not only was a higher degree of technical skill attained, but the work could be executed more quickly than by monks, whose labours were subject to frequent interruption by their religious observances. The famous Missal made for abbot Litlington of Westminster in 1383-4 was the work of a Thomas Preston, who was paid £4 plus £1 for expenditure on his clothing. He was lodged in the abbey, and the year after the completion of the Missal, which cost the enormous sum of £34 14s. 7d., Preston entered the convent as a novice.

[1] Preserved at Longleat. Transcribed from the Latin by Dom A. Watkin, and published in three volumes by the Somerset Record Society, 1947-59.

II. English Monachism through the Centuries

~~~~~~~~~~~~~~~~~~~~~~~~~~~~~~~~~~~~~

The Sources of Saxon Monachism—Pope Gregory's Mission in the South—The Abbey of S. Peter and S. Paul, Canterbury—The Rule of S. Benedict—Daily Life of the Religious—Prayer, Labour, Study—Celtic Monachism from Ireland in the North of England—The Work of Columba and Aidan—Double Monasteries for Monks and Nuns—The Synod of Whitby, 664—Benedictinism planted in the North—Scanty Knowledge of Saxon Foundations—The Monastic Revival of the Tenth Century— Edgar the Peaceable and the great S. Dunstan—The Regularis Concordia —Famous Monasteries of this Period—Canute and Edward the Confessor —The White Robe of Churches in the Eleventh Century—The Revival of Benedictinism in Normandy—Its Influence in Post-Conquest England— The Great Wave of Monastic Building in England—Archbishop Lanfranc's Policy—Saxon Abbots displaced by Normans—Thurstan at Glastonbury—Anglo-Norman Cathedral-Priories—The Status of the Bishop —Priors and Bishops at Variance—Enmity at Durham—Founding of Daughter Houses by the Greater Abbeys—Cluniac Priories—The Preeminence of the Benedictines overthrown in the Twelfth Century—The Orders of Regular Canons—Augustinian, Premonstratensian, and Gilbertine—The Cistercian Order and its Rapid Growth in the First Half of the Twelfth Century—The Knightly Orders; Templars and Hospitallers—Lesser Orders and their Few Houses—The Carthusians and their High Ideals—The Severe Austerity of their Eremitical Life—Monastic Expansion in the Twelfth Century—The Arrival of the Mendicant Orders—Their Missionary Work in Populous Towns—Corporate Control of Benedictine Monasteries by Papal Decree—General Chapters— Colleges founded for Monks at Oxford—The Statute of Mortmain, 1279—Benefactions and Endowments for Colleges in the Fourteenth Century—The decline of Monachism—Dives and Pauper—Its condemnation of Monastic Avarice—Order of Knights Templars abolished in 1312— The Black Death, 1349—Mortality in the Greater Abbeys—Decay of Fervour in the Franciscan Order—The Bill of 1410 to Transfer Monastic Property to the Crown—Alien Priories in England—Dependencies of Foreign Abbeys—Their Position in Times of War with France—Control by the Crown—Charters of Denization—Revenues of Alien Houses to endow Charterhouses and Royal Colleges—Suppression of some Smaller Monasteries in Henry VII's Reign—Cardinal Wolsey's Suppressions for the Endowment of Colleges at Oxford and Ipswich—Thomas Cromwell.

~~~~~~~~~~~~~~~~~~~~~~~~~~~~~~~~~~~~~

IN MEDIAEVAL ENGLAND there were at one time and another monasteries of a dozen or more different Orders, each with its own ideals and code of observances. The monachism that ran its course in this country for nearly a thousand years derived in the first place from two independent sources, Rome and Ireland.

In the south the earliest religious houses, founded in the seventh and eighth centuries, sprang from Pope Gregory's mission to Kent headed by S. Augustine, himself a monk. The abbey of S. Peter and S. Paul at Canterbury, founded by King Ethelbert of Kent *c.* 605, was described by successive Popes as 'the first and chief mother of monasteries in England'.[1] In those early times the spread of the Christian faith was largely the work of monks, for every monastery was a mission-station and every mission-station a monastery. The way of life observed by the brethren of S. Augustine's abbey and of other houses inspired by the Roman mission was based on the Rule of S. Benedict, subject as it was to considerable latitude and variations.

The great S. Benedict, 480–534, may be regarded as the father of Western monachism, and the succession of the various religious Orders in Western Christendom throughout the Middle Ages begins with the monastery he founded *c.* 529 at Monte Cassino, near Naples, afterwards the most famous in Italy. Here he composed the Rule that subsequently became the code of monachism in Western Europe. There were Christian monks before his time and many others after him who were not bound by his Rule, but by the end of the seventh century Benedictinism was supreme.

The Rule made provision for the division of the monk's day into three periods, to be devoted to prayer, to study, and to manual labour. Of prime importance was the *Opus Dei*, the duty of offering up prayer and praise in the church; at fixed times the brethren were to occupy themselves in sacred reading, the *Divine Lectio*. The pursuit of learning and literature was expressly enjoined, and as 'Idleness is the enemy of the soul', says S. Benedict, 'therefore let the brethren devote certain hours to work with their hands'. There was nothing austere or exacting in the Rule. It was 'a very little Rule for beginners', and the abbot of a Benedictine house could exercise his discretion in applying it to the conditions and circumstances of his own convent. 'Let all things be done in moderation on account of the faint-hearted.'

A monastery was to be arranged so that everything necessary— water, a mill, a garden, a bakery—should be available, and there should be 'no need for monks to wander about outside'. No one in the monastery was to follow his own inclinations, but was to subject himself to the discipline of the Rule. Whenever matters of

[1] After the burial of S. Augustine in the abbey church, the monastery was known as S. Augustine's abbey.

importance arose in the convent, the abbot was to summon all the brethren and 'take counsel'. If a brother was disobedient or insubordinate, proud or a grumbler, he was to be privately admonished; and if he did not amend or was incorrigible, he was to undergo corporal punishment or take his meals alone. The abbot was to treat defaulters 'with all prudence and diligence'. More than anything was 'the vice of property to be cut off root and branch'. A monk should have nothing at all, neither a book, nor tablets, nor a pen. All things were to be common to all, as it is written 'Let not any man presume to call anything his own' (Acts, iv, 32). Regulations were drawn up fixing the hours of the day and night offices to be recited in the church, for 'Seven times in the day do I praise Thee' (Psalm 119, v. 164). Each monk was to 'discipline his body in respect of food, drink, sleep, chatter and mirth'. The brethren were to sleep in one room and in separate beds; they were to sleep clothed, girdled with belts or cords, but without knives at their sides, lest they injure themselves in sleep. For the daily meal at the sixth or ninth hour there were to be two cooked dishes, 'so that he who cannot eat of one may make his meal of the other'. For the brethren who were engaged in unusually heavy labour, extra allowances of food might be made at the abbot's discretion, but 'all must abstain from the flesh of four-footed beasts, except the delicate and sick'. One pint of wine was allowed each monk at meals, but if the nature of a brother's labour or the heat of the day required, he might take more. All guests were to be received as Christ himself, in accordance with the Gospel, 'I was a stranger and ye took me in' (Matthew, xxv, 35), and fitting honour was to be shown to all. The prior was to receive visitors 'with inclined head, or with prostrating of the whole body on the ground. . . . The abbot as well as the whole congregation shall wash the feet of all guests'.

The spirit of moderation and the reasonableness underlying the Benedictine Rule was responsible for its pre-eminence from the eighth century onwards. From their habit, which consisted of a black cape and hood over a cassock of black, white, or russet with white or black fur, the Benedictines were commonly known as Black Monks.

Before the advent of S. Augustine in 597, Celtic monachism emanating from Ireland had already gained a footing in the north of England. A great number of monastic oratories existed in Ireland in the sixth century, whence monk-missionaries were despatched to Scotland and Gaul; for the Celtic Church, like that of the south, was essentially a missionary Church and was monastic in its organisation. Whether Irish monachism was of Egyptian or

Eastern origin, or was of indigenous growth is a matter of uncertainty. In the year 563 the Irish monk Columba settled in the desolate isle of Iona off the west coast of Scotland and he there founded a monastery peopled by monk-missionaries who with Columba set themselves the task of Christianising the north. The monk Aidan of Iona, 'the apostle of Northumbria', worked unceasingly in the area between the Forth and the Humber, where in due course a number of Celtic monasteries were established. His name is closely associated with Lindisfarne, the original headquarters of the Celtic Church in the north, where a see was attached to the monastery, Aidan himself being the first bishop.

Columba is not known to have composed a written Rule for his brethren, although a document under that name compiled by one of his community at a later date (Appendix B) shows that Celtic monachism had much in common with the Rule of S. Benedict that became paramount in Western Christendom by the end of the seventh century.

The religious houses of Celtic origin in this country were frequently double monasteries, i.e. for monks and nuns, such houses being presided over by an abbess. This was the custom in the Irish convents of S. Bridget. 450–523. Hilda's abbey at Whitby, founded c. 657, and that of Wimborne in Dorset about fifty years later[1] were double communities of the Celtic type, which however were not looked upon with favour by the Roman Church.

At the Synod of Whitby in 664 the Church in the north became united with that of the south in the customs and usages of Latin Christianity, and thenceforth monachism throughout the whole country tended to approximate more closely to the Benedictine model.[2] Before the end of the seventh century Lindisfarne had adopted the Benedictine code, and the famous Wilfrid, originally a monk of Lindisfarne and the leader of the pro-Roman party at the Synod of Whitby, planted the Rule of S. Benedict in the monasteries of Ripon and Hexham. A few years afterwards the two important houses of Wearmouth (674) and Jarrow (681) observing the same Rule, were founded by Benedict Biscop after his return from Italy, where he had visited many monasteries.

Little is known of the conventual life or of the buildings of Anglo-Saxon foundations of the seventh and eighth centuries, for scarcely any of them survived the devastations wrought by the Danish invasions of the ninth and tenth centuries. Abbeys and churches were pillaged, precious libraries destroyed, and the in-

[1] Celtic monachism was implanted mainly in the north, but under its influence a few houses such as Wimborne and Glastonbury sprang up sporadically in the south.
[2] A. H. Thompson, *English Monasteries*.

I. The northern Gatehouse, Bury S. Edmund's Abbey.

II. The Gatehouse, Worksop Priory.

III. The Great Gatehouse, S. Albans.

IV. The Gatehouse, Thornton Abbey (inner face).

V. South cloister walk, Gloucester.

VI. East cloister walk, Lacock Abbey.

VII. Interior of the lavatorium, Gloucester.

VIII. Night-stairs, Hexham Priory.

IX. Night-stairs, Bristol Cathedral.

X. Chapter house portals, Kirkstall Abbey.

XI. Chapter house doorway and day-stairs, Cleeve Abbey.

mates put to the sword. The real history of English monachism begins in the second half of the tenth century, when the Rule of S. Benedict was generally imposed upon the religious houses of the land, the chief promoter being the great S. Dunstan, Archbishop of Canterbury, minister and counsellor to Edgar the Peaceable, 958–75. The King had declared that 'All the monasteries in my realm to the outward sight are nothing but worm-eaten and rotten timber and boards; and that is worse, they are almost empty and devoid of Divine service'. In the work of re-organisation Dunstan was assisted by Ethelwold, Bishop of Winchester, and Bishop Oswald of Worcester, who had made his profession abroad in the newly-formed abbey of Fleury or S. Benoit-sur-Loire. The abbot of S. Benoit was invited to England to help in the task, and in order to ensure a uniformity in the observance of the Benedictine Rule, King Edgar convened a synod at Winchester, c. 965, at which a Customal was prepared by S. Dunstan, known as the *Regularis Concordia*. Intended to govern the lives of all English monks, it was a code that set the standard for Benedictine religious life, prescribing one customary *Use* for the whole of the kingdom. No general scheme of government or control was formulated in the Concordia. Strictly speaking the Benedictines never constituted an Order, for each abbey was autonomous, owing no allegiance to a central authority or governing house. In the Concordia emphasis was laid on the association of the King with monastic life and Rule. The election of abbots and abbesses was made subject to royal confirmation, a measure that was designed to free monasteries from interference by lay magnates. Of significance is the wording of a document in which King Edgar confirmed the privileges of Romsey abbey in 966. 'To the nuns I concede for ever the liberty of monastic privilege. . . . The whole congregation of the aforesaid monastery, electing as the Rule of the blessed S. Benedict appoints, shall elect an abbess rightly out of the same company of sisters. Nor may anyone from outside, trusting to tyrannical contumacy in the aforesaid monastery taking it by force, exercise the right of power in the aforesaid monastery.'

During and after the episcopate of S. Dunstan, several important religious houses were founded or refounded, work in which Ethelwold and Oswald took an active part. Winchester, Worcester, Evesham, Abingdon, and Pershore were outstanding centres of the monastic revival. By the end of the tenth century thirty or more monasteries and six nunneries had been founded or restored, including the abbeys of Ely and Ramsey in the Fens, Peterborough and Westminster, the last-named being peopled by S. Dunstan with monks from Glastonbury. This was the finest age of Saxon monachism. On the accession of Ethelred an unhappy era set in, for the descent of the mighty Sweyn and his Danish hordes early in the eleventh century brought disaster in its train. However, after Sweyn's son, Canute, had embraced the Christian faith, he became an avowed friend of the Church and bestowed benefactions on many religious houses. Later, the rebuilding of the abbey of S. Peter, Westminster, by Ewdard the Confessor was the harbinger of the wave of monastic building that swept over England after the Conquest.

In the first half of the eleventh century the Church in Western Christendom, under a strong monastic impulse, sprang into a new vitality, that expressed itself in an enormous activity in the building of churches. Raoul Glaber, a monk-historian of the great abbey of Cluny, wrote c. 1030: 'It was as if the whole world had thrown off the rags of its ancient time, and had arrayed itself in a white robe of churches.' A momentous revival of Benedictinism in Normandy was heralded in the year 1002 by the arrival in the Duchy, at the instance of Duke Richard II, of a body of Burgundian monks from Dijon. The abbeys of Fécamp, Jumièges, and Bernay, that were to rival those of Burgundy, were the centres of the revival, and at the time of the Norman Conquest the Benedictine Order was flourishing in Normandy.

When Duke William landed on these shores in 1066, there were about fifty Benedictine monasteries in England, nine of which were nunneries. No sooner was the Conqueror firmly established here than abbots and ecclesiastics poured into this country from across the Channel, bringing with them the culture, the ritual, and liturgical observances of the great Benedictine abbeys of Normandy such as Jumièges, Caen, and Bec. They served the political ends of William and satisfied the claims of the next world by rebuilding many Saxon monasteries and founding large numbers of others. Under the system of feudal tenure, the Norman barons and nobles became possessed of vast estates in England, from which they bestowed lands upon the Church for the founding of religious houses, and also made gifts of land to houses in France.

In the year 1070 Stigand, the Saxon Archbishop of Canterbury, was deposed and was replaced by the able and far-seeing Lanfranc, a Benedictine monk who had been the prior of Bec and the abbot of S. Étienne, Caen. To Lanfranc was entrusted the task of reorganising the English Church. Being a monk he had the monastic revival at heart, and as a result the Saxon abbots and superiors almost without exception were evicted in favour of foreigners. Paul at S. Albans, Flambard at Durham, Walkelyn at Winchester and Serlo at Gloucester, to name a few, responded nobly to the demands of the Conqueror and Lanfranc. The ejection of Saxon abbots, a reminder of the fallen fortunes of the conquered race, undoubtedly met with opposition in some houses. Glastonbury is a case in point. There, the resentment of the Saxon brethren on the removal of abbot Ailnoth was aggravated by the arrogance of his successor, Thurstan, who was determined to impose the ritual of Normandy upon the convent. In a body the monks refused to accept a chant of foreign origin for use in the Divine offices, whereupon Thurstan sent for a number of armed men who burst into the church 'and slew some of the monks, and wounded many more, so that blood ran down from the altar on to the steps and from the steps to the floor. . . . Three were smitten to death and eighteen wounded'. Thurstan was removed from Glastonbury for a time, but purchased his re-instatement by a gift of five hundred pounds of silver to William II, although peace was not restored to the convent until after his death.

Amongst the many changes effected by Lanfranc in his scheme of re-organisation was the conversion of several of the secular cathedrals into cathedral-priories, a practice that was unusual on the Continent. Following his installation at Canterbury Lanfranc planned a monastery of Benedictine monks as part of the cathedral establishment, the cathedral serving as the conventual church. The union of monastery and cathedral occurred in eight English sees in the second half of the eleventh century, viz. Canterbury, Bath, Coventry, Durham, Norwich, Rochester, Winchester, and Worcester, though in the two last-named no radical change took place in their constitution, as they had both been monastic before Lanfranc's reform.[1] In these cathedral-priories the bishop of the see was given the honorary recognition due to an abbot, but he was not a member of the convent nor had he any voice in the chapter. The head of the monastery was the prior, who presided in chapter and governed the affairs of the house. There were occasions when the prior and the bishop as titular abbot were at variance concerning their respective rights and possessions. For more than a century there was continual dissension between the two parties at the cathedral-priory of Durham. In the year 1197 Bishop Philip of Poitou, whose abbatial authority was contested by the monks, excommunicated the prior, cut off the supplies of food and water from the monastery, and broke down the ovens, and when the prior was about to celebrate mass the bishop's men broke into the cathedral and seized the altar linen, whereupon an unseemly

---

[1] In 1109 the famous Benedictine abbey of S. Etheldreda, Ely, was made the seat of a bishop, and the house of Augustinian canons at Carlisle was raised to cathedral rank in 1133.

struggle took place in the choir. At length the dispute was settled, and to quote the monk-historian 'there was a great calm'. Until the early part of the fourteenth century, successive bishops of Durham were in a state of enmity with the convent on matters connected with the election of the prior and the right of visitation, contentions that were destructive of the spiritual life and morale of the brethren.

In course of time many of the greater abbeys in which the number of monks exceeded the accommodation sent out twelve brethren with a thirteenth as abbot to colonise daughter houses. Thus S. Albans founded no fewer than eight dependent houses, of which Tynemouth, Binham, and Hatfield Peveril were the most important. Tynemouth priory, *c.* 1090, was generously endowed by Robert de Mowbray, Earl of Northumberland, and became as wealthy as many abbeys, though in the fourteenth century it was reduced to such poverty by the Scottish wars and by costly hospitality that the monks could hardly find the means to live. A letter from a monk of S. Albans who had been exiled to Tynemouth priory is not without interest. 'Our house', he wrote, 'is confined to the top of a rock, surrounded by the sea on all sides but one. Day and night the waves break and roar, thick sea frets roll in wrapping everything in gloom. Dim eyes, hoarse voices, sore throats are the consequence. Spring and summer never come here. The north wind is always blowing, and it brings with it cold and snow or storms of wind. No ring-dove or nightingale is here, only grey birds whose screaming denotes a storm. See to it brother that you do not come to so comfortless a place.' Other dependencies of S. Albans were the nunneries of Sopwell and S. Mary de Pré.[1]

The monks of Durham thought otherwise of Finchale priory, one of the seven cells of the cathedral-priory. From the fourteenth century Finchale served as a holiday home for jaded brethren of the mother house, four at a time being allowed to spend three weeks there, during which they were relieved from the rigid observance of the canonical hours.

S. Mary's abbey, York, had seven dependencies and from Norman times the priories of Great Malvern, Hurley, and Sudbury were cells of Westminster abbey. A number of Benedictine priories were subject to foreign abbeys. Shrewsbury was colonised by monks from S. Martin Séez *c.* 1083, S. Neot's was a daughter house of Bec, and Hatfield Broadoak was a cell of S. Melaine, Rennes.

---

[1] S. Albans was originally a house of Benedictine monks and nuns, until in 1140 the convent established a priory at Sopwell for the nuns; and *c.* 1325 the hospital for leprous women at S. Mary de Pré was converted into a dependent priory of S. Albans.

By the end of the eleventh century the number of religious houses in England had risen to about a hundred and thirty, of which forty-five were independent abbeys, twenty-nine were cells of parent monasteries, forty-five were alien priories (p. 51), in addition to many nunneries. All of these were Benedictine with the exception of five Cluniac houses which were subject to the reformed Benedictine abbey of Cluny in Burgundy (Chapter VIII). Within a century of its foundation in 910, Cluny was second only to Rome as a centre of ecclesiastical Christendom. Unlike Benedictine monasteries which were independent, those of the Cluniac Order were under the control of the abbot of Cluny. The chief English house of the Order was the priory of S. Pancras, Lewes.

In the twelfth century the structure of English monachism took on a more complex pattern. The predominance of the Benedictines was overthrown by the spread and popularity of other Orders that struck root on English soil, in particular the regular canons and the Cistercians, whose houses multiplied with rapidity in the first half of the century. The Canons Regular, of which there were three Orders, Augustinian, Premonstratensian, and Gilbertine (Chapter X), were communities of priests who were also monks observing a discipline and living a common life that in many respects resembled that of Benedictinism. Foremost were the Augustinian Canons who first appeared in England in 1100; by the end of the century there were nearly a hundred and forty of their establishments, mostly priories, in England and Wales. More rigorous and ascetic in their observances were the Canons Regular of Prémontré, whose earliest English foundation was in 1143; in all there were thirty-one Premonstratensian houses in this country. The priories of the Gilbertine Canons, the only religious Order founded in England, were served by canons and nuns and numbered twenty-seven.

The most important and far-reaching influence in English monachism of the twelfth century was that of the Cistercian Order, whose ideals aimed at a strict observance of the Benedictine Rule and a rigid simplicity and uniformity in their way of life (Chapter IX). The first house was Waverley in Surrey, founded in 1128, and this was followed in three or four years by Rievaulx and Fountains, whence brethren were sent forth to colonise. Within twenty-five years of their arrival, fifty Cistercian monasteries had come into being, most of them deriving from the three early foundations.

In contradistinction to the Benedictines and Cistercians as regards the principle of enclosure within monastic precincts, were the two military Orders, the Knights Templars and Knights Hospitallers, warrior-monks that formed the standing army of the

Crusaders (Chapter XI). The Templars established their first house in London, in the year 1128, and the Hospitallers in 1180. The patronage of the great S. Bernard in their early days ensured the Knightly Orders a popularity that was maintained for a century and a half.

Represented by only three priories in this country was the little-known Order of Grandmontines, an offshoot of the Benedictines that took its name from the parent house of Grandmont in the diocese of Limoges, founded in 1046. Of the English houses, which were situated in remote spots, two were confiscated as alien priories in the fifteenth century and the third, Grosmont, Yorkshire, became denizen.

Other lesser Orders of French origin, of which there were few English convents, were the Savigniacs, the Tironensians, and the Order of Fontevrault. The Order of Savigny was founded in 1112 at the abbey of that name near Mortmain in Normandy, which became the parent house of twenty-three monasteries. Furness abbey, c. 1127, was largely responsible for the spread of the Rule in England and Wales, where there were ten of their houses. The priories of the Order of Fontevrault, which came into being in 1110, were served by nuns and priests who followed the Benedictine Rule. The four English houses, of which the most famous was Nuneaton, c. 1155, were transferred to the Benedictines in the fifteenth century. The Order of Tiron was so-called from the parent house in the diocese of Chartres, where *tirones* (apprentices) settled to pursue their crafts in the service of the Church.[1] Of the five priories on this side of the Channel, S. Dogmell's in Pembroke was autonomous and was made an abbey in 1120, the other houses being dependencies of Tiron.

Of the many religious Orders in mediaeval England the Carthusians alone preserved the high ideals of their founder through the centuries, and kept to the literal interpretation of the Rule.[2] Their first settlement was at Witham in Somerset in 1181, but the eremitical life of the fathers and the severe austerity of the Rule failed to attract many votaries and of the eight other English Charterhouses seven were not founded until the fourteenth century (Chapter XII).

Remarkable is it that the monastic expansion of the twelfth

---

[1] A. H. Thompson, *English Monasteries*.
[2] Significant of the shortcomings of other Orders in this respect is the colloquy between Richard I and the Frenchman Fulke, just before the King set out on the Crusade in 1189. 'You have three daughters', said Fulke, 'pride, luxury, and avarice, and as long as they remain with you, you cannot expect favour from God', to which Richard replied, 'I have already given away those daughters in marriage—pride to the Templars, luxury to the Black monks, and avarice to the White.'

century continued unchecked during the internecine wars of Stephen and Matilda. In the nineteen years of the struggle, when 'men said openly that Christ slept, and his saints', no fewer than a hundred and nineteen religious houses were founded. This was the very period when the Cistercian Order was spreading far and wide throughout the land; and in the reign of Stephen's successor, Henry II, another hundred and thirteen abbeys and priories were established. But by the end of the century the monastic impulse had spent itself, and afterwards few Benedictine or Cistercian houses were founded. The Augustinian canons continued to flourish, eighty of their priories being founded after the year 1175.

The decline in monachism was furthered by the arrival of the Mendicant friars, notably of the Franciscan and Dominican Orders (Chapter XIII). Missionaries in the true sense of the word, their aim was to minister to the poor, the outcast, and the sick in cities and populous places. Despite the difficulties they encountered on their first arrival in 1221, the Mendicants multiplied to such an extent that by the middle of the thirteenth century, the Franciscans possessed forty-nine friaries in London, York, Bristol, and elsewhere; and they enjoyed the patronage of royalty, nobles, and wealthy merchants. In no country was the influence of the Mendicant Orders more powerful in the thirteenth century than in England, and it remained so with little diminution until the Suppression.

Early in the thirteenth century a Papal decree was issued to effect some control over Benedictine monasteries, which unlike the Cluniac and Cistercian establishments were subject to no central and governing authority. Bishops held the right to conduct visitations of all the Benedictine houses, with a few exceptions, in their respective dioceses;[1] their inquiries being directed to the discipline and the internal affairs of the convents. A form of corporate control came into being in the year 1215, when the Fourth Lateran Council under Pope Innocent III decreed that in every Benedictine province or kingdom a chapter of abbots should be held every three years in some conveniently situated monastery. Inexperienced in the methods of conducting such chapters, they

---

[1] The English exceptions were S. Augustine's Canterbury, Evesham, Westminster, Bury S. Edmunds, and S. Albans. Exemption was a favour granted by the Pope, and the first house to be so honoured was S. Albans in 1155 by Adrian IV (Nicholas Breakspear), as a token of his affection for the house where he had wished to be professed. Eight years later at the Council of Tours, S. Albans was acknowledged to be the premier Benedictine abbey of England, a status that was contested by the monks of Westminster. In the councils of the Church, the abbot of S. Albans took precedence over all other English abbots.

were advised to co-opt two Cistercian abbots of the neighbourhood to advise them in matters of procedure, for 'the Cistercians have long been accustomed to holding such chapters'. In association with two Benedictine abbots the two Cistercians were to preside at the first chapter, and thereafter four Benedictines were elected, their resolutions being binding on all. For a long period the north and south provinces of England held their chapters independently, but in 1336 they were united to form one national assembly that generally met at Northampton. Two abbots were chosen annually by the chapter to conduct visitations of Benedictine houses. In 1279 the General Chapter held at Abingdon decided that all the houses of the Order within the province of Canterbury should pay a yearly tax equal to one-eightieth of their revenue for the maintenance of a hostel at Oxford, where brethren of those houses should be fittingly lodged and boarded for the purpose of study at the University. Before the levy was imposed, the convent of S. Peter, Gloucester, was given a site at Oxford for the proposed college founded by their benefactor, John Giffarde, Baron of Brimsfield. Primarily intended to accommodate thirteen monks, Gloucester Hall was thrown open to all Benedictine houses, each having to bear the cost of maintaining its own students. Before the end of the thirteenth century another college was founded at Oxford by the cathedral-priory of Durham.[1]

In the year 1257 a house of the Order of Bonshommes (*Boni Homines*) was founded at Ashridge in Buckinghamshire by Edmund, Duke of Cornwall, brother of Henry III. The brethren observed the Rule of the Augustinian Canons, and a century passed before the only other establishment of the Order, viz. Edington, Wiltshire, was founded. The church originally belonged to the nuns of Romsey, who in 1351 surrendered it to Bishop Edington of Winchester, who proposed converting it into a chantry college, and rebuilt it for that purpose. At the instance of the Black Prince, the foundation was transferred to the Order of Bonshommes, the nave being reserved to the parishioners. Both Ashridge and Edington were richly endowed by Prince Edward.

In the course of their existence, many of the monasteries came into possession of vast landed estates that had been purchased, bequeathed, or bestowed upon them as endowments, and the

---

[1] The bull *Summa Magistri*, issued in 1336, required that one in every twenty monks should reside at the University for the study of Holy Writ, theology, or canon law. In 1437 Archbishop Chicheley of Canterbury founded S. Bernard's college at Oxford for Cistercian monks. All the monastic colleges were suppressed at the Dissolution. Durham was refounded as Trinity college, Worcester college, Oxford, is the successor of Gloucester Hall, and S. John's occupies the site and part of the buildings of the college of S. Bernard.

alienation of such properties deprived the Crown or the feudal lord of the escheats, wardships, death dues, and services belonging to the lands. Accordingly the Statute of Mortmain was passed in 1279, which controlled the alienation of lands and rents in such wise that they should come into mortmain, 'for a dead hand [*mortua manus*] yieldeth no service'. Henceforward any alienations that took place without licence were forfeit to the Crown. Before a benefactor could bestow property upon a religious house, a commission was issued to the sheriff of the county directing him to summon a jury to determine whether the revenue of the Crown would suffer by the transfer. In after days the heads of monasteries were often required to produce their licences and substantiate their claim to the properties they held. The Statute was rigidly enforced when land became a common form of chantry endowment (p. 86).

Very few religious houses came into existence in the fourteenth century. Benefactions which in the past had been generously heaped on monastic establishments were now directed to some specific purpose such as the endowment of chantries (p. 86), or to the founding of colleges and schools. Adding acre to acre the larger houses had become wealthy in landed properties, in revenues issuing from leases and rents, as well as in worldly goods; and many of their abbots lived in a state of affluence that was far removed from the poverty enjoined by their Rule. The anonymous friar who wrote *Dives and Pauper*, c. 1400, spared no words in his condemnation of monastic avarice. 'They [the monks] show well that all their business is to spare, to purchase, to beg of lords and ladies and of other men lands and rent, gold and silver; not for help of the poor, but to maintain their pride and their lust fare. By such hypocrisy under the cover of poverty, they maintain their pride and their avarice and occupy greater lordships than do many dukes, earls and barons, to great hindering of the land and great disease of the poor people. . . . For goods of the religious should be more common than other men's goods, to help the land and the poor people. . . . It is a shame that an over-great abusion, that a man of religion shall ride with his tenth sum or with his twenty sum [i.e. with a train of ten or twenty people], on a horse of ten pound, in a saddle all gold-begone, and for poverty that he bindeth him to in his profession, as they say, he may not give an halfpenny for God's love, nor help his father or mother at need without asking leave of his sovereign.'

In 1312 the Order of Knights Templars, possessed of enormous riches but serving no sufficient purpose now that the Crusades were at an end, was abolished by Pope Clement V. Most of their

D

houses in this country were transferred to the Knights Hospitallers (p. 200).

The greatest calamity that befell the monasteries prior to the Dissolution was the pestilence known as the Black Death, 1349. This terrible scourge, the bubonic plague, came from the Far East by way of Constantinople and the Mediterranean ports, and towards the close of 1348 appeared in Dorset, whence it spread to all parts of the land. The population then numbered about four million, of which more than a third perished; and the principal monastic centres of the Benedictines, the Cistercians, and the Mendicants were visited with extreme severity. The abbot of Westminster and twenty-six monks, one half of the convent, were victims of the scourge; in the south walk of the abbey cloister is a large marble slab that covers the grave of the brethren. The register of the Cistercian monastery of Newenham, Devon, records that 'in the time of this mortality there died in this house 20 monks and 3 lay-brothers; and Walter the abbot and 2 monks only were left alive there after the sickness'. At S. Albans, abbot Mentmore, the prior, and forty-six of the convent perished, and at the Cistercian abbey of Meaux all but ten of the forty-two monks together with seven conversi were carried off. The nunneries suffered in the same way; at the House of the Grace of the Blessed Mary, Aldgate, twenty-seven of the minoresses died, besides a number of lay-servants. In some houses there were but two or three left, so that the offices in the choir were discontinued.

Bishop Edington of Winchester enjoined the monks of the cathedral-priory to assemble 'every Sunday and Wednesday all of you . . . in the choir of your monastery, say the seven penitential Psalms and the fifteen gradual Psalms on your knees humbly and devoutly; also on every Friday together with these Psalms, we direct that you chant the long Litany, instituted against pestilence of this kind by the Holy Fathers, through the market place of our city of Winchester, walking in procession together with the clergy and people of the city'.

After the terrible plague the monastic houses were never again what they had been. A Franciscan annalist attributed the decay of fervour in his Order to the frightful mortality of the Black Death. 'The masters of regular discipline', he wrote, 'and the seniors of experience being carried off, the rigours of discipline being relaxed, could not be renewed by the youths received without the necessary training to fill the depopulated houses.' The religious never recovered from the effects of the calamity; conversi no longer formed part of the personnel of Cistercian abbeys, and like other great landowners, the monasteries were forced to cut up their large farms that had hitherto been managed by bailiffs, into smaller ones that could be let out on short leases. For there were no longer labourers to till the soil, and wages soared to un-heard-of heights despite the Statute of Labourers that was passed to regulate them.

Further outbreaks of the plague in 1361 and 1368 rendered the plight of the monasteries more desperate; so much so, that many of the convents, reduced to small numbers of brethren, appealed to Pope Urban V for faculties to admit to the priesthood monks who were below the canonical age.

In the year 1410 a Bill was brought before Parliament providing that the temporal lands that had been bequeathed to the Church should be alienated to the Crown, a measure that aroused alarm and opposition amongst the religious Orders, who 'determined to assaie all waies to put by and overthrow this bill'. The opening scene in Shakespeare's *Henry V* is in part a discussion between the Archbishop of Canterbury and the Bishop of Ely, concerning the Bill which

> 'Was like, and had indeed against us pass'd,
> But that the scambling and unquiet time
> Did push it out of further question.'

The year 1414 witnessed the end of all the alien priories in England, mainly houses that were dependencies of Cluny, La Charité-sur-Loire, and S. Martin des Champs in Paris; and the Benedictine priories that were cells of parent houses in Normandy and Anjou. Many of the alien cells, priories only in name, were not conventual but were merely manors and granges owned by some foreign abbey and occupied by two or three monks who collected the rents and revenues of the properties. The priors of alien houses were always foreigners appointed by the head of the parent abbey, to whom they were required to make an annual payment in recognition of their dependence.

The status of alien priories first became the concern of the Crown in 1295, when Edward I was forced into a war with France to recover Guienne from King Philip. The existence of foreign houses on English soil being regarded as a menace to the safety of the realm, their temporalities were seized by the Crown, and restrictions were imposed upon the members of the convents. Foreign monks dwelling within thirteen miles of the coast were ordered to be removed and sent to a place at least twenty miles distant.[1] In some cases alien priories secured exemption from Crown control by undertaking to withold the dues payable to

[1] Rose Graham. *Journal of the British Archaeological Association*, 1948.

their parent houses, and by the annual payment of a heavy fine. The outbreak of the Hundred Years War with France in 1337 placed them again in a precarious position; for Edward III gave orders to the sheriffs 'to seize the priories and benefices, their goods and chattels, i.e. horses and animals, money, jewels, gold and silver vessels, and growing corn, saving reasonable maintenance for monks and servants', and the priors were summoned to appear before a council at Westminster. Victims as they were to severe restrictions and heavy taxation, many of the alien priories found the money to purchase charters of denization from the Crown. The Cluniac priory of Lewes, one of the most important of the Order in England, together with her six daughter houses, thus secured naturalisation in 1351, and thereafter only Englishmen were installed as superiors of those convents. In 1376 Parliament petitioned that the priors and brethren of all Cluniac establishments should be Englishmen, and that the Frenchmen should be compelled to return to their own country. In 1403 the large sum of £106 13s. 4d. was paid by the prior of Barnstaple to secure the denization of his house, a dependency of S. Martin des Champs, Paris.

A great part of the revenue of the alien priories seized by the Crown went to provide endowments for the six Carthusian houses established between 1343 and 1414. In the year 1399, only a few months after Mount Grace priory had been founded, Richard II gave the fathers the alien houses of Hinckley, Wareham, and Carisbrooke, as well as all the lands belonging to the priory of S. Mary de Lire, the parent house in Normandy. These properties were to be held by the convent of Mount Grace as long as war continued between England and France.

The end of all the remaining alien priories was not far distant. In 1414, the year after the accession of the warlike Henry V, an Act was passed by the Parliament at Leicester surrendering all alien houses and confiscating their property, the bulk of which was subsequently set aside for the endowment of religious houses and of colleges of royal foundation. In 1421 the Charterhouse of Mount Grace was further enriched by the possessions of three alien priories that had belonged to the abbeys of Savigny and Cherbourg in Normandy; and Wareham and Carisbrooke were finally made over to Sheen, another Carthusian establishment. The unworldly Henry VI endowed the royal collegiate foundations of S. George's Windsor, Eton, and King's College, Cambridge, with property derived from the suppression of alien priories.

Long before the end of the fifteenth century a large number of the smaller monasteries and nunneries had fallen into decay, and were reduced to the borderline of poverty; their inmates were few in number and were hard put to it to find the means to live. The first of the Tudors and the ecclesiastics who held high office in the Church deemed that the revenues of such houses, small though they might be, could be put to more useful purposes. But Papal sanction, the permission of the patron, and royal licence were essential preliminaries before a religious house could be suppressed and its revenues and properties appropriated. Bishop Alcock of Ely had little difficulty in acquiring the nunnery of S. Radegund, Cambridge, in order that he could found Jesus College, Cambridge. The house was not fulfilling its purpose, for there were but two inmates, against whom the Bishop trumped up a charge of immorality. Accordingly in 1497 Henry VII granted him licence 'to expel the prioress and nuns of S. Radegund . . . which had become reduced to poverty and decay by reason of the dissolute conduct and incontinence of the prioress and nuns on account of their vicinity to the University of Cambridge, so that they cannot maintain Divine service or hospitality or other works of mercy and pity according to their foundation, or support themselves which are two in number, one of whom is professed elsewhere, and the other an infant'. Similarly the poor nunneries of Higham and Bromhall were suppressed in 1524 to enrich S. John's college, Cambridge, that had been founded by Henry VII's mother, Margaret, Countess of Richmond. When Henry VII undertook the building of the magnificent Lady Chapel at Westminster abbey in 1502, he obtained Papal sanction to dissolve the small monastic houses of Mottisfont and Suffield, the revenues of which partly furnished the endowments of the royal chapel; and in 1509, the last year of his life, he appropriated the revenues of some small religious houses for the purpose of erecting a hospital at Bath.

Suppressions on a much larger scale authorised by a Papal bull were carried out by the Lord Chancellor in Henry VIII's reign. In the year 1519, after Wolsey had been created Cardinal Legate, Pope Leo X issued a bull empowering him to reform the monasteries of this country, and to this end the Cardinal summoned a General Chapter of the Benedictines to meet under his presidency at Westminster. The measures he advocated to restore discipline were considered impracticable by the religious of all Orders, and the task proving to be beyond his powers Wolsey and his high-handed agents, John Allen and Thomas Cromwell, who were not above accepting bribes, undertook the visitation of certain monasteries, for the sole purpose of suppressing them and seizing their properties for the endowment of the Cardinal's colleges at Oxford and Ipswich. Empowered by a Papal bull of 1524, Wolsey set to work dissolving no fewer than twenty-two monasteries and three nunneries, houses in which the number of inmates was fewer than twelve. The manner in which the doomed houses were suppressed is described in Hall's *Chronicle* (1809). The Cardinal's commissioners, he tells us, 'Suddenly entered the said houses and put out the religious, took all their goods and movables, and scarcely gave to the poor wretches anything, except it were to the heads of the houses'. By this means the Augustinian priory of S. Frideswide, Oxford, was transformed into Cardinal College, the endowment of which issued from the suppression of twelve other Augustinian establishments, six Benedictine priories, three Benedictine nunneries, two Cluniac priories, and the Premonstratensian abbey of Bayham. The fall of these houses, wrote Fuller, 'made all the forest of religious foundations in England to shake, just fearing that the King would fell the oaks, when the Cardinal began to cut the underwood'. Certainly the experience gained by Thomas Cromwell in effecting Wolsey's seizures served him in good stead when as the King's Vicar-General a dozen and more years later he organised the general Dissolution of the monasteries.

III. *The Cloistral and Conventual Buildings*

~~~~~~

The Monastic Precinct—Areas enclosed by the Walls—Great Gate-houses—Some Notable Examples—Battlemented Gateways—Benedictine Influence in Planning—Water Supply and Drainage—Wibert's System at Canterbury—Conduits and Springs—Varying Dimensions of the Monastic Cloister—The Normal Lay-out of Conventual Buildings—The Cloister-walks—The Scriptorium—Carrels at Durham—Book-recesses and Libraries—Doorways from the Cloister to the Church—Western Walk for Novices—The Weekly Maundy in the South Walk—The Eastern Cloistral Range—Chapter Houses and their Varying Forms—The Vestibule—Polygonal Chapter Houses—The Vestry and Slype—The Sub-dorter and Locutorium—Day-stairs to the Dorter—The Calefactorium or Warming House—Arrangement of Beds in the Dorter—The Night-stairs to the Transept—The Norman Dorter at Canterbury—The Fourteenth-century Dorter at Durham—The Necessarium or Rere-Dorter —The Monks' Frater—Lavatoria at Durham and Gloucester—Towel Cupboards—Seating of the Brethren in the Frater—The Abbot's Table at S. Albans—The Reader's Pulpit—Kitchen and other Offices—The Cellarium and Outer Parlour—The Farmery and its Buildings—Minutio—Arrangement of the Beds in the Farmery Hall—The Flesh-frater or Misericord—The Abbot's Lodging—Cheyney Gates, Westminster Abbey —Guest Houses—The Provision for Persons of Various Degrees—Hospitia at Christ Church, Canterbury—The Almonry—Buildings in the Outer Court—Minor Changes in the Arrangement of Cloistral Buildings in the Later Middle Ages.

~~~~~~

THE MONASTIC PRECINCT, within which the church and the conventual buildings were situated, was generally shut off from the outside world by walls in which was the great gatehouse. Where there were no walls the boundary was marked by a ditch. In the larger monasteries there were two or more gatehouses, and often an outer court in which stood the workshops, stables, and offices where outside labour was employed. The area enclosed by the walls varied considerably. At Battle abbey, where some 700 feet of the walls remain on the north, the precinct was twenty acres in extent; at S. Augustine's, Canterbury, thirty; and at Westminster a little less than forty. The Cistercian abbey of Tintern covered twenty-seven acres, that of Furness sixty-three acres, and at Fountains the outer walls enclosed an area of ninety acres.

Several noble examples of monastic gatehouses of the Norman and the Gothic periods have been preserved, often large and imposing structures two or more stories in height. Those of the twelfth and thirteenth centuries such as Bury S. Edmunds and Gloucester had a single wide and lofty archway, that was used alike by mounted and foot passengers and by wheeled traffic; but later the main archway was flanked by a smaller doorway for those on foot, as at S. Albans and Battle. On one side of the great archway, which was generally roofed with a stone vault, was the lodging for the gate-keeper, and the chambers on the upper floors were put to various purposes. Often there were a chapel, a prison, a lodging for a corrodian or for a visitor arriving at a late hour. A notable gate-house of the twelfth century is that at Bury S. Edmunds, a massive building of four stories with bold pilasters at the angles, that, but for the large windows on each floor, might well be a Norman keep. Of the same period was the gatehouse of S. Augustine's, Bristol, though it was practically rebuilt in the sixteenth century; and that at Peterborough is also a Norman building, though faced with a front of the Decorated period. A beautiful specimen of Decorated Gothic is the northern gatehouse at Bury S. Edmunds that gave entrance to the outer court, and retains a façade adorned with arcadings and niches for figure sculpture (Pl. I).

In the fourteenth century the abbots of the greater monasteries, assuming the state of baronial magnates, obtained licences to crenellate their walls and gatehouses. A battlemented gatehouse was in the nature of a defensive work, for aggressive townspeople as well as wandering bands of marauders were a menace to the peace and security of the convent. Further, the fronts of the gate-houses were enriched with the heraldic shields of founders and benefactors. Above the wide arch of the ruined gatehouse of Kirkham priory are still to be seen the arms of the Scrope, de Roos, and Espec families. Larger and more lofty gatehouses appeared in the same century, as for instance the Ely Porta, c. 1396, and that at S. Albans, built c. 1365, the sole remaining one of the four that once opened into the precinct (Pl. III). The latter is a three-storied building with turreted stairways to the upper floors, and below ground level are dungeons wherein the law-breakers of the town, over which the abbot had civil jurisdiction, were imprisoned after trial. Eighteen of the rioters who stormed the abbey during Wat Tyler's rebellion in 1381 passed their last days in these dungeons. Other gatehouses of the fourteenth century include those of Battle and Worksop. The first-named, dating from 1338, is about thirty feet square and has an octagonal turret at each angle, and the front of Worksop gatehouse, which is two stories in height, is divided by stout buttresses into a wide central portion containing the archway, and a wing on either side (Pl. II).

The gatehouse of Thornton abbey is *par excellence* the greatest of all in this country, a fortified house rather than the entrance to a monastery. It is built of brick and was begun after the licence to crenellate was granted in 1382. The outer façade has turrets at the angles and two intermediately; the intervening walls are without windows but are faced with tall tabernacled niches, the three above the archway containing figures representing the Coronation of the Virgin. The inner face of the gatehouse presents the aspect of a fortress, with four large turrets rising from the ground to the parapet. In the two floors above the archway are several apartments that served as the abbot's house (Pl. IV).

Two of the last gatehouses to be erected were those at Christ Church, Canterbury, and S. Osyth's, Essex, both excellent examples of Perpendicular Gothic. Prior Goldstone's gatehouse at Canterbury, the main entrance to the precinct, dating from 1517, is a lofty three-storied structure with octagonal stairway turrets at the angles. Above the archway is a row of heraldic shields newly coloured and another band with angel supporters runs beneath the windows of the top stage. Of an entirely different character is the battlemented gatehouse of flint and stone at S. Osyth's priory, commenced *c.* 1525. Exceptional are the massive polygonal towers at the angles; and the whole surface of the building is faced with flushwork, a common form of wall enrichment in East Anglia.

The most important building within the precinct of a religious house was the church, the very centre of monastic life, for nothing was allowed to interfere with the many services that took place in the choir and the celebration of masses at the High Altar. The general planning of the church, and the arrangements and furniture of the interior are dealt with at length in a later chapter.

Being a self-contained community, the inmates of a monastery needed living and sleeping apartments, a great hall where they dined in common, a kitchen, and other domestic offices. The obedientiaries who were responsible for the internal administration, for clothing and feeding the brethren, and supplying their material wants, had their own storage departments and offices.

The Benedictine monks from Normandy who settled in this

country after the Conquest brought with them a perfected plan for the conventual buildings, the main features of which were never departed from. With the exception of the houses of the Carthusians, the Gilbertine canons, and the Mendicants, the arrangement of the buildings within the precincts of English monasteries followed closely that of the Benedictine establishments, the layout being determined by the requirements of the Rule. Necessarily there were variations occasioned by the exigencies of the site, and in Cistercian houses by their peculiar constitution (p. 157). The disposition of the conventual buildings at the Cluniac priory of Wenlock, at the Augustinian priory of Repton, and at the Premonstratensian abbey of Halesowen show a close approximation to the normal Benedictine method of planning.

'In choosing the site of a monastery, the first consideration was the water supply. The domestic needs of the house, the mill and the sanitary arrangements all depended on this, and the whole disposition of the buildings was regulated by the relative positions of water and site.'[1] In their methods for ensuring an adequate water supply and effective drainage, mediaeval monasteries were far in advance of the outer world. An elaborate system for the supply and distribution of water was inaugurated at Christ Church, Canterbury, by prior Wibert, 1151-67. Two contemporary drawings inserted in a Great Psalter, now preserved at Trinity College, Cambridge, depict the Norman buildings of the priory in a sort of bird's-eye view, and show the course of the water from its source to the City wall. A document of Edward II's time records that prior Wibert 'caused to be made the conduits of water in all the offices within the court of the priory, and that water taketh its source about a mile out of the City, which wholly under the ground by pipes of lead he caused to come into the church'. From springs situated in the 'North Holmes' the water was conveyed by a pipe to a circular conduit-house and then to the City wall, passing in succession five settling tanks. An aqueduct crossed an orchard belonging to S. Gregory's priory, whose brethren were allowed to use a cock in the Christ Church main that was carried across the City moat and entered the precinct at the north-east corner of the Green Court (Fig. 2). From there the water passed underground to the water tower in the small cloister, and thence to the kitchen of the monks' infirmary and to the lavatorium in the main cloister. From the water tower it was conveyed through the domestic offices, the kitchen and scullery, and across the Green Court to the brewhouse and bakehouse on the north, afterwards turning westwards to a laver beneath the porch of the

[1] W. St John Hope, *Journal of the Derbyshire Archaeological Society*, VI.

guest-house or Aula nova. In all these places the water was drawn from stand-pipes. The disposal of waste water was planned on as elaborate a scale; after passing beneath the monks' necessarium, the great drain was carried under the Green Court and emptied into the City ditch. In the fifteenth century alterations and improvements were effected in the drainage, but the system was never superseded and remains in part today.

To serve the domestic and sanitary requirements of Beaulieu abbey, water was brought by an underground conduit from a spring a mile distant, and the water supply at Tintern abbey derived from a spring to the south of the precinct, whence it was conveyed in lead pipes to the various offices. The great drain there discharged the waste into the Wye on the north. To the west of the abbey church of Rievaulx was a conduit-house from which pipes distributed water that came from springs in the hillside; and at Westminster water was conveyed in lead pipes to the abbey from springs at the southern end of the Serpentine in the convent's manor of Hyde, now Hyde Park.

The main buildings for the housing of the monks were the apartments ranged round the cloister, a square or rectangular enclosure or garth, surrounded by four covered walks that afforded easy access from one apartment to another. The size of the cloister depended upon the wealth and importance of the foundation, and the number of monks it was intended to house. At Christ Church, Canterbury, the cloister measured 144 feet square, and slightly larger were those of Durham, Ely, and Gloucester; at Fountains the cloister was 125 feet square, at Byland 145, at Bury S. Edmunds 157, and at Glastonbury, unusually large, 221 feet. On a smaller scale were those at Tintern, 110 feet; at Castle Acre 100, at Barking nunnery 99, at Lacock nunnery 90, and at Tynemouth priory, 82 feet by 79. The average width of the cloister walks was 11 or 12 feet.

The cloister was the centre of the monks' daily life. Within the covered walks the brethren studied, wrote, and copied manuscripts, when they were not reciting the sacred offices in the church or engaged on duties assigned them by the abbot or one of the obedientiaries.

In order to secure the maximum light and warmth, the closter was usually built to the south of the nave of the monastic church, which at the same time afforded protection from the cold north winds to those monks whose duties lay in one or other of the cloister walks (Figs. 1, 17). There were exceptions. Owing to the restricted nature of the site, the cloister at Rochester stood to the south of the choir, and that at Waltham north of the choir. To simplify the discharge of drainage into the Wye at Tintern, the cloistral buildings were planned north of the nave (Fig. 16), a position they also occupied at Canterbury, Gloucester, and Chester, where they would be remote from the noise and bustle of the City.

The cloister walls bounding the garth were opened up in Norman times with arcades of small semi-circular arches carried by slender shafts standing on dwarf walls; but in the Gothic centuries, the walks were more adequately lighted by traceried windows. The four alleys were covered with lean-to roofs, and after the Norman period were invariably vaulted in stone. The lierne vaults in the cloister walks at Canterbury are notable for the 811 carved bosses which display the heraldic arms of benefactors and of persons and places associated with Christ Church priory. No less remarkable are the hundreds of carved bosses in the fourteenth-century cloister walks at Norwich.

The walk adjoining the church was set aside as the scriptorium and place for reading and study, and sometimes was enclosed by timber draught-excluding screens at each end; and the floor or pavement was strewn with straw or hay as a creature-comfort for studious monks. The north walk at Durham was fitted up with thirty small cubicles, or *carrels*, each with its own desk and door. 'In every windowe were iij pewes or carrels, where every one of the old monks had his carrell, severall by himselfe, that when they had dynd, they dyd resorte to that place of [the] cloister, and there studyd upon there books, every one in his carrell, all the after nonne unto evensong tyme. This was there exercise every daie. All there pewes . . . were all fynely wainscotted and very close, all but the forepart which had carved wourke that gave light in at there carrell doures of wainscot. And in every carrell was a desk to lye there books on.'[1]

The carrels at Gloucester were of a more permanent form. In the lower part of the cloister-windows next the church (Pl. V) are still to be seen ten arched recesses, each of which was divided into two little studies. The books and manuscripts were kept in wooden presses that usually stood against the inner wall of the cloister-walk. Often there was a book-recess in the west wall of the transept. The *Observances of Barnwell* advised that 'the press in which the books were kept should be lined with wood, so that the damp of the walls may not moisten or stain the books . . . and should be divided by sundry shelves on which the books may be ranged so as to be separated from one another'. In course of time when monastic libraries increased in size, special chambers were built

[1] *Rites of Durham.*

for the purpose. At Tintern, Beaulieu, Fountains, and other Cistercian houses the library occupied part of the vestry adjoining the transept (Figs 16, 17). The scriptorium at Norwich was probably the chamber over the north walk of the cloister, and the library of the Franciscan priory of Christ Church, London, was a long apartment that extended over one of the cloister-walks. At the cathedral-priory of Worcester, the library, mentioned in the archives of 1377, was housed in a chamber above the south aisle of the nave. In the fourteenth century the monks of S. Albans built a separate scriptorium and library, although the position is not known.

The rule of silence being strictly enforced in the scriptorium as in the cloister, the *Customary of Cluny* ordained that if a monk-scribe wished the attendant to bring him a Christian work or manuscript he moved his hand as if turning the leaves of a book; but if a pagan author was required, he scratched his ear in the manner of a dog, because 'unbelievers may well be compared with dogs'.[1]

In the days when every book was the work of a laborious scribe and was not easily replaceable, the monastic librarian took every precaution against loss. In the Constitutions of Archbishop Lanfranc instructions were issued concerning the use of the library at Christ Church, Canterbury: 'On Monday before the first Sunday in Lent, before the brethren come into the chapter house, the librarian shall have a carpet laid down and all the books got together upon it, except those which a year previously had been assigned for reading. These the brethren are to bring with them when they come to the chapter house, each with his book in his hand. . . . As each brother hears his name pronounced he is to give back the book that has been entrusted to him, and he whose conscience accuses him of not having read the book through he had received, he is to fall on his face, confess his fault and entreat forgiveness. . . . The librarian shall then make a fresh distribution of the books, namely a different volume for each brother for his reading.'[2] Amongst the Cottonian MSS. in the British Museum is a catalogue of books at Christ Church, Canterbury, of the time of prior Eastrey, 1284–1331, in which are enumerated 1,831 volumes dealing with theology, canon law, history, and the classics. It is not known where this collection was housed. In earlier days the slype between the north transept and the chapter house at Canterbury (Fig. 2) was furnished with book presses, but the space there was necessarily limited, and before the middle of the fifteenth century a separate apartment, or *bibliotheca*, was built over the prior's

[1] Martène, *De Antiq. Monach. Ritibus.*
[2] Woodruff and Danks, *Memorials of Canterbury Cathedral.*

chapel on the south side of the little or farmery cloister. The book presses were arranged at right angles to the walls, eight on either side with desks and benches for the readers. Of the same period was the bibliotheca at Titchfield abbey, in which there were four presses each with two shelves marked alphabetically to indicate the subject classification.

At the eastern end of the north walk of the cloister was the main entrance to the church from the conventual buildings, and at the western end of the same walk was a doorway opening into the nave and used for processional purposes. At S. Augustine's, Bristol, and at Canterbury the chief cloistral doorway opened into the transept. Built into the wall on either side of the doorway at Canterbury is an elbow-seat, that was used by the 'spies of the cloister' appointed by the prior to maintain discipline in the cloister-walks.

The west walk was appropriated to the novices, of whom there were usually six or more, and who received their training under the supervision of one of the senior monks. At Durham 'there was a fair stall of wainscot, where the novices did sit and learn, and the master had a pretty stall adjoining . . . and there he sat and taught the novices both forenoon and afternoon, and no persons were allowed to trouble him; and a porter was appointed to keep the cloister door for that purpose'. Although the minimum age was supposed to be seventeen years, there is evidence that frequently boys of a more tender age, who naturally could not put all childish things behind them, were received as novices. Incised in the stone benches of the cloister-walks at Gloucester, Canterbury, and Norwich are traces of the game-boards cut by youthful novices for playing fox and geese, and nine-men's morris, in their idle moments. Any of the novices who showed marked ability as scholars might eventually be sent to one of the Benedictine colleges at Oxford. The audit Rolls of various houses have entries relating to the expenses of monks at the University.

The south walk of the cloister was the scene of the weekly Maundy or washing of the feet of the poor. After an early mass, the almoner went to the gate of the abbey and selected a number of the poor awaiting alms, whose feet were to be washed by the abbot or by a monk deputed by him. On the Great Maundy in Holy Week, it was the custom in most Benedictine houses to admit as many poor folk as there were brethren in the convent. Placed opposite each other in two rows in the south cloister-walk were the poor men on one side and the monks on the other. After certain appropriate psalms and collects had been recited, each brother crossed over to his poor man, knelt before him and washed his feet; then rising, he kissed him on the mouth and eyes, sat him down to meat and ministered to him. At Abingdon abbey there was a daily Maundy of three persons.

The eastern range of cloistral buildings, extending north or south of the transept as the case might be, was two stories in height, the chief apartments being the chapter house on the ground level, and the dorter or monks' dormitory on the whole of the upper floor. Every morning before High Mass the brethren assembled in the chapter house to transact the business of the convent and to deal with all matters concerning its administration (p. 109). In the chapter house too the bishop and his officers conducted their inquiries on the occasion of an episcopal visitation.

On plan the chapter house was generally an oblong apartment projecting eastwards from the cloistral buildings (Fig. 17).[1] The entrance doorway was in the middle of the west wall and was flanked by an open arch or a window on either side. Chapter houses of the Norman period were often planned with an apse at the east, as at Durham, Norwich, and Reading. The importance attached to the chapter house by the Normans is indicated by the ornate treatment of the interior walls. At S. Augustine's, Bristol, the internal walls are faced with tiers of arcading and interlaced lattice-work; and even more elaborate in its ruined state is the interior of the chapter house of Wenlock priory with its triple tiers of intersecting arches that spring from wall-shafts.

With a few exceptions chapter houses were roofed at the same level as the adjoining apartments on the ground floor of the eastern cloistral range, in order that the dorter above could be carried up to the transept. The chapter house at Christ Church, Canterbury (Pl. XIV), was built the full height of the eastern cloistral block, and the dorter therefore did not communicate directly with the church. At S. Werburgh's, Chester, and S. Augustine's, Bristol, the chapter house stands to the east and clear of the cloistral range and is entered by a vaulted vestibule beneath the dorter.

The English chapter house attained its most glorious expression in the unrivalled series of polygonal buildings, many of them triumphs of structural skill, erected in the thirteenth century. Standing free of the eastern cloistral range, the sides of polygonal chapter houses were opened up with large windows that flooded the interior with light, and a vestibule was essential (Fig. 1). Unfortunately only two monastic examples have survived, viz. Westminster and Cockersand. The prototype was the circular chapter house of the cathedral-priory of Worcester dating from c. 1120

---

[1] In Cistercian monasteries the chapter house was usually divided into three aisles (p. 160).

but made ten-sided in 1400. The polygonal form was adopted by the Cistercians at Margam and Abbey Dore (twelve-sided); by Augustinian canons at Carlisle and Bolton (octagonal), and at Bridlington (ten-sided); by the Premonstratensian canons at Cockersand (octagonal); and by the Benedictines at Evesham (ten-sided) and Westminster (octagonal), (Fig. 1).

At Battle, Furness, Waverley, Castle Acre, and a few other houses the chapter house immediately adjoined the south transept of the church; elsewhere, as at S. Albans and S. Mary's, York, a narrow space intervened that served as a *slype* or a vestry. The slype was a through passage from the east cloister-walk to the monks' cemetery that lay to the south of the choir. There the rank and file of the convent were laid to rest.

Before it became the practice to bury abbots and priors in their conventual church, they were interred in the east walk of the

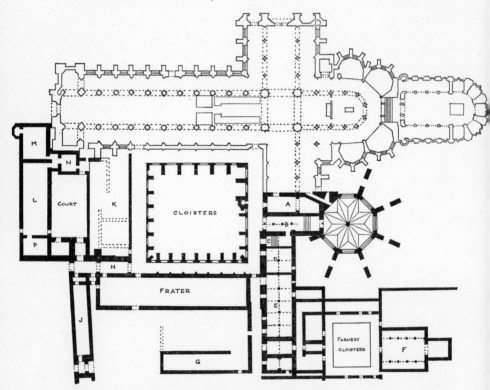

1. WESTMINSTER ABBEY

A. Revestry. B. Vestibule to chapter house. C. Day-stairs to dorter. D. Pyx chapel. E. Calefactorium. F. Farmery chapel. G. Prior's lodging. H. Outer parlour. J. Calbege. K. Old cellarium. L. Abbot's hall. M. Jerusalem chamber. N. Ante-room or Jericho parlour. P. Abbot's kitchen.

cloister or in the chapter house. Abbot Byrcheston of Westminster, who fell a victim to the Black Death in 1349, was buried in the east cloister-walk which he had just built, and beneath the wall-bench in the south walk close by are grave-slabs with effigies in low relief of three Norman abbots of Westminster. In the chapter house at Fountains nineteen abbots are recorded to have been buried, thirteen of whose gravestones are still to be seen.

In most Cistercian abbeys, e.g. Beaulieu and Tintern (Fig. 16), the space between the chapter house and the transept served a double purpose, the eastern half being utilised as a vestry, and the western part cut off by a wall serving as the library. This was the original arrangement at Fountains, but subsequently the chamber was converted into a slype. The long narrow chamber in the same relative position at Canterbury in which were kept the book presses of the priory, was reconditioned and converted into a chapel for the chantry of Archbishop Warham in 1506. It was entered from the transept by a small doorway, now blocked up, in the transept wall. The present chapel of S. Faith opening from the south transept in Westminster abbey (Fig. 1) was the *revestry*, where copes and vestments were kept hanging on 'cranes of wood'. The altar at the east end, the dedication of which is original, was set up from the first.

On the other side of the chapter house the eastern range, two stories in height, extended some distance to the south (or north) beyond the cloister. The ground floor or sub-dorter was divided into two aisles by a central range of columns and was vaulted throughout. Usually it was seven or eight bays in length, that at Furness of fourteen bays being abnormally long. A notable survival of the eleventh century is the seven-bayed sub-dorter of Westminster abbey.[1] The bay adjoining the chapter house on the side remote from the transept was the monks' parlour or *locutorium*, where conversation was permitted at stated hours, silence being enjoined in other parts of the house; and close by was a stone stairway known as the day-stairs, by which the brethren reached the dorter in the day time. At Westminster the day-stairs now lead to the library. Those at Chester are constructed in the thickness of the wall dividing the sub-dorter from the east cloister-walk at its northern end. The long flight of steps thus runs parallel to the walk. A similar arrangement obtains at Lacock abbey, where the stairs are within the wall dividing the sacristy from the east cloister-walk, but unlike those at Chester they adjoin the conven-

---

[1] Two bays walled off at the northern end were the treasury or the chapel of the Pyx (Fig. 1) so named from the pyx or chest in which were kept standard specimens of the gold and silver coinage. Against the east wall the original stone altar remains *in situ*.

E

tual church (Fig. 41). In the earliest Cistercian abbeys the day-stairs occupied the normal position in the middle of the sub-dorter, but later they were built at the south-east angle of the cloister and parallel with the dorter, as at Furness and Tintern. In other houses this was a passage in alignment with the east walk of the cloister.

The rest of the sub-dorter was divided by a partition wall into a common room for the professed monks and a day-room for the novices. The common room was termed the *calefactorium* or warm-ing-house, the only place where a fire was allowed other than the kitchen. Heat was provided by a brazier of charcoal. At Rievaulx the common room originally occupied the northern half of the sub-dorter and had fireplaces in the east and west walls, but later, when the calefactorium was transferred to the southern range, the apartment was probably made over to the novices. Once a year the calefactorium at Durham (Pl. XIX) was the scene of a monas-tic feast. 'Within this house did the master thereof keep his *O Sapientia* once a year, namely between Martinmas and Christ-mas, a solemn banquet that the prior and convent did use at that time of the year only, when their banquet was of figs and raisins, cakes and ale; and thereof no superfluity or excess, but a scholasti-cal and moderate congratulation amongst themselves.'

The whole of the upper floor of the eastern cloistral range was the monks' dorter. The Rule of monastic life enjoined that the brethren should all sleep in the common dormitory, which origin-ally was open from end to end, the beds being ranged against the wall, as in a hospital ward. In course of time, when the Rule re-laxed, the abbot dwelt apart, and to afford the monks greater privacy, the dorter was subdivided by wooden partitions into a number of cubicles on each side, with a passage down the middle. In the dorter at Durham every cubicle was fitted with a desk beneath a window so that during the afternoon rest-period, a monk could read or study without disturbance. There is no evidence that this was general in other houses. At the transept end of the dorter was a doorway that opened on to a flight of stairs in the transept, known as the night-stairs. When roused in the middle of the night for the first office of the day in the choir, the brethren could thus enter the church without having to descend to the cloister, a great advantage in the winter months. At Hexham priory the stone night-stairs built against the west wall of the south transept are in a perfect state of preservation (Pl. VIII), as also are those in the north transept at Tintern (Fig. 16). At West-minster abbey a bridge spanning the west end of the revestry formerly led to the night-stairs, a spiral structure of timber no

longer existing. The night-doorway in the end wall of the south
transept is hidden by the Argyle monument. The night-stairs at
S. Augustine's, Bristol (Pl. IX), are in the thickness of the end wall
of the south transept, and at Hayles abbey in the western wall of
the south transept (Fig. 22).

Of special interest was the early Norman dorter of Christ
Church, Canterbury, a vast building adjoining the chapter house
on the north (Fig. 2). From north to south it measured 148 feet
and was 78 feet wide. A massive wall pierced by twelve arches[1]
divided it longitudinally into two apartments and supported a
double roof; the sub-vault of each half was divided into three
aisles which were vaulted throughout. As the chapter house intervened between the dorter and the transept there were no night-
stairs, and for the night offices in the choir the monks had to pass
from the dorter along a gallery of the farmery cloister to a doorway in the choir transept. At Gloucester the dorter and its sub-
vault were planned at right angles to the east cloister-walk. The
dorter at Durham extends over the whole of the building on the
west side of the cloister. In Norman times it occupied the normal
position in the eastern block, and was transferred to the west in
1398. The sub-dorter, that is divided into two aisles by an arcade
of circular columns and is roofed with ribbed vaulting, is in a fairly
perfect condition. The most northerly bay, walled off from the
common room, was used as a muniment room and treasury. The
lofty and spacious dorter above is 194 feet in length and is now
entered by a stone stairway that replaced the day-stairs used by
the monks. The sub-prior whose duty it was to maintain discipline
had a chamber by the door, and his office was 'to go before mydnyght and after mydnyght to every monncke's chamber and to
caule at his chamber door upon him by his name, to see that none
of them should be lacking or stolen furth, to goe about any kind of
vice or nawghtyness'.

Attached to the dorter, generally at right angles or near the
southern end, was a long narrow building, two stories in height,
the upper floor of which was the *necessarium* or rere-dorter. Within
was a row of wooden seats separated by partitions, and the drain
enclosed by the wall was flushed by running water. At Castle
Acre, Westminster, and Kirkham, the rere-dorter extended across
the end of the dorter; at Fountains (Fig. 17) and Rievaulx it projected from the south-east, and at Furness, where two rows of seats
backed a central wall, the rere-dorter stood parallel to the eastern
cloistral range. The Norman necessarium at Canterbury had a
frontage of 155 feet. It was planned at right angles to the dorter at

[1] In the plan (after Willis) only ten bays are shown.

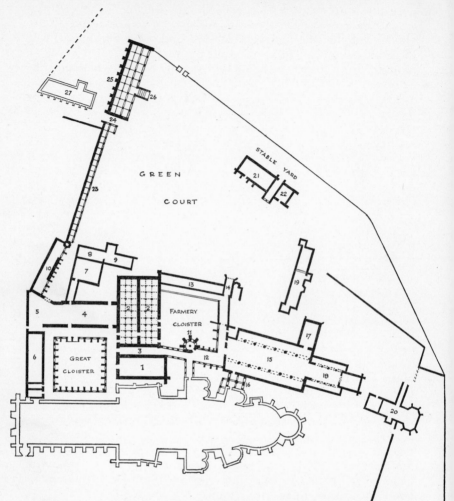

2. CHRIST CHURCH PRIORY, CANTERBURY

1. Chapter house. 2. Sub-dorter. 3. Passage to farmery. 4. Frater. 5. Buttery.
6. Cellarium. 7. Kitchen. 8. Guest chamber. 9. Larder. 10 Cellarer's hall.
11. Water-tower. 12. Sub-vault of prior's chapel. 13 Rere-dorter. 14. Prior's
gateway. 15. Farmery hall. 16 Treasury. 17. Table hall or flesh-frater. 18.
Farmery chapel. 19. Prior's lodging. 20. Meister Omers. 21. Bakehouse and
brewhouse. 22. Granary 23. Pentise. 24. Court Gate. 25. Aula nova. 26. Norman
staircase. 27. Almonry chapel.

the north-east corner and contained fifty-five seats. In the undercroft a series of thin arches spanned the great drain from end to end,
each supporting a wooden partition that divided the seating above.

In line with the east cloister-walk was usually a passage that led to the outer court of the monastery, or to the farmery, the abbot's lodging, the barns and stables, and other buildings. Over the archway of the 'dark entry', as the passage is called at Westminster, is the blocked-up window of a chamber from which the sub-prior kept a watchful eye on the monks as they passed to and fro.

The southern block of cloistral buildings consisted mainly of the monks' refectory, or *frater*, which except in Cistercian abbeys ran parallel to the church. In some instances it was raised upon a vaulted cellar in which provisions were stored, as at Rievaulx and Easby. On plan it was a rectangular hall, entered from the south walk of the cloister by a doorway near the western end. Near the doorway was the *lavatorium*, at which the brethren washed their hands before and after meals. Often it consisted of a tank with water cocks set within a wall recess in the south or west walk. At Durham and Wenlock the lavatorium was an octagonal building projecting into the garth from the south walk. That at Durham is described in the *Rites* as 'a fair laver or conduitt for the monks to wash their hands and faces at, being made in form round, covered with lead and all of marble save the outermost walls. Within . . . the laver of marble having many little conduits or spouts of brass', and above was 'a faire dove-cotte both fine and costly'. On either side of the entrance to the frater at Durham were cupboards or almeries in which the monks kept their towels 'to drie there hands on when they went to dine. All the fore part of the almeries was thorowgh carved worke, for to give ayre to the towels'. The lavatorium at Gloucester is the best-preserved example in the country (Pl. VII). It is 47 feet long and projects into the garth some 8 feet. Entered from the cloister by eight tall arches, it is lighted by two-light windows in the outer wall. Within is a broad flat shelf on which stood the leaden cistern with a row of taps, and in front a hollow trough in which the monks washed. The little structure is roofed with fan vaulting. In the wall opposite the lavatorium is an almery or recess where the towels were kept. The monks of Christ Church, Canterbury, had two lavatoria; one for use in the day time projected into the cloister garth between three buttresses of the north walk (Fig. 2), and a second, where the brethren performed their ablutions on their way from the dorter to the choir for matins, was in the upper story of the circular conduit or water-tower off the south alley of the farmery cloister (Fig. 2). The tank is described in an Account Roll of the treasurer as 'lavertorium electri juxta vetus dormitorium' (the brazen laver near the old dormitory), and is said to have weighed no less than 710 lb. Formerly a conduit house stood in the middle of the cloister garth at Sherborne abbey. It was a hexagonal structure with traceried openings on five sides, the sixth being the entrance, and in 1560 it was removed to its present site in Cheap St, Sherborne.

More generally the lavatorium was placed in a wall recess near the door of the frater. In the Cistercian abbeys of Rievaulx, Tintern, and Fountains it extended each side of the door; elsewhere it was constructed in the wall of the western cloister-walk, as at Norwich, Kirkham, and Worcester.

The western end of the frater was often screened off to make a passage to the kitchen and larder. The arrangement of the tables was similar to that in the college halls of our universities. On a dais at the east end was the high table for the abbot and the obedientiaries, the other tables running lengthwise in the body of the frater, the novices being seated near the door. In the frater at S. Albans there was 'an ascent of fifteen steps to the abbot's table, to which the monks brought up the service in plate, and staying at every fifth step, which was a landing place . . . they sung a short hymn. The abbot usually sat alone in the middle of the table; and when any nobleman or ambassador, or stranger of eminent quality came thither, they sat at his table, towards the ends thereof. After the monks had waited awhile on the abbot, they sat down at two other tables, placed along the sides of the hall, and had their services brought in by the novices, who when the monks had dined, sat down to their own dinners.'[1]

On the wall above the abbot's table was a painting of the Rood, the remains of which are yet visible in the frater of Cleeve abbey, Somerset. In the same position at Worcester was a sculptured reredos painted and gilded, representing Christ in the act of benediction with the four Evangelists.

Corbelled out from the south wall of the frater near the high table was the reader's puplit, from which a homily or a portion of a devotional work was read during meals by one of the convent. The pulpit, which was built of stone, was entered by a stairway constructed in the thickness of the wall, as in the perfect examples still to be seen at Chester (Pl. XV) and Beaulieu (Pl. XVI). Traces of others remain in many ruined abbeys, e.g. Tintern and Fountains (Pl. XVII).

At meal times the brethren were summoned to the frater by a bell, and after they had washed their hands at the lavatorium, they entered the frater in double file. When they were seated at table, the prior or the senior monk struck the *skilla* or gong on the high table, and after grace had been sung the reader began his lection.

[1] F. Grose, *Antiquities of England and Wales.*

Towards the end of the Middle Ages when the number of monks had declined in many houses, the frater was used only on great occasions and on Feast days. At Westminster, Durham, and Easby, a solar or loft over a chamber at the south-west end of the frater was used as a dining hall; that at Westminster is spoken of in a post-Reformation document as 'the chamber called the misericorde'.

The kitchen, together with the pantry, the larder, and scullery, was necessarily connected with the frater, but except in Cistercian monasteries these offices were not entered directly from the cloister-walk, but stood at the rear of the frater to the south-west, lest the smell of cooking should reach the church. Preserved in its entirety is the great fourteenth-century kitchen at Durham, a detached building at the south-west of the frater, with which it was connected by a covered passage. It is a massive square structure with fireplaces in the angles, above which arches support intricate vaulting, and it is crowned with an octagonal louvre for ventilation and light. Of a similar type is the kitchen at Glastonbury, and there were others at Christ Church, Canterbury, and Ely.

The two-storied building on the west side of the cloister was the *cellarium*, the great cellar of the monastery, that was divided into a number of store-rooms where were kept the goods and commodities needed for the maintenance of the brethren. Between the cellarium and the church was a passage known as the outer parlour, where contact was made with the outer world. There a monk might be visited by his kinsfolk, and there the obedientiaries received merchants who came 'to utter their wares', and other layfolk concerned with the business of the convent. The outer parlour at Westminster is a vaulted passage that continues westwards from the south cloister-walk, and at Lacock it ran about mid-way through the western range (Fig. 41).

In the wall near the portal of the cellarium that opens into the north cloister-walk at Canterbury is an octagonal aperture about 16 inches in diameter which was part of a contrivance called the *rota*, by means of which a monk could obtain a cup of beer from the cellarer on a hot summer afternoon. The cup was placed in a vertical cylinder that turned on its axis and delivered the refresher to the thirsty monk without his being seen by the cellarer.

When it became the practice for the head of a religious house to live apart from the monks, the upper floor of the cellarium in the smaller houses was made the abbot's lodging or camera, with a hall for his guests. In Cistercian abbeys the western block was the house of the conversi, and the cellarer's stores were kept in the undercroft of the frater (p. 161).

Of the many buildings beyond the cloister, the most important was the farmery or *infirmitorium*, where accommodation was provided for sick brethren and for the aged and infirm who could no longer comply with the exact observance of the Rule nor lead the normal daily life in the convent. A Cistercian monk who had been professed for fifty years earned the privilege of permanent residence in the farmery, and there he passed his last days in comparative comfort. In addition to the sick and aged, the inmates of the farmery included those monks who had subjected themselves to the periodical blood-letting or *minutio*, and there they enjoyed a welcome break from the monotony of the daily routine and were allowed a flesh diet. Blood-letting was common in all mediaeval monasteries, and was a weekly or fortnightly occurrence, each monk taking his turn every two or three months. All religious houses except those of the Carthusian Order had a farmery, and in Cistercian abbeys a separate farmery was built for the lay-brothers or conversi.

The farmery buildings were generally situated beyond the eastern cloistral range, notable exceptions being Furness and Haughmond, where they lay to the south; Durham, where they were at the west; and Easby, where owing to the slope of the land at the east the farmery was built to the north of the church and was reached by a long passage from the north transept. In the smaller abbeys the farmery consisted of a rectangular hall in which the beds were placed in rows as in the dorter, a chapel, a misericord or flesh-frater, a kitchen and a rere-dorter. The farmery hall at Furness, where the beds stood in wall-recesses, had an upper floor and at the east end was a chapel flanked on the north by the buttery; farther east lay the octagonal kitchen.

From the twelfth century the farmery hall in the greater abbeys was planned with side-aisles for the beds. Embedded in the walls of post-Reformation houses at Westminster and Ely are the circular and octagonal columns of the Norman arcades that divided the nave of the farmery hall from its aisles. The hall at Ely, 105 feet long and 44 feet wide, was planned in nine bays, and the octagonal columns are set with their angles foremost, a peculiarity they share with those at Westminster. In the farmery hall at Canterbury are five Norman columns and arches of the south arcade, though nothing remains of the clerestory wall they carried. At the east end the hall opens into the ruined chapel, four bays in length with north and south aisles and a small rectangular chancel. These buildings stood to the east of the small farmery cloister of the same period (Fig. 2). The six arches that remain in the eastern walk of the cloister must be the earliest piece of cloister-arcading in the country (Pl. XXII). The Norman farmery at Westminster, entered from a passage through the sub-dorter, was similarly planned, with an aisled hall and a chapel dedicated to S. Katherine. 'Hither', wrote Dean Stanley, 'came the processions of the convent to see the sick brethren, and were greeted by a blazing fire in the hall, and long rows of candles in the chapel. Here, although not only here, were conducted the constant bleedings of the monks. Here the invalids were soothed by music. Here, in the chapel, the young monks were privately whipped. Here also lived the seven *sympecta*, the elder monks who after they had passed fifty years in the monastic profession were exempted from all the ordinary regulations, were never told anything unpleasant, and themselves took the liberty of examining and censuring everything.' In the fourteenth century, however, the hall was taken down and in its place was built a small square cloister surrounded by a number of chambers. A diminutive cloister stands at the west end of the remains of the thirteenth-century farmery hall at Gloucester.

In the fifteenth century in order to make the farmery hall more comfortable, it became the custom to wall off portions of the aisles and divide them into separate rooms furnished with fireplaces. This was done at Canterbury, Ely, Peterborough, Fountains, and Kirkstall. There is evidence that the aisles of the farmery hall at Fountains, which measured 170 feet in length and was 70 feet wide, were partitioned into a dozen or more rooms during the rule of abbot Huby, 1494–1526.

The flesh-frater, or misericord, where the inmates took their meals occupied no fixed position in the farmery buildings, though it was generally within easy access of the hall. At Tintern and Canterbury (Fig. 2), it projected from the north aisle of the hall at the east end, and at Kirkham it adjoined the kitchen at the southern end of the hall.

The farmery buildings at Lewes were marked by a peculiarity that derived from the parent house of Cluny. There, the hall lay to the east of the dorter range, but the chapel, which was detached, stood at the south-east of the priory church. Like that at Cluny the chapel had a square chancel flanked on either side by an apsidal chapel.

The farmery was an essential in a mediaeval nunnery as it was in a house of monks. At Barking abbey the farmery buildings lay to the north of the choir and were approached by a passage from the eastern cloistral range. The hall, a rectangular apartment, stood north and south, the chapel projecting from the south-eastern angle. The nuns' misericord was an apartment at right angles to the west wall of the hall.

In theory the regular observance of the monastic Rule was based upon the principle of a common life, so that even the head of the house, abbot or prior, should live with his brethren, dine with them in the frater and have his bed in the dorter. In early days this was the general custom, but before the end of the twelfth century abbots took to living in their own lodging, or *camera*, often on the upper floor of the cellarium. Although they retained their own bed in the dorter, they rarely slept there, and as time went on the abbot's lodging developed into a separate house with hall, solar, bedroom, kitchen and other apartments, attached to which was a staff of lay servants. That the father of the house should dwell apart and draw upon the resources of the convent for the maintenance of his household was contrary to the monastic ideal, and the separation of incomes often gave rise to friction between the abbot and his flock. The site chosen for the lodging in the precinct varied considerably. At Battle it stood west of the monks' frater; at S. Albans it was on the north side of a courtyard adjoining the guest-house west of the cellarium; at S. Bartholomew's, Smithfield, the lodging of the prior stood in an inner court south of the choir. The present deanery at Gloucester, west of the cloister from which it is separated by a small court, was formerly the abbot's lodging, consisting of a hall, a solar, a chapel, and living apartments, together with chambers for the abbot's guests. Early in the fourteenth century a new and magnificent house for the abbot of Gloucester was erected some distance north of the cloister, where the bishop's palace now stands, and the old lodging which still retains many Norman features was assigned to the prior. Late in the fifteenth century the prior of Castle Acre extended his lodging at the northern end of the cellarium, by adding a two-storied building at the west that remains *in situ*. The lower floor was a cellar, above was the solar, and adjoining it over the outer parlour was the prior's chapel.

A site in proximity to the farmery was favoured by many abbots, probably on account of the quietude. The prior's lodging at Wenlock, a long two-storied building, was situated north of the farmery cloister. In a fine state of preservation to-day, it is noteworthy for the range of thirty or more closely-set Perpendicular windows that light each floor (Pl. XVIII). At Kirkham the prior's lodging adjoined the farmery cloister, a similar position being chosen for the abbot's house at Rievaulx and Haughmond. Most unusual was the arrangement at Easby, where the abbot's lodging was incorporated in the extensive farmery buildings north of the church. The hall, solar, and other chambers occupied the upper floor and the kitchen was common to both.

The abbot's lodging at Westminster abbey, which narrowly escaped destruction by enemy bombing during the Second World War, affords a good example of a mediaeval house of the fourteenth century, its apartments being grouped about a quadrangular courtyard (Fig. 1). With the exception of the parlour on the north side, Cheyney Gates, as the house was called, was built by abbot Litlington between 1360 and 1386. The earlier lodging of the abbot, above the outer parlour of the abbey, was quite inadequate to the needs of Litlington, upon whom fell the burden of entertaining the overflow of guests from the king's palace on great occasions. As a mitred abbot he was a person of some consequence, and a commodious self-contained house befitting his dignity was long overdue. Cheyney Gates was built west of the old cellarium which was absorbed by the new building. The cellarer's quarters were removed to a long two-storied building spoken of as the *calbege*, on the east side of what is now Dean's Yard. On the west of the courtyard of Cheyney Gates are the hall and kitchen with Jerusalem chamber at the northern end. The ante-room known as Jericho parlour, with chambers above and below, was added by abbot Islip early in the sixteenth century.[1] The prior of Westminster had his own lodging south of the frater where Ashburnum House now stands.

In the monastic cathedrals such as Ely, Winchester, and Canterbury, the prior being the head of the establishment had a lodging as splendid and commodious as the head of other houses. At Ely it was situated south of the cloistral buildings, and the hall divided into two aisles and vaulted stands on the east side of a courtyard. Adjoining it on the south is the beautiful prior's chapel over an undercroft, a valuable specimen of Decorated Gothic erected by prior Crauden, 1321–41. Opposite is the prior's guesthouse, to which was attached a square kitchen, and the apartments west of the courtyard were also used for entertaining guests.

An essential part of every large abbey was the *hospitium* or guest-house, which was situated where it would not disturb the daily routine of monastic life, 'so that the guests may not disquiet the brethren by their untimely arrivals'. In the smaller houses the guest-chamber adjoined the abbot's camera on the upper floor of the cellarium. Even in Cistercian monasteries, which were never

---

[1] On the accession of Henry VII, Elizabeth Woodville, the widowed Queen of Edward IV, obtained a forty years' lease of Cheyney Gates, but it is doubtful whether she ever took possession, for she was soon afterwards sent to Bermondsey abbey where she died in 1492. Both Litlington and Islip died in the abbot's manor house at Neate by the riverside in Chelsea, a favourite country resort of the abbots of Westminster. When the abbey was refounded as a collegiate church, Cheyney Gates became the deanery, and the great hall is used today as the dining hall of Westminster school.

open houses to all and sundry, provision was made for receiving visitors and wayfarers, whose stay was generally limited to two days and nights, as in the houses of other Orders. At Fountains there were two guest-houses some distance west of the cloistral buildings, the earlier dating from 1148. They were both two stories in height, the upper floors being dormitories. The hospitium at Durham 'on the west side towards the water' is described in the *Rites* as 'a goodly brave place much like unto the body of a church, with very fair pillars supporting it on either side, and in the midst of the hall a most large range for the fire. The chambers and lodgings belonging to it were sweetly kept, and so richly furnished that they were not unpleasant to lie in, especially one called the King's chamber, deserving that name, in that the King might very well have lain in it, for the princely linen thereof.'

As there were guests of all classes who could not be ushered indiscriminately into one lodging, the greater monasteries had several places for their reception and entertainment. Honoured and distinguished guests were accommodated in the abbot's or prior's house; the less important were assigned to the cellarer's hospitium, and near the gatehouse of the monastery was a lodging for poor strangers. Hospitality was planned on a generous scale at Christ Church, Canterbury, whither vast crowds flocked to visit the shrine of S. Thomas. Normally there was ample room for all pilgrims in the hospitate buildings within the precinct, but on the occasion of the Jubilee of the Translation the convent was hard put to it to find accommodation for everyone, and large numbers were foisted upon S. Augustine's abbey and other religious houses in the neighbourhood. The most ancient hospitium at Christ Church, a great part of which is still standing, is the Aula nova, the great hall next the Court Gate, an attractive Norman building raised on a vaulted undercroft (Fig. 2). On its eastern side is an external stairway with Norman columns and arcadings that leads to the hall above. Originally the Aula nova was 154 feet long and was used as a dormitory and refectory for the poorer guests. Royalty and persons of distinction were entertained by the prior in a house known as Meister Omers that stands to the east of the farmery hall (Fig. 2). The largest hostel in the precinct of Christ Church was that allotted to the cellarer, a three-storied building called Chillenden's Chambers, in the south-west corner of the Green Court and near the monks' kitchen. Extending from the Court Gate to this building was a covered way or pentise of timber dating c. 1394, parts of which are preserved in gardens on the site. Close by the Great Gatehouse in Mercery Lane was 'the Chequers of the Hope that every man doth know', a huge tenement with a large chamber known as 'the Dormitory with a hundred beds', that was used by those pilgrims for whom there was no room in the hospitia of the priory. It was owned by the convent and was repaired on a big scale by prior Chillenden early in the fifteenth century.

Outside the precincts of the greater abbeys and generally near the gatehouse was the almonry, where the dole of broken meat from the frater and the abbot's table was distributed to the needy poor in search of relief. The almonry at Westminster stood outside the precinct wall on the west. The ancient buildings that constituted the almonry in Mint Yard beyond the Court Gate at Canterbury were demolished in 1859 to make room for the enlargement of King's School; in the fourteenth century a chapel, dedicated to S. Thomas and served by six priests, was erected in the almonry. At Evesham the almonry is all that remains of the conventual buildings of that great Benedictine abbey. It stood outside the western gatehouse and is partly half-timber in construction. The almoner's Rolls of Durham cathedral-priory for the fourteenth century afford evidence that a farmery for the sick poor was attached to the almonry, £5 6s. being expended annually on shoes and garments for the inmates.

In the outer court of a monastery were various buildings for providing and storing the commodities necessary for the support of a self-contained community. The smallest house had its granary, bakery and brewery, and in the larger abbeys were workshops, a mill, a laundry and stables for the horses of the abbot and his obedientiaries, who journeyed at times to distant farms, manors, and properties owned or leased by the convent. Very few outbuildings of this kind have survived. On the north side of the Green Court at Canterbury is a rectangular block of buildings, with a gateway projecting from the front that gives entrance to what was the stable yard with servants' offices beyond. In a Norman drawing of the priory at Trinity College, Cambridge, the western portion of the long building on the site is labelled *bracinum* (brewhouse), and the eastern *pistrinum* (bakehouse). Next to these is the granary. Under the heading 'New Buildings and Repairs' in a document amongst the muniments at Canterbury appear the entries: '1285-90. Great barn for hay; 1301. New stable for the treasurer, with upper chamber and small granary; 1303. New granary in the brewhouse or malthouse; 1317. For the new brewhouse and granary, with chimney etc.' And in prior Chillenden's list of 'Repairs in the Curia', c. 1400, mention is made of repairs to the brewhouse, a new tailor's shop, a new stable for the prior and a new barn for the prior's hay. Although greatly damaged by enemy bombing in 1942, these buildings have now been entirely restored.

Amongst the Harleian MSS. in the British Museum is a plan of Chester cathedral and monastic buildings as they were less than a century after the Suppression. On the plan is an area to the north-west of the cloister and about four times as large, that is marked 'the Abbey court'. The entrance to the Court is by a gatehouse on the western side, with the porter's lodge and the abbot's kitchen adjoining it on the south. A long building north of the gatehouse is named 'the great kill and drying floors'. Bounding the Court on the north is a range divided internally into the brewhouse, store-house, and bakehouse 'with two ovens'. The buildings on the eastern side consisted mainly of the cellarium, and the kitchen and pantry attached to the monks' frater. The southern range of two stories was apparently the hall and apartments of the abbot's camera, the lower floors being rooms, cellars, and 'the serving men's hall'.

The planning and arrangement of the conventual buildings of all Orders, particularly the apartments grouped about the cloister, remained much the same from post-Conquest days to the Suppression. Gatehouses were enlarged or rebuilt, hospitia were added to as circumstances required, and separate lodgings erected for the abbot or the prior; but the chapter house, dorter, frater, and cellarium occupied a standard position throughout the cen-turies from the time of the earliest Norman abbeys such as Battle and Lewes. Minor variations that occurred were in general occa-sioned by the exigencies of the site. Excavations at Lewes have shown that unlike the generality of examples, the cloister was not square but oblong, measuring about 140 feet east to west and 100 feet north to south. Originally the cloister there was square, but in the middle of the twelfth century, owing to the increase in the number of monks, a larger cloister and a more commodious frater were needed. To tear down the old frater and rebuild it farther south would have been a costly undertaking. Instead, the cellarium and the adjoining walk of the cloister were moved westwards, and the frater was lengthened in that direction by about 40 feet.[1]

When the Cistercian abbey of Cleeve in Somerset was rebuilt in the fifteenth century, except for the frater which was planned on an east-to-west axis, the cellarium and the west cloister-walk, the arrangement of the buildings followed that of the twelfth century.

It is not without interest, however, that the traditional planning seems to have been abandoned when Bath abbey was reconstruc-ted in the early years of the sixteenth century. No provision was

[1] *Sussex Archaeological Collections*, Vol. XXXIV.

made for an eastern dorter-block attached to the south transept, and the abbey church 'was designed from the first as a free-standing building, except where the old cellarer's range abutted on to it'.[1]

[1] R. Gilyard-Beer, *Abbeys*, H.M.S.O.

IV. The Conventual Church

~~~~~~

A House for the High Altar—The Need for an increasing Number of Altars—General Lay-out of a Monastic Church—The Sanctuary and High Altar—The Pyx, Frontal, and Retable—Notable Reredoses—Sedilia—The Ritual Choir and Pulpitum—Choir Stalls and Misericords—Bishop's Throne in Cathedral-Priories—The Rood Screen—Choir-arm fenced with Lateral Screens—The Ritual Choir at Canterbury—Shrines—The Revestry or Sacristy—Henry III's Sacristy at Westminster—The Purposes of Transepts—Night-stairs—The Transept Galleries at Boxgrove Priory—The Nave for Processions and Altars—Rise of the Chantry Movement—Chantries in Monastic Churches—Forms and Positions of Chantry Chapels—The London Charterhouse and its Chantries—Parochial Rights in Monastic Churches—Relations between the Laity and the Brethren at Wymondham, Rochester, Dunster and Chester—Parish Churches attached to Monasteries—Others within Monastic Precincts—Detached Bell Towers.

~~~~~~

THE HEART OF the monastery was the church, wherein the brethren were under the obligation of performing perpetual celebration of the divine service, the Opus Dei, before the High Altar. Every duty and occupation of the monks was subordinated to the Opus Dei, the *raison d'être* of the whole establishment. In the choir of the conventual church they spent the greater part of their waking hours. The church was a house for the altar, and all through the centuries the utmost skill and ingenuity were exercised by the foremost masons of the age upon its design, construction, and embellishment.

To the west of the High Altar accommodation had to be provided for the brethren during the recitation of the masses and the canonical hours (p. 107). In addition, lesser altars were needed at which the monks who were in holy orders could sing the daily mass their office required. Until the early part of the fourteenth century the great body of monks were unordained but amongst them were a number of priests who ministered to their spiritual needs and celebrated masses in the church. In 1311, however, the Council of Vienne made it compulsory for all monks to take priestly orders to provide for the ever-increasing masses that were endowed on behalf of the many benefactors of their house; and henceforward more altars were required for soul-masses. At Westminster abbey it became the custom for a complimentary present of bread and wine to be given a monk after he had celebrated his first mass as an ordained priest. Further, provision had to be made for the procession that took place in the church on Sundays and festivals, and for shepherding crowds of pilgrims in those churches that possessed the shrine of a saint.

The largest monastic churches were those of the Benedictine cathedral-priories, all of which excepting Norwich and Worcester were the resort of pilgrims. In general the church was a cruciform building, consisting of an eastern choir-arm, north and south transepts and a long nave usually flanked by aisles. At the crossing rose a tower, and in the large churches there were twin towers at the western end.

In the sanctuary or presbytery that occupied three or four bays at the eastern end of the choir stood the High Altar, raised on one or more steps, and some distance to the west were the stalls for seating the monks during the various offices. The choir-arm was a chapel reserved exclusively for the brethren and was closed at the west by a solid screen. Between the two ranges of choir stalls was a raised lectern, from which the lessons were chanted, and there the precentor or his assistant conducted the singing. Situated about midway between the lectern and the High Altar was the matins altar for the first office of the day. The High Altar, that consisted of a monolith slab of stone or marble (*mensa*), was always covered with a cloth and draped with a frontal, the colour of which varied according to the seasons and festivals of the church;[1] and on either side were *ridels* or curtains hanging from metal rods that projected from the screen behind the Altar. Above the High Altar was a wooden tester or canopy, from which was suspended the pyx, a vessel containing the reserved Sacrament. At the back of High Altar was a painted retable or reredos, or more often a stone screen. Preserved at Westminster abbey is a painted retable of wood, 10 feet long and 3 feet in height, that was made for the High Altar of the reconstructed choir *c*. 1270, and was intended to resemble a piece of enamelled gold-work. It is faced with several panels painted with incidents from New Testament history,

[1] The frontal of the High Altar in Westminster abbey was a gold cloth embroidered with precious stones, and took three women nearly four years to make.

F

the central compartment having figures of Our Lord, the Virgin Mary, and S. John, and the field between the panels is filled with strips and pieces of glass to resemble enamels, the frame being inlaid with imitation gems. At Norwich cathedral is a painted reredos that may once have backed the High Altar.

In those churches where the shrine of a saint stood behind the High Altar (p. 131), a stone screen was erected with doors on either side of the Altar, by which monks could pass into the saint's chapel from the sanctuary. The Neville screen at Durham is a notable survival, though now shorn of all the images that once filled the niches. By far the most splendid mediaeval reredoses extant in this country are those of the High Altars in the monastic churches of S. Albans, Winchester, and Southwark. Rising the full height of the east wall of the sanctuary, they are designed in three tiers of tabernacled niches, originally peopled by figures of kings and saints resplendent in colour and gold, with a crucifix as the centre-piece. That at S. Albans was erected in 1484, and those at Winchester and Southwark date from the early years of the sixteenth century.

To the south of the High Altar were the sedilia or seats for the priest-celebrant and his assistants during the singing of portions of High Mass. Generally they were stone structures, with three or four seats surmounted by canopies or tabernacling, as at Gloucester (Pl. XXXI) and Chester. At Durham there are sedilia of four seats on each side of the sanctuary, and in the adjacent piers are small recesses or aumbries for 'the chalices, the basins and the cruets . . . that they did minister withal at the High Altar, with locks and keys for the said almeryes'. The sedilia at Selby abbey are of exactly the same design as those at Durham. On the backs of the wooden sedilia in Westminster abbey, dating *c.* 1308, are the remains of paintings of the founders of the abbey, Sebert and Edward Confessor, with other kings and saints, and on the inside are figures of Henry III and Edward I in fair state of preservation. In the canted bay of the apsidal choir at Tewkesbury (Pl. XXIII) are the mutilated remains of beautiful sedilia of the Decorated period, with richly carved foliage in the gabled canopies, formerly coloured and gilded. In the ruined presbytery of Furness abbey are sedilia of four seats set within canopied niches of the Perpendicular period. The undersides of the canopies are vaulted with ribs and bosses. There, as elsewhere, is also a niche for a piscina, a basin with a drain-hole for rinsing the chalices after mass.

In monastic churches of any size the ritual choir in which the stalls were set up intruded into the nave two or three bays west of the crossing, an arrangement that still obtains at S. Albans and

Westminster (Fig. 1). It was closed at the west by a deep screen known as the pulpitum, with a loft above from which the Epistle and Gospel were read on certain festivals. The stalls were arranged in two or more rows on either side of the choir, slightly raised one above another. The senior monks sat in the back rows and the juniors and novices in the front. The abbot occupied a return stall against the pulpitum on the south side of the doorway, and on the north side was the prior's stall. At the celebration of High Mass the abbot and prior moved to seats near the altar. Each of the monks' stalls was furnished with a tip-up seat or misericord and a broad arm-rest. On the underside of the seat was a projecting ledge, so that when the seat was turned up the occupant could assume a half-sitting position and yet remain on his feet, thereby complying with ancient discipline. The ledges of the misericords were usually carved with clumps of foliage or with sacred subjects, with animals or grotesque creatures, or with representations of the common activities of mediaeval life. The monastic churches of Gloucester, Ely, Winchester, and Norwich each have sixty or more mediaeval misericords. Choir stalls as permanent fixtures were not in general use until the fourteenth century. The fine series at Winchester, the earliest of their kind, date from c. 1308, and thenceforth taber-nacled canopies above the back stalls became an essential of stall-design in monastic and other large churches.

In the churches of cathedral-priories the throne of the bishop of the diocese was installed in the choir at the east end of the southern range of stalls. A notable example, unique in character, is the throne at Durham, built by Bishop Hatfield, 1345–81. With two seats on either side for the bishop's chaplains, the throne is raised on a gallery above a small chantry chapel containing the tomb of the prelate. The lofty tabernacling that surmounts the five seats is similar in design to the reredos of the High Altar and is of the same period.

Two bays to the west of the pulpitum was the rood screen, so called from the large Rood or crucifix suspended above, with attendant figures of S. Mary and S. John. The noble rood screen at S. Albans, erected 1363–5, spans the nave at a point three bays west of the crossing. It measures 43 feet long and 22 feet high, and in front of it was an altar dedicated to Our Lady, flanked by a processional doorway on each side. Although it is now divested of its statuary and colour, the screen remains a priceless relic of mediaeval monasticism.

Spanning the aisles and in line with the rood screen were screens of iron or timber to exclude all but the monks from the eastern arm of the church. The main doorway from the cloister being in the south aisle of the nave east of the screens, the brethren were able to enter the ritual choir without passing through the nave. Both the sanctuary and the ritual choir were fenced laterally by screens along their entire length, and were entered from the transepts by doors in the screens known as *ostia chori*.

The arrangement of the ritual choir in the nunnery church of Romsey was similar to that in monks' churches. The nuns' stalls intruded into the nave; in the second bay west of the crossing stood the pulpitum and a bay farther west was the rood screen. The church of Barking nunnery, where the nave was eleven bays in length, furnished another example.

In several conventual churches, however, the stalls were confined to the eastern arm, the pulpitum being placed beneath the eastern arch of the crossing, and the rood screen beneath the western, as at Durham, Canterbury, Tynemouth, and Crowland (Pl. XXVIII).[1] It could not have been otherwise at Canterbury, as the eastern arm is raised on a lofty crypt and the pavement level is several feet above the nave. There, the inordinate length of the choir-arm afforded ample space for the stalls at the western end. In an almost perfect state of preservation is the pulpitum at Canterbury, approached by a flight of steps in the crossing. Of unusual form was the rood screen that remained *in situ* at the east end of the nave until 1750. It consisted of a lofty grate of iron, through which people entering the church at the west could catch a glimpse of the shrine of S. Thomas reared high beyond the High Altar.

The acquisition of relics of the saints and the setting up of shrines to contain them brought great changes in the planning of monastic choirs (p. 131). Usually the shrine was erected in a chapel behind the High Altar, access to which was provided by continuing the aisles eastwards, thus forming an ambulatory that also led to the Lady Chapel at the extreme east (p. 132).

From early morn masses were sung at various altars in the monastic church, for which the celebrant-priests clad themselves in appropriate vestments in the revestry or robing-room. For convenience it was generally attached to the south side of the choir. That at Durham extended almost the entire length of the south aisle and within was an altar that was used for the training of mass-priests. A small chamber above the revestry at the western end was occupied every night by two monk-watchers. For no apparent

---

[1] At Christ Church priory, Hampshire, the pulpitum, which is nine feet deep and much restored, now stands at the entrance to the choir-arm; but when first erected in 1380 it spanned the first bay of the nave. At Tynemouth and Crowland the rood screens in their ruined state remain *in situ*.

reason it was demolished in 1802 but the entrance doorway is still to be seen in the aisle wall.

In the outer wall of the small sacristy off the south choir-aisle at S. Augustine's, Bristol, are three niches, one of which contains the hearth where the altar-breads were baked, and above is the flue. In one corner is a long narrow recess in which the abbot's crozier was kept. In addition to the revestry, now the chapel of S. Faith adjoining the south transept at Westminster, a large sacristy was built by Henry III *c.* 1250 in the angle of the north transept and the north aisle of the nave. It has long since disappeared but the foundations, unearthed in 1860, reveal that it was a narrow building parallel to the north aisle and extending to the transept. About 120 feet in length, it was separated from the aisle by a small courtyard. Excavations disclosed the remains of two stairways, showing that the sacristy was a two-storied building. It was entered by a doorway in the north aisle of the nave.

In Cistercian churches the sacristy usually occupied the eastern half of a narrow chamber adjoining the transept, as for instance at Netley, Tintern (Fig. 16), and Rievaulx.

The transepts of monastic churches served several purposes. Structurally they afforded abutment to the central tower on the north and the south. Deep transepts also provided space for lesser altars, especially where there were eastern aisles, each bay being fenced off with timber or stone screens to form chapels. The north transept at Westminster abbey (Fig. 1) has aisles to the east and west, the latter serving as a passage-way for pilgrims who entered the church to visit the shrine of the Confessor.

For the first office of the day, between midnight and 2 a.m., the monks made their way from the dorter to the choir by the night-stairs in the north or south transept (p. 66). In the daytime they used the doorway in the north-eastern angle of the cloister, which being east of the aisle-screen was safe from the intrusion of lay-folk. A unique feature marks the transepts of Boxgrove priory church, each having an upper floor or gallery open to the church and dating from the fifteenth century. The purpose of these galleries has never been satisfactorily explained. That in the north transept has a stone fireplace and a doorway that originally opened into the monks' dorter. It may be that in the winter months the brethren recited the early offices there, rather than descend to the chilly choir.

That part of the nave west of the rood screen was a vast vestibule to the choir, used for the processions that took place on Sundays and such festivals as Christmas, Easter, Whitsun, and Corpus Christi. In Cistercian churches the western part of the nave was the choir of the conversi (p. 157). For ritualistic purposes the only other use of the nave by the convent was to furnish room for altars, where there was no space elsewhere in the church. On the western face of six piers of the north nave arcade at S. Albans are still to be seen the painted reredoses of mediaeval altars, and in the *Rites of Durham* mention is made of five altars that stood in the nave of that mighty church.

In the greater monastic churches the need for a large number of altars became more urgent from the beginning of the fourteenth century for more than one reason. After the year 1311 all the religious were required to take Holy Orders after a probationary period. Each of them was then under the obligation of reciting a mass every morning before noon. In a monastery where there were more than a dozen brethren, the individual masses were not easy to arrange unless there were many minor altars in the church; and where the monks numbered thirty or more it was quite impracticable for all to fulfil their obligations unless there was a multiplicity of altars. Further, the rise of the chantry movement necessitated still more altars. The belief in the efficacy of intercessions on behalf of benefactors led to endowments for the recitation of specific masses for the good estate of the founder during his lifetime and for his soul after death. From the end of the thirteenth century the piety that had hitherto manifested itself in the founding of religious houses was directed to the more personal endowments known as chantries, bequests being made for the purpose of securing prayers for the testator after death. This cult of soul-masses was the motive underlying chantry endowments, and during the fourteenth century the movement established itself as the foremost manifestation of Christian belief in this country. Royalty, the nobility, abbots, ecclesiastics and wealthy merchants in their turn sought the spiritual and posthumous benefits that the endowment of soul-masses would confer upon them. Often the founder of a chantry stipulated the altar, dedicated to a particular saint, at which the masses should be celebrated. The dedications were innumerable; saints of the Gospels, apostles, evangelists, and martyrs; saints of the English Church such as S. Cuthbert, and founders of the monastic Orders such as S. Benedict.

The nature of the chantry depended largely upon the value of the endowment. Often a chantry was of limited duration, viz., for two or three years; a moderate endowment would ensure the singing of a soul-mass on the first, the third, the seventh and the thirtieth day after the death of the founder. Less costly was an obit, a mass that was recited on the anniversary of the death for a few years or in perpetuity. The endowment of a perpetual chantry was the privilege only of the wealthy, and often included the building of a special chapel that was reserved solely for masses on behalf of the founder and his family. In the Benedictine monasteries and cathedral-priories such as Westminster, Tewkesbury, and Winchester a great many chantries were founded, and there were a goodly number in the great Augustinian and Mendicant churches. As one might expect, they were less common in the churches of Cistercian abbeys and in those of the unworldly Carthusians.[1]

The vast majority of chantries in monastic and other churches were founded at existing altars; members of the royal family, bishops, abbots, and wealthy patrons often erected chapels during their lifetime for perpetual chantries in churches with which they were closely associated. These chapels vary considerably in form. The most splendid of all was Henry VII's chapel at Westminster, built as an eastern annexe to the royal abbey, and in a similar position is the Percy chapel at Tynemouth priory. A more common type took the form of an enclosure of stone screens, pierced with open traceried panels, usually rectangular on plan and built between two piers of a choir or nave arcade. A stately example is that of Prince Arthur, son of Henry VII, in the choir of Worcester cathedral. For chantry chapels of this type a favourite site was on the north or south side of the High Altar, as for example that of abbot Ramryge at St. Albans. The sanctuary at Tewkesbury abbey is encircled with chapels and tombs of noble benefactors (Fig. 13). In churches where there was a saint's chapel, preference was for a position near the shrine. Within a few feet of the shrine

---

[1] The complete isolation of the Carthusian fathers from the world and the exclusion of the laity from their precincts would seem to have precluded the founding of chantries in their churches, though the fathers were in a special degree responsible for masses for their benefactors. By his will dated 1371, Sir Walter Manny, one of the founders of the London Charterhouse, desired to be buried 'in the midst of the choir . . . but without any great pomp, and I will that my executors cause twenty masses to be said for my soul and that a tomb of alabaster with my image as a knight and my arms thereon should be made for me'. A Memorandum *Concerning the Chantries of the Charterhouse, London,* dated *c.* 1431, gives a list of the benefactors for whom the fathers were to celebrate masses, and the gifts they had made. 'The indented writings having been carefully examined, by which we and our successors are bound and held to certain definite chantries perpetually to be continued by our brethren-priests for certain of our great benefactors, who at their costs built the cells in this cloister . . . we have inserted them in this page as follows.' Amongst those enumerated are Adam Franceys, one-time Mayor, d. 1374, who gave 1,000 marks for the founding of five cells, and the more famous Mayor, Sir William Walworth, who did the same. Neither of them stipulated that masses should be sung for their souls, an omission that called for remark in the Memorandum. 'Neither of them by any writing has bound us, yet out of good conscience, those dwelling in the said cells which they built . . . are bound specially to pray for them as their founders.' The same conditions obtained at Mount Grace priory, Yorkshire, also Carthusian, the foundation charter of which enjoined that prayers should be offered up for the founders and post-mortem masses said for their souls.

of S. Swithun at Winchester were erected the chapels of Bishops Fox and Gardiner, and in the retrochoir some yards distant are the chapels of Cardinal Beaufort and Bishop Waynflete. In the nave of the cathedral is the noble chapel of Bishop William of Wykeham, who was largely responsible for transforming the Norman nave into the Perpendicular building now standing. Less costly was a chantry chapel built between a pair of deeply projecting buttresses of an aisle, the construction of which entailed little more than erecting an outer wall at the extremities of the buttresses and then covering the space with a roof or vault. A notable instance is Henry IV's chapel off the ambulatory of the saint's chapel at Canterbury. An altar was always set up in the chapel against the east wall, and invariably provision was made for the erection of the tomb of the founder in the middle of the chapel.[1]

In the churches of many Benedictine and Augustinian houses, the nave was used for parochial worship, the altar for the laity being set up against the rood screen, between the two processional doorways. The origin of this is in many instances obscure. If the site required for a monastery was in part occupied by a parish church which had to be swept away, the convent was under the obligation of providing facilities for parish worship, either by granting the laity the nave or an aisle of their church, or by building them a new church on another site. At a visitation of the cathedral-priory of Ely in 1315, complaint was made that the parochial altar was so close to the High Altar in the monastic choir, that the services often clashed; and the convent were enjoined to provide a church for the parishioners at a convenient distance from the choir. About the year 1355 a church dedicated to S. Cross was erected north of the nave of the monastic church, between the main and the western transepts. It was, however, taken down in the reign of Elizabeth I, and then the Lady Chapel of the conventual church was made over to the parishioners.

It has been estimated that in 119 Benedictine churches and in thirty-seven of the Augustinian canons, the nave or one of its aisles was parochial.[2] This accounts for the survival of a great many monastic naves at the Dissolution. By asserting their vested and traditional right, parishioners succeeded in saving the nave, but the choir and transepts for which they had no use were demolished (p. 257).

---

[1] The tomb of Henry IV is not in his little chapel, but stands on the north side of the shrine of S. Thomas; and the tomb of the Black Prince, d. 1376, is immediately opposite, though his chantry chapel is in the crypt of the cathedral.

[2] *Archaeological Journal*, Vols XLI, XLII, and XLIII.

XII. Chapter house, Valle Crucis Abbey.

XIII. Chapter house, Lacock Abbey.

XIV. Chapter house, Canterbury.

XV. Reader's pulpit in the frater, Chester.

XVI. The frater, Beaulieu Abbey, now the parish church.

XVII. Entrance to the stairway up to the reader's pulpit in the frater,
Fountains Abbey.

The existence of a parochial altar in a monastic church did not always make for harmonious relations between the lay-folk and the monks. There was serious trouble at Wymondham abbey in the fifteenth century concerning the bells. Those in the central tower were rung night and day for the religious offices of the monks, apparently to the annoyance of the parishioners, who wanted their own bells for other occasions. The quarrel only came to an end when the present tower at the west end of the church was built by the laity to hold the parish bells. The ringing of bells was the cause of an acrimonious dispute between the citizens of Bath and the brethren of the cathedral-priory. The prior forbade the parishioners to use their bells until after those of the abbey had been rung; and the quarrel was not settled until 1421, when as the result of an appeal to the Crown, the claim of the prior was upheld.

The church of the cathedral-priory of Rochester was parochial from Norman times, the laity using an altar dedicated to S. Nicholas that stood against the rood screen in the nave. In 1312, when alterations were taking place in the nave, an agreement was made by virtue of which the parishioners would relinquish all claim to an altar in the church if the convent built them a separate church outside. Until then they demanded free access to the nave by day and night. On Trinity Sunday 1327, 'the men of Rochester conspired to despoil the cathedral church under pretence of having access to the church, to minister the Reserved Sacrament to the sick, and being denied entry they broke the doors of the church, and throughout the night and until terce the next day besieged the monks.' The convent agreed 'to make for the said parishioners an oratory . . . beside the north door, with a door and window on the outer side of the said church, to place the Corpus Domini in, to minister to the sick during the night hours at all future times, with free entry and exit to the said oratory.'[1] A century passed before the parish fold had their own church of S. Nicholas, built by the monks 'in the cemetery commonly called Green Church Hawe', and dedicated on 18th December 1423.

Frequently monks and parishioners were at variance over their respective rights in a conventual church. The unusual position of the rood screen in Dunster church, Somerset, bears witness to such a dispute. For centuries the laity had worshipped at an altar in the nave of the church of the Benedictine priory, although their rights therein were ill-defined. As the result of a controversy in 1498 the matter in dispute was referred to the abbot of Glastonbury, who pronounced that the choir and transepts should be used solely by the monks, and the nave by the parishioners. The

---

[1] W. St John Hope, *Architectural History of Rochester Cathedral.*

laity had little to complain of, for the nave was more than half the total length of the church. Even so, they wanted a chancel as well as a nave, and to this end they set up the rood screen two bays west of the crossing and carried screens across the aisles. The nave was shut off from the crossing by screens and the monks similarly screened their choir and its aisles at the west, so that the transepts served as a no-man's land.

Parishioners of the Middle Ages seemed to be fully aware of their rights when a monastic building-scheme robbed them of their church. Chester furnishes a typical instance. In 1325–30 the monks of S. Werburgh abbey swept away the church of S. Oswald to make room for the spacious south transept of the abbey church. When it was finished the parishioners claimed it as their own, and made an entrance door in the west wall. The convent opposed the claim, and nothing would do but to build a church for parochial use near-by. The laity however re-asserted their right to use the transept in the fifteenth century, and it was partitioned off from the rest of the abbey church and served for lay-worship until 1880.

In many cases a parish church was attached to the fabric of a monastic church, an arrangement far less likely to cause friction between the laity and the religious. At S. Albans the church of S. Andrew flanked the great nave of the abbey church at the north-western end; at S. Mary Overie, Southwark, the parish church of S. Mary Magdalen stood in the angle of the south transept and the choir; at the nunnery church of Romsey, S. Lawrence church lay to the north of the nave, the north transept of the conventual church serving as the parochial chancel (Fig. 40).

A dispute between townsfolk and monks over their respective rights led to disastrous consequences at Sherborne abbey, the nave of which was parochial until the middle of the fourteenth century, when the church of All Hallows was built at the west end of the abbey church. In the year 1436 the parishioners were at variance with the convent concerning the parish font, which the monks refused to surrender for baptisms in All Hallows. Driven to desperation by their arrogance the vicar shot a fiery shaft into the thatched roof of the abbey church, and within a short time the greater part of the building was reduced to a smoking ruin.

When a parish church was a separate building within the precinct of a religious house, disputes were less likely to occur. The nuns of Barking abbey, within whose walls stood the church of S. Margaret, allowed the parishioners the use of the Curfew Gate-house for their bell-ringing until they added a western tower to their own church for that purpose. Only a few yards north of Westminster abbey stands the church of S. Margaret, a descendant of the parish chapel that was taken down when Edward the Confessor rebuilt the abbey church. Throughout the Middle Ages the almoner of the abbey was the rector of S. Margaret's, and when the chancel was rebuilt in 1517–18 the convent bore most of the cost.

In the churches of S. Lawrence and All Saints that stood within the confines of the great Benedictine abbey of Evesham, stone chantry chapels were built and endowed by abbot Lichfield, 1514–39, an indication of the happy relations that existed between himself and the lay-folk; and within the precinct walls of the equally famous abbey of Bury S. Edmund's were two churches for lay-worship. That dedicated to S. James was erected by the monks for the townspeople who had hitherto used the nave of the abbey church; and S. Mary's church was a gift of the sacrist of Bury.

Bells were being rung at all hours of the day and night in mediaeval monasteries to summon the brethren to the offices in the choir. As a rule the central tower of a church was unsuitable as a belfry, for swaying bells endangered the stability of a tower carried by more or less isolated piers at the crossing. Owing to unsound methods of construction, central towers were a constant source of anxiety and frequently collapsed without warning, particularly those of the Norman period. In the interests of safety therefore it was by no means uncommon for a detached bell-tower to be erected in the precinct. On the site of the present Middlesex Guildhall at Westminster once stood a belfry that formed part of Henry III's great reconstruction of the abbey. It was a massive stone tower, 75 feet square, supporting a timber bell-cage and surmounted by a lead-covered spire, and it was used as a belfry until the western towers were built (in part) early in the sixteenth century. At S. Augustine's abbey, Canterbury, a William Berne made a bequest of £9 in 1461 'towards the rebuilding of the bell tower of this monastery', and other sums were given for the 'new steeple in the churchyard'. There was an isolated tower at Romsey to the north of the nuns' church, taken down in 1625, and another at Tewkesbury in a similar position survived until 1817. The *clocherium* at Worcester, situated to the north-east of the choir and pulled down in 1647, was an octagonal structure with a timber spire that rose to a height of 210 feet.

The finest surviving example is the magnificent tower at Evesham, built in the early years of the sixteenth century at some distance north of the north transept of the abbey church.

V. Internal Administration
of a Monastery

IN ITS CONSTITUTION a mediaeval monastery consisted of an abbot and monks, and was described as *abbas et conventus*. The title abbas (father) expressed the paternal relation that existed between the head of the house and his brethren. Within the jurisdiction of the monastery his authority was supreme, although he was equally bound with the monks to observe the Rule of his Order. On all matters pertaining to the administration of the house he was the sole judge, and though he was enjoined to take counsel with the brethren in matters of importance, he had the final word. He was an absolute monarch, and his subjects, to whom he was not responsible for the management of the house, were on oath to obey implicitly all his dictates; he could not be called to account, except by an appeal to the Pope, the king, or the bishop of the diocese.

The Rule of S. Benedict ordained that as the abbot was 'considered to represent the person of Christ' due reverence was always to be paid him as to the Master himself. When he passed any of the monks in the cloister, they were to stand with heads bowed, and in the chapter house and frater they were not to sit until the abbot had taken his seat.

In the ten cathedral-priories, in houses that were dependencies of parent abbeys, and in most Augustinian establishments, the superior was the prior, whose authority in the domestic affairs of the convent was little inferior to that of an abbot. The bishop had his throne in the monastic cathedral, but was in no way concerned with the internal management of the priory, and any attempt on his part to over-ride the authority of the prior invariably led to strife.[1]

A prior who was the head of a dependent house held his office by the grace and favour of the parent house, and might be deprived at the will of the abbot; and the superior of an alien priory was similarly subject to the mother abbey across the Channel. The Augustinian priors on the other hand were abbots in all but name, and being independent they were free of external control, excepting episcopal visitation (p. 178).

The head of a religious house was formally elected by the brethren, who had perfect freedom of choice; they were not obliged to elect the senior officer, nor was their choice limited to one of their own convent. On an abbacy becoming vacant, the convent had to obtain leave of the king or of the patron of the house to proceed to the election of a new superior. Once the *congé d'élire* was granted, the monks assembled in chapter at an appointed time, and after certain formal preliminaries they decided the particular form the election should take. There were three methods; the most direct was by acclamation, employed only when the brethren were unanimous and when no doubt existed as to who should be elected. A

---

[1] The bishops of the monastic cathedrals were at a disadvantage compared with those of the secular cathedrals such as York and Exeter; for none of the monks of a cathedral-priory were clerks or lawyers in the service of the bishop, as were the canons of the secular chapters. From the thirteenth century some of the bishops of the cathedral-priories founded collegiate churches that were served by clerks of their own choosing. Between 1283 and 1293 Bishop Bek of Durham, who was constantly at loggerheads with the monks, converted three parish churches in his diocese into collegiate establishments, all of which were served by canons, and were in the nature of rival corporations to the monastic chapter of Durham.

second mode was *per viam scrutinii*, i.e. the recording of votes by all the professed monks; but probably the most common method was that known as *per compromissum*, i.e. the appointment of a small committee of four or five monks who should make the choice in the name of the whole assembly. The election was subject to confirmation by the king and the bishop of the diocese, or in case of exempt houses by the Pope,[1] all of whom had to be furnished with documentary proof that the election had been regular. The confirmation was followed shortly afterwards by the installation of the abbot-elect. On the day appointed for the ceremony, he was received at the door of the abbey church, barefooted, and singing the Te Deum the monks led him to the High Altar and there handed him the keys of the church. Then one by one they knelt before their new master and received from him the kiss of peace. The ceremony ended with the abbatial blessing of all the convent from the steps of the High Altar.

In the monastic cathedrals the prior owed his appointment to the bishop, although the brethren had some voice in the election of their superior. At Christ Church, Canterbury, it was customary for the archbishop to summon the whole convent to the chapter house for the purpose of recording their votes, after which he retired for consultation with his officers and subsequently returned to announce the name of the prior-elect in these words: 'In the name of the Lord and of His Most Glorious Mother, of the Holy Trinity, and of all the Saints, we nominate, appoint, and give you as prior the religious man, brother N, one of the monks of this church; and we enjoin you, in virtue of your holy rule, to give him obedience in things both spiritual and temporal.'[2] Then the ring of his office was placed on the prior's right hand and all went in procession to the choir where a solemn Te Deum was sung, after which the prior was installed in his seat on the north side of the choir.

In monasteries that were subject to episcopal jurisdiction and visitation, a newly-elected abbot had to make profession of canonical obedience to the bishop of the diocese. Amongst the muniments

---

[1] The abbots-elect of exempt houses had to journey to Rome to obtain Papal confirmation, an expedition that lasted several months and swallowed up large sums in travelling expenses and in Papal fees. On his accession to the abbacy of S. Augustine's, Canterbury, William Welde sent one of his monks to Rome to secure confirmation, but without success. The abbot was compelled to present himself in person and the fees then demanded amounted to more than £280, a very considerable sum. When he returned in 1389 the abbey had been without a head for more than two years. The abbot-elect of Westminster, John Estney, in 1474 was more fortunate, for by the payment of a fine of £30 to the Papal agent in London, he was excused the journey to Rome; and four years later he obtained an indulgence granting a similar privilege to his successors on their payment of a sum of 100 florins.

[2] Woodruff, and Danks, *Memorials of Canterbury Cathedral.*

at Canterbury cathedral are originals of some early 'professions' made by abbots of the adjacent abbey of S. Augustine. That of the first Norman abbot runs: 'I, Scotland, Abbot-elect of the Church of the blessed Apostles Peter and Paul and S. Augustine, do promise to the holy church of Canterbury and to the vicars thereof, canonical submission (*subjectio*).'[1]

The conferring of the mitre, ring, gloves, and sandals upon an abbot was an honour much coveted in the Middle Ages. Originally the insignia were regarded as a monopoly of bishops, but they came to be granted by the Pope to abbots who were important and sufficiently wealthy to pay for such an honour. The earliest instance was in 1063 when Pope Alexander II conferred the mitre upon abbot Egelsin of S. Augustine's, Canterbury. There were privileges attached to the status. A mitred abbot was exempt from episcopal visitation and control and was subject only to the Pope. Further, he possessed quasi-episcopal jurisdiction over a whole district. As a spiritual lord he was entitled to a seat in Parliament, but in the days when roads were bad and progress was slow, and the retinue for a journey to Westminster was a costly affair, a seat in the House of Lords was perhaps regarded by an unambitious abbot as a somewhat doubtful privilege.

The abbots who sat in Parliament far outnumbered the bishops. In 1272, fifty-seven abbots and priors were summoned to Parliament by Edward I, but in later times the number of monastic superiors in the Lords included twenty-five abbots of the greater houses such as S. Albans and Westminster and the prior of Coventry, all of whom were accounted barons of the realm. The privilege of wearing the mitre was possessed by twenty-nine abbots.[2]

Often an abbot or a prior was appointed by the Crown to serve on the commission of peace for the county in which his house was situated; and when a tax was levied by the Crown on ecclesiastical property, the task of collecting it was frequently assigned to the head of an important monastery in the area concerned.

Except in the smaller houses, the abbot was assisted by a prior (*praepositus*), whose special duty was to maintain discipline and to ensure the observance of the Rule by all the inmates of the convent. Usually he was nominated by the abbot for the office, and

---

[1] In 1176 however, abbot Roger gained exemption from primatial authority for S. Augustine's abbey.

[2] Of these, Beaulieu, Fountains, and S. Mary Graces at Tower Hill were Cistercian; Cirencester, Thornton, and Waltham were houses of Augustinian canons; and twenty-three were Benedictine, viz. Abingdon, Bardney, Battle, Bury S. Edmunds, Crowland, Evesham, Glastonbury, Gloucester, Malmesbury, Peterborough, Ramsey, Reading, S. Albans, S. Augustine's Canterbury, S. John's Colchester, S. Mary's York, Selby, Sherborne, Shrewsbury, Tavistock, Tewkesbury, Thorney, and Westminster.

was formally elected in chapter. In the thirteenth-century Customary of abbot Ware of Westminster it was ordained that the prior was 'to admonish the rebellious, encourage the timid, sustain the weak, be long-suffering with all, and in general be a true physician of souls'. It was the prior's duty to take a lighted lantern to the monks' dorter to see that all had risen for the first office of the day in the church, and after compline he was to make sure that all the monks had retired for the night. Then he went the round of the cloister with a lantern and made fast the doors of the church. He was responsible for the attendance of all the brethren at the many services by day and by night in the choir. In the absence of the abbot he acted as head of the house, and he was often assisted by a sub-prior or cloistral-prior who kept a watchful eye upon monks in the cloister. In early days the prior dined in the frater and slept in the monks' dorter but in the later Middle Ages he had his own *camera* or lodging within the precinct.

In addition to the abbot and prior there was a large staff of other officers known as obedientiaries, each of whom was responsible for some department of the monastery. The Rule of S. Benedict, compiled *c*. 540, contemplated only four officials as in the main responsible for the administration viz., the abbot, prior, cellarer, and porter. In the course of natural development, the number of inmates was ever on the increase and additional obedientiaries became necessary. In the *Constitutions* of Archbishop Lanfranc mention is made also of the sacrist, the precentor or cantor, the infirmarer, guest-master, and almoner; and subsequently other officers and assistants were appointed to manage various departments of a monastery.

The bodily needs and the general well-being of the brethren depended to a large extent upon the cellarer, who was the housekeeper, the chief of the commissariat and the purveyor of all the food and drink, not only for the monks but for the guests and the many lay-servants and dependants of the house. He made all the necessary purchases of provisions, stores, and furniture at neighbouring fairs and markets; he had to provide fuel and utensils for cooking and cleaning, as well as materials such as timber, glass, roofing tiles and iron that might be needed for repairs to the conventual buildings. The 'charthe longynge to the office of celeresse' at Barking abbey laid down in great detail her duties in catering for the nuns, and 'thanne sche must see that all manner of howses within her office be sufficiently repayred as well without at hyr fyrmes [farms], manners [manors], as within the monastery'.

All the lay-servants were engaged, supervised, and fed by the cellarer, who could dismiss them if need be. A special duty of his was to see that the meals were properly and punctually served in the frater. The cellarer at Westminster was in charge of the abbey mill and the riverside wharf where were unloaded goods and merchandise needed for the convent. When he had occasion to visit the abbey's farms and granaries to procure supplies of grain and vegetables, he was excused attendance at the canonical hours in the church but was to say them privately if possible.

So multifarious were the duties of the cellarer that he had an assistant, the sub-cellarer, whose special task amongst many others was to ensure that the bread and beer were in condition before they were served in the frater.

Closely associated with the cellarer was the granger (*granatorius*) who received and checked the supplies of corn, attended to the milling, and issued the flour to the bakehouse. In the summer and autumn he visited the farms that supplied the grain in order to estimate the yield of the various crops.

Of no less importance was the fraterer, the officer responsible for everything in the monks' dining hall, for the tables, the seating, the cloths and napkins, the cups, jugs and dishes, and the straw that was strewn on the floor of the refectory. He also had to superintend the laying of the table-cloths and the service of the monk-waiters. Cups and spoons had to be counted every day by the fraterer[1] and he was also responsible for the supply of clean towels in the aumbries near the monks' lavatorium.

In charge of the kitchen and of the officers attached to it was the kitchener, who superintended the work of the cook and his assistants. He was to 'have a sparing hand in supplying his own needs, and a prodigal one where others were concerned'. The quantity and quality of the food at each meal were his special concern, and he was to see that it was not served in broken dishes or in vessels that were dirty underneath, lest they soiled the table-cloths. Whilst the monks were at table the kitchener was to prevent any unnecessary noise and clatter in the kitchen. Under his supervision were the brethren who served in the frater and worked in the kitchen and larder. On the last evening of their week's duty, it was the custom for them to wash the feet of the abbot and the monks in the south walk of the cloister, a ceremony that was known as the Weekly Maundy. In early times each of the monks in turn acted as cook (*coquinarius*) for a week, but later, although the office was nominally held by one of their number, the preparation and the cooking of food was done by lay-servants.

---

[1] At Westminster a quantity of valuable plate belonged to the frater, including a silver cup with lid, weighing 30 oz., the gift of Henry III; and in 1378 abbot Litlyngton presented sets of trenchers, chargers, and salt-cellars for daily use in the frater and the misericord.

G

The obedientiary who was responsible for the clothing and foot-wear of the brethren was the chamberlain (*camerarius*), who also supplied the linen for the frater, and the blankets and the straw for the mattresses in the dorter. He was assisted by the sub-chamberlain, and in his employ were a number of lay-workers, such as tailors, laundresses, bath-attendants, and a barber. At Abingdon abbey there were eight assistants in the tailor's shop, where new garments were made and old ones repaired. Materials of all kinds were purchased by the chamberlain, including lamb-skins and furs for lining winter garments, and other skins for making summer and winter boots. The laundresses were required to mend as well as wash the shirts, surplices, sheets, underwear, and socks of the monks, and if any article were lost through negligence, they had to make them good out of their wages. One of the duties of the chamberlain was to arrange for the shaving of the monks' heads every three weeks. This took place in the south walk of the cloister, where the brethren sat in two rows facing each other, the senior monks being treated first. Three or four times a year the monks took baths in the warming-house, the chamberlain providing the soap, the fuel for heating the water, and the hay that was spread round the tubs for the monks to stand on.

Any of the brethren who were sick or infirm were entrusted to the care of the *infirmarer*, an office that demanded sympathy and patience to a pre-eminent degree. The farmery or sick-ward was completely self-contained, having its own kitchen, offices, and chapel (p. 72), and the infirmarer as the medical officer had his own lodging in or near the farmery. He not only ministered to the bodily needs of his patients, but sang mass for them, and if they were unable to recite their office he said it for them. Out of the revenues of his office he provided food, medicines, and comforts suitable to his charges; under his direction medicines and syrups were made up, often of plants and herbs grown in the herbarium. Such things as liquorice, ginger, and cinnamon were kept in a cupboard, so as to be at hand if a sick monk were 'stricken by a sudden malady'. The patience of the infirmarer must have been sorely tried at times. In 1334 one of the monks in the farmery at Westminster complained to the abbot that he could not drink the beer provided ('So he says' occurs in the farmerer's record), and wine had to be purchased for him. If a sick brother needed cheer-ing up at S. Augustine's, Canterbury, he was taken into the chapel of the farmery, and when the doors were closed, a monk or servant played the harp 'for his delectation'.

As regards hospitality and entertainment the reputation of a monastery depended almost entirely upon the cellarer and the guest-master or hosteller (*hospitarius*). The provision of food and drink was the concern of the cellarer, but the guest-master was responsible for all the arrangements in the hospitium for feeding and lodging visitors of all kinds. The monastic Customals insist upon the discharge of this obligation with all courtesy and kindness, and enjoin on the hosteller the primary duties of having everything ready, sweet, and clean in the guest-house or the appointed chambers, such as wood for the fire, straw for the beds, water for the jugs and basins, rushes for the floor, and candles for the lighting. Guests were to be supplied if possible with better food than the ordinary monastic commons. From the cellarer the guest-master obtained the food and the fuel; from the fraterer, cups, platters, and spoons for the use of visitors; and he attended to the stabling and if necessary the shoeing of the travellers' horses, especially those belonging to pilgrims and to monks from other houses. Before the departure of guests the hostellers inspected the chambers they had occupied to make sure they had left nothing behind or taken away anything belonging to the convent.

The Customaries lay down the most careful directions as to the office of the almoner (*elemosinarius*), whose chief function was to distribute the alms of the house to the poor. Amongst his other duties was the visiting of the sick, the infirm, the blind, and the bed-ridden poor in the neighbourhood of the monastery. Two servants usually accompanied him on his errands of mercy, carrying with them medicines to relieve suffering. In the almonry he supplied the necessitous with clothing, and at Christmas time he laid in a store of stockings, that were given as presents to widows, orphans and poor clerks. The Rolls of Durham cathedral-priory of the fourteenth century show that the convent maintained an infirmary in the almonry for the destitute poor, the annual cost for the garments and shoes for the inmates being £5 6s., a sum equal to more than £300 of our money. The almoner supervised the daily Maundy, i.e. the washing of the feet of the poor by one of the monks; and he also attended to the obituary rolls brought by messengers from other houses, and prepared the mortuary rolls of his own house which were despatched to other monasteries in spiritual fraternity.

Of the utmost importance was the training of the novices, a task that was entrusted to one of the senior monks, a man experienced in the Rule and in the practices and customs of religious life. The master of the novices, a person of judgment and sympathy, had full control over all the postulants; they were constantly under his watchful eye and were trained by him in the usages of the house; and were even clothed by him. In the school in the west walk of the cloister they learned how to conduct themselves properly in the church, the dorter, and the frater, and how to behave in the presence of officers and superiors. There they received instruction in everything pertaining to the Rule, the observances of the canonical hours, processions, feasts, and fasts of the Church, and were taught singing and chanting as well as Latin, an essential for an understanding of the services in the choir. Part of their training was the learning of the Psalms by heart, for these figured largely in the canonical hours.

In charge of the church were the precentor and the sacrist, together with their assistants. The precentor (*cantor*) was the choirmaster, who directed all the services in the church, the chants and the music. He assigned to individual monks the singing of the lessons and responses, and with his assistant the succentor, he arranged and supervised the processions in the church and cloister. The devotional passages that were read in the frater at mealtimes were chosen by the precentor. In most houses he combined with these duties that of librarian (*armarius*), and as such was responsible for the preservation and repair of the books and manuscripts in the scriptorium. He furnished the monk-scribes with pens, inks, and parchment and any other materials they required; he was one of the three custodians of the convent seal, holding one of the three keys of the chest containing it, an indication of the importance of his office in the internal management of the house. In the presence of the brethren in the chapter house, the librarian affixed the wax seal of the convent to any document needing it.

The sacrist was responsible for furnishing all the accessories of Divine worship, and for the care of the fabric of the church. He had to see that the appropriate vestments, altar-cloths, plate, and lights were used in the choir in accordance with the Church calendar. He it was who timed the ringing of bells during the monastic day; he had to ensure that the church was kept clean, that the altars were prepared for the several masses, and on Feast days he furnished the hangings for draping the altars, and supplied the extra candles needed. If the choir was unpaved, the sacrist was to provide hay or rushes to be strewn on the floor. He bought the incense, and the wax and oil for candles and lamps. Expenditure on wax and candles was always a considerable item in the accounts of the sacrist. Candles were needed to light the church for the night offices, for the masses, obits, and anniversaries of the dead that were celebrated at minor altars, for the processions, for lighting the dorter and farmery, for the lanterns used by the prior or sub-prior on their nightly rounds, and for the lodgings of the abbot and prior. In the year 1496 the sacrist of Christ Church,

Canterbury, spent £29 13s. 4d. (say £1,500 in modern values) on the purchase of 1,256 lb. of wax for the making of candles. Vested in albs the sacrist and his assistants made the altar breads, psalms being sung during the baking. When a monk died the sacrist furnished everything for the obsequies, and he was in charge of the cemetery south of the choir, and had to keep it trim and free of weeds. By day and night watch was kept in the church lest any valuable ornaments should be stolen, and for this purpose the sub-sacrist and one or two of the monks slept in the church. For repairs to the roofs, water-pipes, windows, and so on, outside labour was generally employed, the sacrist paying the wages of the workmen. In a sacrist's Roll of the late fifteenth century at Westminster abbey appears an entry recording payment for 'clearing away snow fron the church roof, and scattering the crows and pigeons that strove to nest there'.[1] In addition to the sub-sacrist there were other assistants in his department, notable the *revestiarius* and the treasurer, and often a warden of the Lady Chapel.

The revestiarius was entrusted with the care of the vestments, copes, altar-cloths, draperies, and hangings belonging to the choir, which he had to have in readiness as occasion required. The treasurer had charge of the plate and sacred vessels, the reliquaries and the treasures of the convent, and at times he assisted the sacrist in minor duties such as preparing the lights for the first office of the day.

In monasteries such as S. Albans and Westminster that possessed the shrine of a local saint, one of the brethren held the office of keeper of the shrine (*custos feretri*), whose duty was in the main to supervise the monk-guards who maintained a twenty-four hours' watch in the saint's chapel, lest any of the treasures or jewels attached to the shrine should be stolen. On occasion of a pilgrim-visitation he doubtless attended to the shepherding of the crowds that surged into the church, and he or one of his assistants discoursed upon the virtues of the saint and on the benefactors who had enriched the shrine.

The large number of obedientiaries holding office in houses of any size was a measure of the high state of organisation that characterised monastic life in the Middle Ages. In the Customary of Westminster abbey *c.* 1266 the number of obedientiaries is given as fourteen, and to these must be added many sub-officers who acted as assistants or deputies. Besides the abbot and prior at S. Augustine's, Canterbury, there was a sub-prior, a third and fourth prior, a precentor, a succentor, a sacrist and sub-sacrist, a cellarer and sub-cellarer, an infirmarer and fraterer, a chamberlain, two

---

[1] H. F. Westlake, *The Last Days of Westminster Abbey.*

treasurers, a guest-master, an almoner and sub-almoner, a master of the novices, a vestiarius, wardens of the Lady Chapel and the crypt, and two chaplains of the abbot. In addition there were monk-bailiffs who managed the manors and estates belonging to the abbey. Almost every monk there had some special duty assigned him, which undoubtedly relieved the daily routine of its dull monotony. Each of the administrative departments of a convent derived its income from rents and revenues issuing from lands and properties specially assigned to it, and the obedientiaries had to submit a Roll or account of their receipts and expenditure for an annual audit. The Rolls that have survived shed much light on the activities of the officers and on the internal economy of a religious house. In the muniments of Westminster abbey are preserved more than three thousand such accounts, many of which furnish in great detail the expenditure in certain departments of this royal foundation.

From early times lay-servants were employed by the obedientiaries for the domestic work and the menial tasks of their several departments, a practice that was frowned upon by visiting bishops. At the time of the Dissolution, the number of hired workers in most houses exceeded the number of monks. In the year 1100 there were fifty-five brethren at Evesham abbey and sixty-five paid servants, of whom five served in the church, seven worked in the bakehouse, five in the kitchen, two in the pantry, four in the brewhouse, two in the farmery, and five in the vineyard; of the others there were four fishermen, two shoemakers, three gardeners, eight employed in the abbot's household, and four who accompanied the monks when they journeyed abroad. At the cathedral-priory of Norwich there were at one time 146 lay-servants as against sixty-two monks.

The lay-servants were not all necessarily resident within the precincts, nor were the agricultural labourers, shepherds, carters, and other hired servants who were employed on the home-farms attached to many religious houses.

The successful management of a monastery called for organising ability, tact, and self-sacrifice on the part of the superior, whose judgment was exercised in the choice of suitable brethren to act as obedientiaries. The spiritual and temporal affairs of the house needed constant supervision, and in a convent of any size the abbot can have had little time for hawking and hunting. Monastic chronicles and the records of visitations in episcopal registers provide evidence that there were capable and incapable abbots, both good and bad. Of abbot Samson who ruled at Bury S. Edmunds strictly, firmly, but with every kindness, one of his monks wrote:

'On the 30th December [1211] at S. Edmunds died Samson of pious memory, the venerable abbot of that place, after he had prosperously ruled the abbey committed to him for 30 years and had freed it from a load of debt, had enriched it with privileges, liberties, possessions, and spacious buildings, and had restored the worship of the church, both internally and externally, in the most ample manner.'

Through the centuries it was inevitable that in the long line of abbots of any one house, there should be one or two who were not proof against worldly distractions. In 1466 the monks of Westminster petitioned the King 'to considre the gret wast and destruccion of your seid monasterie', occasioned by the abbot's lavish entertainment of his friends at his manor of Pyrford. In four years abbot Norwych had incurred debts amounting to more than £2,000, a sum equivalent to nearly £100,000 in modern value. Rather than face an inquiry the abbot resigned and was granted a pension of 100 marks; he died two years later.[1] An even worse case was that of abbot Norreys of Evesham, whose evil ways brought about his deposition by the Pope. Matthew Paris tells of a prior of Thetford, a monk of Cluny, who in 1248 invited kinsmen of his to the house and spent his nights feasting and drinking with them 'till cockcrow' at the expense of the convent. One of the monks attacked the prior with a knife and slew him, and after his arrest was committed to a dungeon in Norwich castle by order of Henry III.

It was fitting and proper that monasteries should be subject to some form of external control. In the Saxon period bishops made periodical visitations to the houses in their dioceses, for the purpose of inquiring into their internal condition and of imposing disciplinary measures where necessary. All the English Benedictine establishments but five (p. 47) that paid fees regularly to the Holy See for the somewhat doubtful privilege of exemption, remained under episcopal control through the centuries. In the case of the exempt houses, the election of a new abbot was subject to Papal confirmation on the payment of heavy fees to the Roman Chancery. In the early years of the sixteenth century the convent of S. Albans were paying £14 annually to the Papal receiver on this account. Visitation of the exempt monasteries could be made by order of the Pope, the king, or the General Chapter of the Benedictines.[2]

---

[1] H. F. Westlake, *Westminster Abbey: the Church, Convent, Cathedral, and College of S. Peter, Westminster.*

[2] In 1268 Cardinal-legate Ottobuoni conducted a visitation of Westminster abbey, and in 1441, at the instigation of Henry VI, the royal abbey was again subjected to visitation, the General Chapter appointing the abbots of Abingdon, S. Albans, Chertsey, and Colchester as the visitors.

After the Norman Conquest, when houses of the reformed Orders were planted in this country, exemption from episcopal control was granted them by the Pope, on the ground that they were units of great corporations each with its own centralised authority. So it was that the abbeys and priories of the Cluniac, Cistercian, and Carthusian Orders, and the houses of the Premonstratensian and Gilbertine canons as well as all the friaries were free from episcopal control, being subject only to their governing houses that appointed their own visitors. The central abbeys of Cluny and Citeaux in Burgundy had powers in this respect throughout Christendom, and though the Premonstratensians were subject to Premontré in the diocese of Laon, it became the practice of the chapter to appoint an English bishop as visitor of all their abbeys in this country. The authority of English bishops was therefore limited to all but a few Benedictine establishments, to Augustine houses, Cistercian nunneries and alien priories.

It was customary for the bishop or his deputy to visit every monastery in his diocese excepting those exempt once every three years, and where he found much amiss the visit was repeated after a short interval. A few days before a visitation was to take place, formal notice was sent to the convent, and on the appointed day the prelate and his entourage, consisting of the arch-deacon, the commissary-general, legal advisers, and clerks, were met at the gatehouse of the abbey by the convent, and went in procession to the church, entering by the west door. High Mass was celebrated in the choir, followed by the Benediction, after which they all made their way to the chapter house where a short sermon was preached by one of the clerks. All the monks then withdrew, and from the abbot to the youngest novice they were examined by the bishop singly and in due gradation, the clerks taking notes of all their depositions. The first to be called was the head of the house who, after producing a certificate of his installation, submitted a report on the financial state of the house, of the properties owned by the convent including an inventory of its plate and treasures, and the number and conduct of the brethren. He was followed by the obedientiaries, each of whom was questioned as to the affairs of his office, and was required to present an account or roll of income and expenditure. After this the rank and file were examined individually, so that they could be perfectly frank and open in their declarations and conceal nothing. When irregularities were brought to light the clerks must have been kept very busy. After the inquiry the findings were summarised and known as *comperta*; injunctions were issued to correct any faults and were ordered to be read frequently in chapter before the whole convent, until all had been rectified.

The records of visitations in the episcopal registers of several cathedrals present but one aspect of monastic life, for the object of a visitation was to detect and correct laxity, indiscipline, and iniquities, not to record the good name and fame of houses 'of virtuous living'. Human nature being what it is, there were certain houses where the life of the inmates left much to be desired; on the other hand there is but incidental mention of a great many monasteries in which nothing called for redress. At the Bodleian is a volume pertaining to the diocese of Norwich from 1492 to 1532, when thirty-four houses were subject to the bishop. Details are given of visitations conducted in Norfolk and Suffolk on 141 occasions, and in the large majority of cases the visitor found nothing that needed reform. In fifteen instances irregularities were brought to light and strict measures were issued to restore discipline. In the archives of Lincoln cathedral are lengthy records of visitations in that diocese between 1437 and 1449, in which period the wealthy Benedictine abbey of Peterborough was visited by Bishop Alnwick on three occasions. The *comperta* present a picture of the disorder into which the convent had fallen under unscrupulous and worldly abbots. Abbot Depyng maintained a costly and numerous household, and two of his kinsmen 'do turn the abbot about at their liking; they make away with wine by skinsful'. On his resignation in 1438 he left the house £4,000 in debt. His successor, abbot Ashton, enjoyed an income of £14,000 a year in modern value; he wasted the property of the monks by fraudulent leases, and he was defamed of adultery with three married women of the town. The monks were allowed £25 a year as pocket-money, and were addicted to wandering outside the abbey much as they pleased, frequenting the taverns of the town. Women had access to the precinct, and some of the brethren danced in public. Many of them absented themselves from the services in the choir, for 'there are not more than ten or twelve in the quire at time of the Divine office, so that secular folk who see these things do speak harm of this scantiness of monks in the quire'. When the younger monks were corrected they became defiant and 'kept weapons of attack and defence in places apart from their cells'. Brother Maksey 'withstood the abbot to his face with a knife in his hand'. In 1446 it was revealed that 'after compline the young monks . . . do set to drinking with the abbot, as freely as if this were allowed them, and so are rendered altogether unfit for matins or for Mass on the day following'.

The visitation of a monastery by any but the bishop of the

diocese or his commissary met with opposition by the convent. In the year 1250 the tyrannical Boniface, Archbishop of Canterbury, claimed the right of visitation of the priory of S. Bartholomew, Smithfield, in place of the bishop. The occasion was marked by a violent scene in the priory church, described by Matthew Paris. Amidst the ringing of bells Boniface was received by the sub-prior and canons in solemn procession bearing lighted candles and was conducted to the choir with his attendants. There, one of the canons, on behalf of the convent, informed the Primate that only the diocesan was privileged to conduct a visitation. Thereupon Boniface in a fit of anger struck the canon several blows, tore the vestments off the sub-prior, trampled on them, and 'rushed like a madman on this holy man'. Coming to his assistance other canons pushed the Archbishop backwards, and as he fell his robes were thrown aside and he was seen to be clad in armour. His followers then attacked the unarmed canons, wounding many of them and throwing them to the ground. News of the affray spread through the City, and the populace rose in pursuit of Boniface as he fled to Lambeth. Safe in the chapel of his palace he pronounced the sentence of excommunication upon the canons of the priory. Appeals were made to Rome, and ultimately the sentence was annulled, but the Pope issued a mandate to the priory confirming the Primate's right of visitation.

The records of visitations afford evidence that where the head of a religious house was found to be incapable or inefficient, the bishop was empowered to appoint an outsider to act as co-adjutor, and any obedientiary who was incompetent could be removed from his charge and replaced by another monk. Further, any of the rank and file who were troublesome or undesirable could be sent to other houses.

Alien priories whose brethren were foreigners from the parent house abroad came under the jurisdiction of the bishop and were subject to visitation. The appointment of an alien prior needed confirmation by the bishop, who also controlled the passing to and fro of foreign monks.

VI. The Daily Life of the Monk

~~~~~~

The Round of Services in the Church—Seven Canonical Hours and High Mass—The Hebdomadarian—The Night Office, Matins—Rousing of the Monks in the Dorter by the Prior—The Circator—The Office of Prime— Family-Mass for the Lay-Servants—Breakfast or Mixtum—Lady Mass —Terce followed by Chapter—Procedure in the Chapter House—The Confession of Faults, and Punishments—Prison Cells at Durham—The Parliament—The Sunday Procession for the Asperging of Altars in the Church—The Route in the Church and Cloister—Stations in the Nave during the Bidding Prayer—Easter Day Ceremonial—The Easter Sepulchre—Dinner in the Frater—The Monastic Dietary—Cellarers' Rolls —The Behaviour of Monks at Table—Signs for Various Kinds of Food —Pittances or Extra Fare—The Pittancer and his Funds—Food Surplus to the Almoner—The Afternoon for Recreation, Study, and Labour— Vespers and Collation—Compline, the Final Office of the Day—The Daily Life of the Conversi in Cistercian Monasteries—Ceremonies on the Death of a Monk—Contact with the Outer World—Procedure for Pilgrim Visitations.

~~~~~~

THE PRIME OBLIGATION of the religious of either sex was the recitation of an incessant round of services in the church every day, beginning with matins and ending with compline, after which the brethren retired to the dorter for the night. In accordance with the psalmist's 'At midnight will I rise to give thanks unto Thee', and 'Seven times a day will I praise Thee', the regula ordained that the twenty-four hours of the day should be portioned out into seven canonical hours, viz., matins and lauds, prime, terce, sext, none, vespers, and compline. The actual hours at which these offices were observed varied according to the season, the daylight hours being shorter in winter than in summer. In addition to the canonical hours there was the important Mass at the High Altar, and a number of early masses sung at the lesser altars by individual priests on behalf of founders and benefactors. Every Saturday evening before vespers, one of the brethren who was in priestly orders took on the duty of hebdomadarian for the following week. He officiated at all the canonical hours and was the celebrant at High Mass every morning; he blessed the holy water for the Sunday procession, in the course of which he asperged all the altars in the church.

On occasion when any of the obedientiaries such as the cellarer were absent from the house on business connected with their office, they were dispensed from attendance at some of the 'hours'; otherwise all the brethren except those in the farmery were required to be present at all the services in the choir.

Usually the first night-office matins was sung between midnight and 2 a.m. Shortly before the appointed hour the sacrist or one of his assistants lighted candles in the choir and in the transept near the night-stairs, and the prior or the sub-prior entered the dorter and gave the signal for rising by ringing a small handbell as he passed between the beds of the sleeping monks. Those who slept heavily might be awakened by the *light* tap of a small rod. Candles or cressets were lighted in the dorter for the monks to dress by. In the winter the brethren were provided with fur-lined boots to wear at the early services in the unheated choir.[1]

When the church bell rang they left the dorter, and preceded by a lantern-bearer entered the transept by the night-stairs and made their way to the stalls in the choir, where they knelt until the abbot joined them. The night-office commenced with the Pater, Ave, and Creed, followed by the recitation of the fifteen gradual Psalms (CXX–CXXXIV) and the reading of the lessons, sometimes as many as twelve in number, each being read by a different monk. After the Te Deum and the Gospels, the office of matins concluded with the prayer for the day. Then followed a short interval, during which the bell was rung for lauds, so-named from the opening words *Laudate Dominum* of the Psalms; and the brethren either remained in their stalls or left the choir to take a brisk turn in the cloister to restore their circulation. Matins and lauds lasted an hour and a half or two hours, during which some of the monks must have found it difficult to keep awake. In some houses a *circator* paced the choir with a lantern, to see that none fell asleep; if he found an offender he held the lantern before his eyes and shook him. At the conclusion of the night-offices the brethren returned in procession to their beds in the dorter for a few hours, before being summoned by the bell for the first office of

---

[1] King Canute is said to have presented the monks of Crowland with twelve polar-bear skins for this purpose, and such was the severity of winter in the Fen district that in the thirteenth century the monks of Peterborough were granted Papal permission to wear caps in church.

the day known as prime. This took place at about 6 a.m. in the summer and at daybreak in winter. After dressing themselves in their day attire, they descended by the day-stairs to the east cloister-walk, entered the church by the eastern portal and took their places in the choir before the bell ceased to ring. The office of prime was not a lengthy one; it consisted of a hymn, psalms, and prayers and was followed immediately by early or family mass for the lay-servants of the house, celebrated in turn by each of the monks who were in priestly orders. On Sundays only were other brethren present to receive communion. On weekdays during the family mass the monks washed themselves at the lavatorium in the cloister. The obedientiaries then went about their respective tasks, the rank and file read and meditated in the cloister and the novices attended their master in the west walk.

The next office was chapter mass, before which the monks partook of a light breakfast known as *mixtum*, consisting of a quarter of a pound of bread and a third of a pint of beer or wine. On fast days there was no mixtum, nor during the season of Lent except on Sundays. A bell then summoned them to chapter mass, or, as it was often called, Lady mass, being celebrated at the altar in the Lady Chapel. This was followed by the short office of terce, succeeded by the chapter, to which the monks went in procession headed by the novices.[1] The abbot or the prior who presided at the meeting occupied a raised seat at the east end with his obedientiaries on either side, and the other monks sat on the stone bench round the walls in order of seniority, the youngest and the novices being at the west end near the door. Above the abbot's seat was a Majestas or a crucifix, and in the middle of the chapter house stood a reading desk. The proceedings were of about twenty minutes' duration. After the abbot had pronounced his blessing on the assembly, the Martyrology, or notice of the saints to be commemorated that day, was read from the lectern by one of the brethren, after which all stood and turned to the Majestas during a short office of prayers on behalf of the convent and their deliberations. Then followed the reading of a portion of the Rule of the Order, and the abbot pronounced 'Loquamur de Ordine nostro' (Let us speak of the affairs of our house), whereupon the novices

[1] In Benedictine and Cistercian houses the chapter was held after prime in the summer time, and was then followed by terce and Lady mass. In the Customs or *Consuetudines* compiled by abbot Ware of Westminster, 1258–84, he described the chapter house as 'the little house in which the convent meets to consult for its welfare. It is well called the *capitulum* because it is the *caput litium* [the head of strifes] for there strifes are ended. It is the workshop of the Holy Spirit in which the sons of God are gathered together. It is the house of confession, the house of obedience, mercy and forgiveness, the house of unity, peace and tranquillity, where the brethren make satisfaction for their faults'.

and any visitors withdrew. The various duties of the day were assigned to individual monks, letters concerning the convent and obits from other houses were read aloud, and then came the confession of faults by any of the erring brethren, and pleas for pardon. Upon those guilty of any misdemeanour the abbot pronounced sentence and imposed penalties, such as fasting on bread and water on certain days, loss of precedence in choir and chapter, and sometimes corporal punishment, which was inflicted there and then in the presence of all the brethren. In the *Customary* of S. Augustine's, Canterbury, we read that while flogging was being administered to one of their number, 'All the brethren sit with bowed and covered heads, and with kind and brotherly affection should have compassion on him'. Serious crimes were punished by solitary confinement, by excommunication, or by expulsion from the Order. In the south wall of the chapter house at Durham was a doorway that led into three small dark chambers that served as a prison for monks who were guilty of light offences. For serious crimes the offenders were imprisoned in the Lyng-house, a vaulted cellar 24 feet in length that stood to the west of the cloistral buildings. There they 'should have sytten for the space of one hole yere in chynes, without any company except the master of the fermery, who did let down there meat thorowgh a trap dour on a corde, being a great distance from them' (*Rites of Durham*).

In the interval between chapter and High Mass, the abbot conferred with the obedientiaries in one walk of the cloister, on matters concerning the business affairs of the house. This meeting was known as 'the Parliament', whence the term came to be applied to the House of our national representatives.

The most important service of the day was the celebration of High Mass, which began at about 10 a.m. On Sundays and festivals of the Church it was preceded by a procession, the purpose of which was the asperging of all the altars in the church with holy water. Vases of water into which salt had been sprinkled were blessed by the hebdomadary or celebrant-priest for the week, and after the High Altar had been 'washed' on all sides with the aspersorium, he proceeded to sprinkle the brethren in the choir. In the meantime, two priests carrying holy water with them visited the apartments round the cloister, which were likewise sprinkled, and two others went to the farmery to asperge the sick and infirm. A procession of all available monks was formed and left the choir by the *ostium chori* on the north side, visiting the altars in the aisles, the Lady Chapel, and the transepts, all of which were duly sprinkled. Anthems were sung during the progress of the procession, which was headed by the priest who asperged the altars; and behind him was the cross-bearer between two monks carrying lighted candles. Then the procession entered the cloister by the main door at the east and passed along the three walks, re-entering the church by the novices' door in the western walk.

From the west end the procession advanced in double file up the middle of the nave, and there took up stationary positions, whilst the celebrant sprinkled the altar against the rood screen and said the bidding prayer on behalf of the Church, the royal family, and all benefactors. Beneath the turf in the nave of Fountains abbey are two rows of stone slabs, twenty-three on each side, running west to east, and indicating the stations made by the monks during the bidding prayer; and at Canterbury two parallel lines incised in the pavement of the nave served the same purpose, but were destroyed when the nave was restored in 1787-8. After the bidding prayer the monks passed through the rood screen and the pulpitum and took their places in the choir for High Mass. The order of the Sunday procession varied in different houses, according to the number and disposition of altars in the church. At Canterbury, after leaving the choir the procession visited the crypt for the altar of Our Lady Undercroft, and thence to the north transept (of the Martyrdom) and into the cloister, re-entering the church by the north-west door of the nave. Royalty were frequent visitors to Canterbury on account of the shrine of S. Thomas, and sometimes took part in the monks' processions. On one occasion Henry VI, who was often there, carried his candle in the procession on Candlemas Day.

On the great festivals such as Palm Sunday, Easter, Ascension Day and Corpus Christi, saintly relics and banners were carried in procession, marked with much ceremonial pomp particularly in Benedictine monasteries. Easter Day was characterised by a ceremony of great solemnity that symbolized the Resurrection. After the Passion had been sung on Good Friday, a receptacle containing the consecrated Host was laid in the Easter Sepulchre, a tomb-like structure that was erected on the north side of the sanctuary. Usually it consisted of a timber frame-work draped with hangings or faced with panels depicting the Entombment and the Resurrection. At Durham the Blessed Sacrament in a crystal container was placed in the breast of an image of the Saviour, and the Easter Sepulchre was watched day and night, the Pascal candle burning before it until Easter morn. Then, between three and four o'clock, 'in honour of the Resurrection two of the oldest monks of the quire came to the Sepulchre all covered with red velvet and embroidered with gold, and then did cense it'; after which the image was removed to the High Altar during the singing of *Christus Resurgus*. Then it was carried round the church in procession beneath a velvet canopy, 'the whole choir waiting upon it with goodly torches and great store of other lights, all singing, rejoicing, and praising God most devoutly, till they came to the High Altar again, whereon they did place the said image there to remain until the Ascension Day' (*Rites of Durham*).

In some churches the Easter Sepulchre was a permanent structure of stone, as for instance that in Lincoln cathedral, on the base of which is sculptured a representation of the sleeping soldiers outside the tomb. A portion of the stone Sepulchre that formerly stood in the sanctuary at Glastonbury shows two Roman soldiers in a reclining position wearing the knightly armour of Henry V's reign; and during the restoration of the Temple church, London, in the nineteenth century, a gilt-brass panel was recovered that is believed to be part of the receptacle of an Easter Sepulchre. Beneath an arcade on the front of the panel are figures in relief of three soldiers in twelfth-century costume. Accounts exist of the expenses incurred in making and painting Easter Sepulchres, in purchasing large wax tapers for burning before them, and in providing bread and ale for the watchers.

After High Mass came dinner, the principal meal of the day, served at about 11 a.m., all the monks washing their hands at the lavatorium before entering the frater, to which they were summoned by a bell. In the frater they bowed before the Majestas above the high table and awaited the abbot or the superior who was to preside at the meal. After Grace when all were seated, the abbot gave the signal to the reader to begin, and when he had uncovered his bread the monks did likewise, and the servers brought in the dishes of food. In the early days the meal consisted of potage, bread, fish, and eggs, and sometimes cheese and fruit. At Christ Church, Canterbury, 'To every two monks, when they had soles, there were four soles in a dish; when they had plaice, two plaice; when they had herrings, eight herrings; when they had whitings, eight whitings; and when they had eggs, two eggs'. The thirty-ninth chapter of the Benedictine Rule forbade the eating of meat or game except by the sick and infirm, but this regulation was relaxed at a Provincial Chapter held at Oxford in 1300. Even so, only on certain days might flesh be eaten, never on fasts or during Lent. The Cluniacs, the Cistercians, and the Carthusians made a point of a more rigid adherence to fleshless diet. At first the Cistercians permitted meat only in the farmery, as was also the case at the wealthy Benedictine abbey of S. Albans until late in the thirteenth century. The Carthusians were absolute in their rejection of flesh-food right up to the Dissolution. The cellarer's Rolls of many houses throw much light on the dieting of the monks and of the expenditure on food-stuffs week by week. At Durham during the week after Martinmas 1333–4, the cellarer purchased a thousand eggs, 6s. 9d; a horse-load of whiting, 4s; seven salmon, plaice and smelts, 4s. 2d; pork and veal, 9s. 0½d; seven sucking pigs, fourteen geese, and seventeen fowls, 7s. 4½d; wild fowl, 3s; butter and honey, 10d; forty-eight fowls, 8s; and seven hundred eggs, 42s. 6d. On the Monday before Christmas Day 1492, the monks of the cathedral-priory of Winchester were served with two dishes of moile, made from marrow and grated bread, tripe, beef, mutton, calves' feet and 170 eggs. The cost of this food amounted to 8s. 4d., or about £14 of our money. Eggs were generally eaten instead of meat, and the great quantity consumed may indicate that most of the brethren abstained from meat. For the year 1333–4 no fewer than 44,140 eggs were purchased by the cellarer of Durham. Such quantities of food were required not only for the monks, but for the lay-servants, the chaplains, the servants of the abbot's and prior's lodgings, the inmates of the almonry, the corrodians (p. 21), and the many guests who knew quite well which houses entertained right royally.

The Customaries and Observances of various houses that have come down to us shed much light on the behaviour expected of monks when at meals. They were not to leave the table and walk about in the frater; they were not to sit with chin on hand, but were to keep arms and elbows off the table; nor were they to indulge in chattering or gazing about. At no time was a monk to make signs to one at another table. Should anyone knock a jug or make any sound to prevent the reader being heard, he was to rise from the table until the abbot or the presiding officer bade him resume his seat. If there were nuts on the menu, a monk was not to crack them loudly with his teeth and so disturb the reader, but to open them privately with his knife. At Barnwell no dishes that were broken or dirty or smeared on the underside were to be used. The brethren 'were not to wipe their noses or rub their teeth on the napkins or tablecloths, nor to staunch blood with them'.

Amongst the MSS. at Lambeth Palace is a treatise bearing the title *De Signis*, a manual in which are given the gestures to be used by the monks of Ely when they sat at table, the rule of silence precluding them from expressing their wants by word of mouth.[1] The treatise resembles one printed in the *Consuetudines Cluniacenses*, and in both are enumerated the signs to be used by the brethren when they wished for different kinds of food, for fish, vegetables, pastry,

[1] D. J. Stewart, *Architectural History of Ely Cathedral*.

H

fruit, bread, cheese, wine, water, or milk. Serving the same purpose was the table of more than a hundred conventional signs that
were used by the nuns of Syon abbey at meal-times. A sister who
wanted fish wagged her hands sideways 'in manere of a fissh taill';
she who needed mustard held her nose in the fist of her right hand
and rubbed it; and for salt, the thumb and fore-finger of the right
hand were 'filliped' over the left thumb.[1]

The apportioned allowance of food for each monk was occasionally supplemented by a pittance (*pietencia*), viz. an extra dish of
flesh, fruit, or some delicacy, for which an endowment or bequest
had been made by some benefactor. It became the custom in some
monasteries, as for instance Durham, for the obedientiaries to give
a pittance to the whole convent on special festivals. The *Customary*
of Barking abbey gives details of various pittances that the cellaress
had to provide for the nuns on certain days of the year, including
wheat and milk for making firmete, fish, chickens, pork, and
bacon, and red wine; and the Annals of S. Albans record lists of
the provisions made for pittances on flesh-days and fish-days.
Endowments for pittances in some houses were so frequent and
considerable that the extra fare bade fair to become permanent
rather than occasional in the daily dietary. In such circumstances
the pittance funds were entrusted to the pittancer (*pittensarius*), who
in accordance with the decision of the abbot and chapter was empowered to allocate part of the endowment to other purposes. Thus
at S. Benet's Holme, Norfolk, the receipts of the pittancer for the
year 1511–12 amounted to £9 17s. 1½d., (equal to £800 today),
of which 16s. were spent on beans and butter, figs and other fruit,
and wine, for the twenty-three brethren of the house, who also
received pocket-money in lieu of the pittance at different times.
The considerable balance was used for the payment of 4s. as a
subsidy to the General Chapter of the Benedictines, for wages and
clothes for the pittancer's servant, for felling trees and making
faggots for fuel, for the repair of broken windows, and for re-
thatching a leaky roof with reeds. Even then the pittancer was left
with 3s. to distribute in alms during Lent.

To return to the frater. At the end of the meal the prior gave
the signal for the collection of the remnants of food on the tables,
by two junior brethren, who later handed over the baskets to the
almoner for distribution to the poor at the gate of the monastery.
Then the monks rose from the tables, and ranging themselves in
two rows facing each other sang Grace. On leaving the frater they
washed their hands again at the lavatorium, a necessary operation
in the days when fingers were used as forks. The brethren who had

[1] G. J. Aungier, *History and Antiquities of Syon.*

acted as servers then took their meal in the frater, the cellarer presiding and the fraterer assisting. After the mid-day repast it was the custom in some houses for the monks to go in procession to the cemetery which they reached from the cloister by the slype in the sub-dorter, and there they stood bareheaded for a time praying for the souls of departed brethren.

In the summer months, to make up for the short nights, vespers and supper being an hour later than in winter, they retired to the dorter for an hour's rest before the next office. The canonical hour of none was recited after the mid-day rest, except on vigils and fast days when it was said before dinner. The afternoon until 4 or 5 o'clock in winter and 6 o'clock in summer was set aside for recreation, for study in the cloister, writing in the scriptorium, or labour in the fields, the workshops, the bakery, and mills; and the obedientiaries attended to the business of their office, such as accounts and requisitions. Labour being all-important in Cistercian monasteries, the brethren worked in the morning after chapter as well as in the afternoon.

At the end of the afternoon the bell rang for vespers, an office that was sung in the choir, and immediately afterwards the monks performed their ablutions at the lavatorium in preparation for supper in the frater, which was taken on all days except on vigils, fast days, and during the season of Lent. Supper consisted of one course, followed by a pittance of cheese, fruit, or nuts. Having given thanks in the church for the meal, the brethren returned to the cloister for the evening collation, a short reading that took place in one walk or in the chapter house. In Cistercian abbeys collation was held in the cloister-walk adjoining the church. About mid-way in the south walk at Tintern an arched recess in the aisle-wall indicates the seat of the abbot during the reading of collation and probably serving a like purpose was the small five-sided alcove at Strata Florida, that projects into the cloister-garth from the middle of the north arcade. When there was no supper the monks could go to the frater and be served with a small portion of bread and a drink, called *potum caritatis*.

A final bell summoned the convent to compline, the last office of the monastic day, which was not necessarily held in the church, and when that was at an end the monks retired to the dorter. Absolute silence was to be maintained, and the doors of the church and cloister were locked until prime.

The daily life of the conversi in Cistercian monasteries differed considerably from that of the choir-monks. They generally rose at dawn after matins and lauds had been sung, and when they had said prime in their choir (p. 157), they betook themselves to their various labours, many of them working at outlying farms and granges under the control of the cellarer. When reciting the offices in their choir they repeated their prayers almost silently lest they should disturb the brethren in the monks' choir. On Sundays and festivals they kept the same observances as the monks, and each of them was required to receive Holy Communion seven times a year, on specified feasts. Three times a year they met in chapter, viz., on the morrows of Christmas Day, Easter Day, and Whitsunday. They dined and supped in their own frater on the ground floor of the domus conversorum (p. 161), their prior presiding at meals. On account of their arduous work they were granted an additional allowance of bread of a coarse kind. As far as was possible they were to observe the rule of silence at their work, but the smiths were allowed to speak because 'they can hardly labour in silence without detriment to their work'.

The last few hours of a monk's life were passed in an atmosphere of much solemnity. The abbot himself, or in his absence the prior, administered Extreme Unction to a dying monk, sprinkled him with holy water and censed him; and as the last moment approached, a tabula or board hanging in one walk of the cloister was beaten with a mallet to summon the convent to the presence of their passing brother. Meanwhile ashes were strewn on the floor in the form of a cross and were covered with a sheet of sack-cloth or a mat, on which the dying man was laid, with his brethren praying around him. After death the body was washed and taken to the chapel of the farmery, where the Litany of the Dying was recited, after which it was sprinkled and censed. It was then taken to the church and, if before dinner, mass for the dead was said and the body buried the same day; but if later, the interment was deferred until the morrow, in which case the body was taken to the church in solemn procession and placed on a hearse, where a number of monks kept a continuous vigil. A requiem mass was said before the dead monk was taken to the cemetery and buried, the church bells being tolled the while. Notice of the death was sent by a special messenger to other houses that were in the 'family' of abbeys, and for thirty days the obit was observed in the church and in chapter; and a portion of food in the name of the deceased was set apart in the frater for distribution to the poor.

Contact with the outer world afforded a welcome break in the daily routine and monotony of life within the convent walls. It was a red-letter day for many a monk when one of his family awaited him in the outer parlour, and there was stir and bustle in the outer court when royalty or members of the nobility arrived for a few days' entertainment, during which the guests would be present at

High Mass and other services. An episcopal visitation undoubtedly provided the brethren with ample food for gossip as they warmed themselves in the calefactorium.

In monastic churches that possessed the shrine of a saint, several of the monks on the occasion of a pilgrimage were assigned duties to facilitate the reception and piloting of the pilgrims. Sight-seers were not allowed to wander at will in the precinct or in the church; they were met at the gatehouse and conducted by certain of the brethren to the saint's chapel in the choir-arm, there to feast their eyes upon the treasures that bedecked the feretrum. Usually they entered the church by a doorway in the transept remote from the cloister. At Westminster abbey the pilgrims' doorway opened into the western aisle of the north transept, whence they were conducted round the north ambulatory of the choir, passing the royal tombs and gaining a glimpse of the Confessor's shrine. Proceeding eastwards they visited the Lady Chapel at the east, after which they completed the circuit of the saint's chapel by way of the south ambulatory, and came to a stop at the iron gates at the west. Retracing their steps they left the church by the portal in the north transept. Only the privileged were permitted to enter the saint's chapel at Westminster.[1] When pilgrims visited S. Albans they entered the precinct by the Wax-house Gate to the north-east of the abbey church, and after purchasing tapers there to burn before the shrine, they made their way to the pilgrims' door that is still to be seen, in the same relative position as at Westminster. At Winchester visitors entered the church by a portal in the west wall of the north transept. Much the same procedure as that at Westminster was followed in other great churches when their doors were opened to pilgrims. Chaucer's and other pilgrims who streamed into the precinct of Christ Church, Canterbury were well repaid for the hazards of the journey, for, in addition to seeing the shrine of Becket, they were shown relics associated with his martyrdom in various parts of the cathedral, including the crypt. This great church was a veritable museum of relics, of S. Dunstan and S. Alphege, and of fragments innumerable, including the arms of eleven saints, the bed of the Virgin Mary, a piece of the rock of Calvary, Aaron's rod, and fragments of the Holy Manger—a heterogeneous assortment that provided the

[1] When royal personages made a pilgrimage to the abbey, they entered by the small doorway now blocked up in the east wall of the north transept and followed the usual route, but after visiting the shrine they passed through the gates in the south ambulatory and left the church by the portal near Chaucer's monument in the south transept. From there a covered way crossed to the palace. On State occasions the royal entry was by the central doorway of the north transept, now the main entrance to the abbey church.

credulous with plenty to see and wonder at. Many monks must have been engaged in conducting the pilgrims to the several places in the cathedral where the treasures were displayed, and others were needed to guard the relics against theft.

The daily routine of monastic life differed but little in the houses of the various Orders, with the exception of the Carthusians, where each of the inmates dwelt in his own cell apart from his brethren (p. 205). Supplementary to the Rule was the *Custumal or Consuetudinary* that was formulated in almost every religious house in which was set forth details of life within the precinct and of the liturgical observances. Those that are extant afford evidence of the similarity in these respects in the establishments of the Benedictines, the Cistercians, and the Regular Canons.

VII. Monasteries and Churches of the Benedictine Order

APART FROM REFERENCES in ancient writings, very little is known of the architectural character of the Benedictine monasteries of Saxon England, for their churches and conventual buildings were swept away almost entirely in the vast rebuilding schemes that followed the Norman Conquest. Little doubt exists that Saxon

abbeys were not laid out on any standard plan as were those of the
Norman and later periods, with a cloister south of the church,
about which were grouped the various living apartments of the
inmates. Rather more is known of the churches.

In the south of England, the church of the Saxon abbey of S.
Peter and S. Paul, Canterbury, *c.* 605, was modelled on the Early
Christian basilican churches of Rome. On plan it was a building
about 58 feet square, divided into a nave and aisles, with an apsidal
sanctuary shut off from the nave at the east by a screen of three
arches. At the western end was a narthex. About 25 feet to the
east of the church stood an oratory with an eastern apse, dedicated
to S. Mary. Towards the end of the eighth century the narthex
was taken down to give place to another built outside the nave at
the west and enclosed within a large courtyard or *atrium*, in the
tradition of the Early Church. The whole structure must have
been built of stone, for it remained unaltered until *c.* 1050, when
the apse of the basilica was removed and a huge octagon erected,
connecting the oratory with the nave. The octagon extended the
full width of the church, the eight columns or piers of the interior
being encircled by an aisle. This Saxon basilica was completely
demolished when the big reconstruction was undertaken by the
Norman abbot Scotland between 1070 and 1085.

A rare example of a Saxon monastic church of the Benedictine
Order that survived the Conquest is that of Deerhurst priory,
Gloucestershire, although the original building is now incorporated
in the enlargements that were carried out in the twelfth and fourteenth centuries (Fig. 3).[1] Here as elsewhere it is evident that the
Roman basilican plan was discarded in favour of a simpler form.
At the time of the Conquest the priory church was a cruciform
building, consisting of a choir terminating at the east in a polygonal apse, an unaisled nave flanked on either side by a square
porticus, or quasi-transept, and a western tower. The apse has disappeared and the transepts have been absorbed into later aisles.
A remarkable feature of the church is the tower, 70 feet in height,
the ground floor of which is divided by a north-to-south wall into
two unequal parts, the western originally serving as a porch.
Attached to the eastern wall of the tower was a small square baptis-
tery, from which the nave was entered by arched openings in the

---

[1] The date of the foundation of the priory is uncertain, but early in the ninth century
it was possessed of extensive landed property. In 1054 Edward the Confessor bestowed
the house upon the French abbey of S. Denis, and as an alien priory it declined in
wealth and importance, owing to the confiscation of its revenues by King John and his
successors. In the reign of Henry VI the convent obtained a charter of denization, and
in 1469 Deerhurst was made a cell of Tewkesbury abbey and remained so until the
Suppression.

western and cross-walls of the tower. The wide arch now filled in at the eastern end of the present church formerly opened into the sanctuary. The quasi-transepts, which were walled off from the nave, were entered by small doorways in the dividing walls.

Beneath the pavement in and near the south transept of Peterborough cathedral, originally a great Benedictine church, are the foundations of the eastern part of a small unaisled cruciform church probably of the tenth century and of a type similar to that of Deerhurst priory.

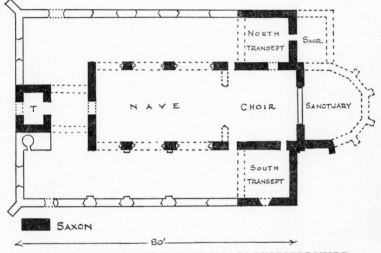

3. DEERHURST PRIORY CHURCH, GLOUCESTERSHIRE

No monastic buildings of these early centuries now exist in Western Christendom, but a most elaborate plan of S. Gall, dating from the beginning of the ninth century, is preserved in the monastery of that name in Switzerland. It is now generally agreed that it does not represent the plan of a monastery that was actually built, but is perhaps no more than a fanciful and ideal conception prepared by a monk. In its comprehensive character the plan was intended to typify a self-contained monastery, comprising the church, the conventual apartments, and innumerable buildings connected with the varied activities of lay-workers and craftsmen within the precinct, thus complying with the Rule of S. Benedict which enjoined that a monastery should contain within its walls everything necessary to the life of the inmates. The S. Gall plan resembles a village laid out on regular and symmetrical lines. Apart from the purely monastic apartments around the cloister, there are mills, a bakehouse and threshing floor, cow-houses and stables, sheep-folds, pig-sties, and fowl-houses, together with workshops and lodgings for goldsmiths, shoemakers, blacksmiths and fullers, tailors and saddlers; and in addition there are lodgings for *scutarii* and *armigeri*, i.e. armed men or retainers who dwelt within the precinct for purposes of security.

Scanty as is our knowledge of the religious establishments of the Saxons, the monastic remains of the post-Conquest centuries in various parts of the country are sufficiently extensive for us to determine with some exactitude the planning and the architectural character of the churches, and of the conventual buildings that were attached to them. Further, excavations carried out from time to time on the sites of monasteries long since destroyed have revealed the foundations of cloisters and buildings that indicate in general the planning adopted by the respective Orders of monks.

The largest mediaeval churches in England today are mainly those of the Benedictine cathedral-priories established by the Normans, most of which were subsequently enlarged; a few retain their cloister-walks but the conventual buildings are less in evidence.

Under the impulse of the Benedictine revival in Normandy (p. 42), a wholesale building and re-building of English monasteries took place in the half century following Duke William's victory at Hastings. Some years before the Conquest the influence of Norman culture and architecture had asserted itself in England, for when Edward the Confessor, who had been brought up in Normandy, embarked upon the re-building of Westminster abbey he imported masons from the Duchy, and the church they erected was planned on the lines of the abbey of Jumièges. An almost clean sweep was made of the Saxon monasteries by the ecclesiastics who followed in the train of the Conqueror, and in their place were reared more spacious and magnificent abbeys and churches, suited to the religious ideals of Normandy. Amongst them were the great Benedictine abbeys of Bury S. Edmunds, Canterbury, Chester, Durham, Ely, Gloucester, Norwich, Pershore, Peterborough, Rochester, Romsey, S. Albans, Tewkesbury, Winchester, and Worcester. A few years passed after the arrival of the Norman abbots and ecclesiastics before any building schemes were put in hand, for they had to accustom themselves to their new environment, lands and sites had to be acquired, and the ecclesiastical system re-organised. The first Benedictine monastery to be founded after the Conquest was the royal abbey of S. Martin, Battle, which in wealth and importance was second to none in the eleventh century. It was built in pursuance of a vow made by

Duke William that if God gave him victory over the Saxon hosts at Senlac, he would found a religious house for Benedictine monks on the site of the battle. The King intended that the abbey should house 140 brethren, but ultimately provision was made for only sixty. Monks were brought over from the Benedictine abbey of Marmoutier, and the Conqueror granted the convent all the land within the radius of three miles of Battle, together with estates in the counties of Kent, Surrey, Essex, Berkshire, Oxfordshire, and Devon. Holding their lands of the Crown *per baronium*, the abbots of Battle were privileged to sit in Parliament.[1]

Despite enlargements of the conventual buildings of Battle abbey in the thirteenth century, the grouping of the domestic apartments about the cloister remained presumably that of the Norman period, no radical change being made in the general lay-out. From the first the cloister lay to the south of the abbey nave; the chapter house and the two-storied dorter block stood on the east side of the cloister; to the south was the monks' frater, and the western range was the cellarium, with apartments for the abbot and his guests on the upper floor. To the east of the cloistral buildings was the farmery. Here was a ready-made plan for a Benedictine monastery; one that was perfectly suited to the needs of the brethren. With minor variations therefore, it was generally adopted for houses of the Order throughout the land. At Westminster abbey are considerable remains of the Norman conventual buildings that were attached to the Confessor's church, in particular the long sub-dorter, a fine example of early Norman work c. 1076, the north wall of the frater, and parts of the farmery hall and chapel. All of these occupy the same relative position as at Battle.

For the planning and building of the new abbeys and churches on English soil, masons from Normandy brought with them the traditions and methods of the Duchy, where several important abbeys had arisen since the Benedictine revival, and others were in course of erection. In general the Anglo-Norman churches, particularly those of the cathedral-priories, were conceived on a far grander scale than those of Normandy on which they were modelled. Cruciform on plan, they consisted of a long nave with north and south aisles, transepts with apsidal chapels at the east, and a short apsidal choir. At the crossing was a low tower and sometimes, as at Durham and Canterbury, there were twin towers

---

[1] Two years before William landed on the Sussex coast he founded the Abbaye aux Hommes (S. Étienne) at Caen, and in 1066 the Abbaye aux Dames (La Trinité) was founded by his wife and cousin, Matilda. Their marriage being within the prohibited degrees, the offending parties had been excommunicated by the Pope, whose wrath was appeased by these acts of contrition.

at the west. In many cases the eastern arm was raised on an extensive crypt, such as those at Winchester, Canterbury, and Worcester. The choirs of S. Augustine's, Canterbury, Bury S. Edmunds, and Evesham, long since destroyed, were also built on crypts. Characteristic of these great Benedictine churches of the eleventh century was the inordinate length of the naves, far exceeding those of the same period in Normandy. The naves of Ely and Winchester were laid out in twelve bays; that of S. Albans in thirteen bays, and of Norwich in fourteen bays, which was surpassed at Bury S. Edmunds by a nave fifteen bays in length. Apart from the massiveness and solidity of the structure the most arresting feature of the interior of these great churches is the bay design of three horizontal stages, viz. nave (or choir) arcade, triforium, and clerestory, well defined as it is, and of varying proportions and architectural design.

Two entirely different methods of planning the choir-arm were employed by the Norman builders. The first and simpler form consisted of an apsidal presbytery of two bays, flanked on either side by a shorter aisle that terminated at the east in an apse. On the chord of the central apse was placed the High Altar, with lesser altars in the lateral apses. This was the plan adopted in the abbey church of Bernay in 1017, and for the choir of the Abbaye aux Hommes at Caen c. 1064, and continued in use in Normandy until the end of the eleventh century. It appeared first in England in the Confessor's church at Westminster, the only pre-Conquest example, although there as in others of the type the lateral apses were squared externally (Fig. 4).[1] Probably Westminster was a copy of Bernay, which is said to have been built under the direction of William de Volpiano, the mainspring of the monastic revival in Normandy.[2]

Of the same type was the Norman church of the cathedral-priory of Canterbury. In 1067 the Saxon church had been destroyed by a disastrous fire, and after the Conqueror had installed

[1] The rebuilding of the abbey was undertaken in pursuance of a vow made by the Confessor during his long exile in Normandy, that he would make a pilgrimage to Rome if ever he were restored to England. On his return as king, the Grand Council of the realm would not hear of it. For their sovereign to undertake so long and perilous a journey was out of the question, as a deputation explained to the Pope. Edward was therefore released from his vow on condition that he refounded the abbey of S. Peter at Westminster. It was commenced c. 1055 and enough of it was completed in 1065 to permit of its consecration in that year. The choir, the transepts and two bays of the nave had been built by that time, but the church and the cloistral buildings were not completed until c. 1163. The total length of the church was about 332 feet. Excavations made in 1930 revealed the footings of five Norman piers at the west end of the present nave.

[2] The three-apsed choir of Bernay was the ancestor of S. Étienne, La Trinité, and S. Nicholas at Caen, and of Cérisy la Forêt, Monteviliers, S. Georges Boscherville, and Lessay.

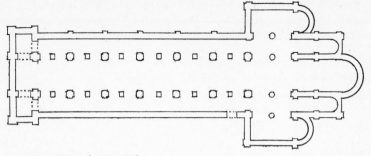

WESTMINSTER (NORMAN)

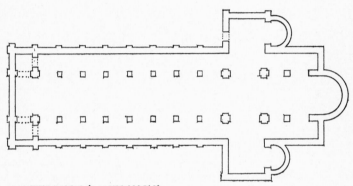

CANTERBURY (LANFRANC'S)

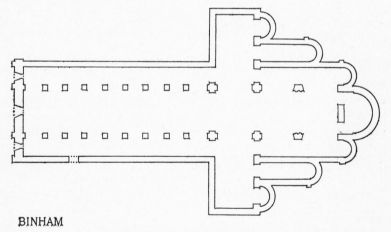

BINHAM

4. EARLY BENEDICTINE CHURCHES

Lanfranc in the arch-see, the site was cleared and Norman masons set to work building the cathedral anew from its foundations. Milo Crispinus tells us that Lanfranc 'caused to be brought over the sea in swift-sailing vessels squared stones from Caen to build with'. In character and dimensions the Norman church at Canterbury was modelled on S. Étienne, Caen, and was put up in great haste, being finished within seven years (Fig. 4). The eastern apses of the choir and of the transepts, the long aisled nave of eight bays with twin towers at the west, the northern of which remained until 1834, were typical of the period. It was by no means a stately or imposing church, being only 285 feet in length.

No complete example of a three-apsed choir remains in this country. Benedictine churches that are known to have been planned in this mode include: Whitby, after 1074; Ely, 1081; Blyth priory, 1087; Durham, 1093; Selby, after 1097; Bath, 1107; Wymondham, 1107; and Peterborough, 1118. A variant occurred at S. Albans, begun in 1077, where the eastern apses and two others in each transept were arranged in echelon, a lay-out that was repeated at S. Mary's abbey, York, in 1089, and again at Binham priory, a cell of S. Albans, in 1100 (Fig. 4). A modified version of the three-apsed choir was that of S. Martin's priory, Dover, c. 1090, where the aisles ended in apses but the presbytery was squared at the east.

The great drawback to the three-apsed choir lay in its inconvenience for processions and for the easy circulation of pilgrims, who might flock to the sanctuary to gaze upon saintly relics that were displayed on or beyond the High Altar. This was a serious consideration in those churches where pilgrimages were all-important and of frequent occurrence. The disadvantage was overcome by adopting the more complex apse-and-ambulatory or peri-apsidal plan for the eastern arm. Around the presbytery which terminated in an apse, the aisles of the choir were continued as a procession path or ambulatory, from which radiated three or more low apsidal chapels. Thus, passing round the ambulatory processions could visit the chapels without having to retrace their steps, and the piloting of pilgrims was a simple matter.

Strangely enough this method of choir-planning was rare in Normandy, where the preference was for parallel apses, but it was quite common in Burgundy, Auvergne, and Poitou, and was probably borrowed from one or other of these districts. The famous pilgrimage church of S. Martin, Tours, which was rebuilt early in the eleventh century may perhaps be regarded as the parent of all the apse-and-ambulatory choirs in England. The plan was certainly not of Norman origin, and it is reasonable to assume that amongst the planners and masons who came here after the Conquest was a sprinkling of Burgundians.[1] Moreover some of the newly appointed abbots were well acquainted with the Romanesque churches of Burgundy of the eleventh century.

The apse-and-ambulatory plan appeared full-blown in two of the earliest Benedictine churches in England, viz. Battle abbey and S. Augustine's, Canterbury, c. 1070 (Fig. 5). Others of the

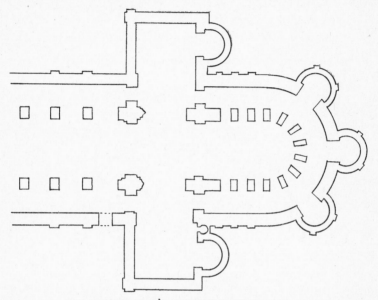

5. AUGUSTINE'S, CANTERBURY, 1070

eleventh century included Winchester, c. 1080; Worcester, c. 1084; Tewkesbury, after 1087; Gloucester, c. 1089; Tynemouth, a cell of S. Albans, c. 1090; S. Werburgh, Chester, 1093; Bury S. Edmunds, consecrated in 1095, and Norwich, 1096. These were followed early in the twelfth century by Crowland, c. 1113; Reading, 1125; Leominster, a cell of Reading, 1125, and the more important 'Glorious Choir' at Canterbury, completed by prior Conrad in 1126, that replaced the three-apsed choir of Lanfranc and doubled the length of the cathedral. A special feature of Conrad's choir

[1] Further evidences of Burgundian influence, if not of actual masoncraft, occur at Gloucester and Tewkesbury, the naves of which are laid out with exceptionally tall cylindrical piers, quite unlike those in the larger churches of Normandy. They seem to have derived from the great eleventh-century church of Tournus in Burgundy, and in all three the capitals are mere circular imposts, rare in Normandy. Again, the chapter house at Gloucester is roofed with a pointed barrel vault that is characteristic of the Romanesque of Burgundy and Auvergne.

was the addition of transepts, each with a pair of apsidal chapels (Fig. 7). The Norman choir of Winchester differed from the normal apse-and-ambulatory type, for in place of the radiating chapels the choir-aisles terminated in square-ended chapels, between which a long apsidal chapel projected eastwards. Today the least altered choir of this kind is that of Norwich, which was erected during the episcopate of Herbert de Losinga and was obviously a copy of Fécamp abbey, of which the bishop had formerly been the

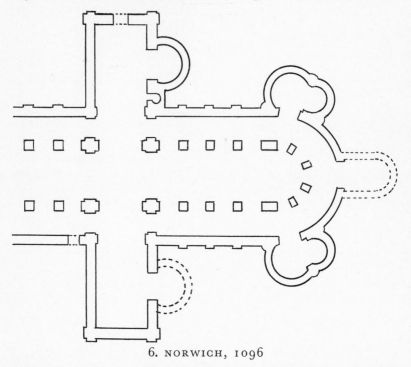

6. NORWICH, 1096

prior (Fig. 6). A peculiarity of Norwich is the double-segmental plan of the north-eastern and south-eastern chapels off the ambulatory.

Of the eight Benedictine cathedral-priories all but Bath, Ely, and Norwich were built with a crypt beneath the eastern arm, the existence of which indicates the plan of the superstructure prior to subsequent remodelling. In this respect the crypts of Winchester, Worcester, and Gloucester in particular are invaluable. The absence of crypts at Ely, Norwich, and Peterborough is due to the marshy nature of the soil in East Anglia.

The building of crypts was a survival of the tradition of the

Early Christian Church in Italy, where it was the custom to bury the bodies of the saints and martyrs in an undercroft beneath the sanctuary. The custom fell into desuetude in this country in the twelfth century, brought about very largely by the murder of Archbishop Thomas Becket in Canterbury cathedral in the year 1170, a tragic deed that established the fame of the priory of Christ Church and brought great wealth to the convent for three centuries or more. In 1173 Becket the martyr was canonised, and the following year the choir of the cathedral was gutted by fire. Rebuilding was undertaken at once, and the French master-mason William de Sens and his successor, William the Englishman, reared a new eastern arm of vast size, embracing a peri-

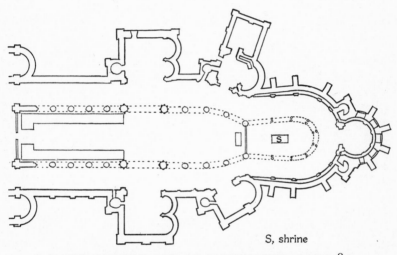

S, shrine

7. THE EASTERN ARM OF CANTERBURY, 1175–84

apsidal extension, specially devised as a saint's chapel to house the shrine of S. Thomas. The shrine was to be translated from the crypt and displayed more worthily above ground in a chapel behind the High Altar, and farther east was a circular chapel or corona to contain relics of the Saint (Fig. 7). The extension was an afterthought inspired by the cult of S. Thomas, an amazing conception that was completed in 1184. It altered the whole trend of choir-planning in the great Benedictine churches, the convents of which made a bid for popularity by installing and displaying their pilgrim-attracting shrines. Every abbey of importance sought to possess the shrine of some wonder-working saint that would add honour and dignity to their house; and the offerings made by pilgrims provided a valuable source of income. Within thirty years

I

of the canonisation of Becket many of the saints of the Saxon
Church were translated to new shrines in famous Benedictine
churches. At S. Albans there was S. Amphibalus; at Ramsey,
S. Ethelbert; at Crowland, S. Guthlac; at Bury S. Edmunds,
S. Edmund; at Tynemouth priory, S. Oswin, and at Winchester,
S. Swithun.

The acquisition of shrines and relics came to be an obsession
with many Benedictine abbots, who sometimes threw all scruples
to the wind to gain their ends. When Benedict, the prior of Canterbury, was made abbot of Peterborough in 1177 he removed two
flagstones from the spot where Becket had been slain, and carted
them off to Peterborough where they were used for the making of
two altars. No less enterprising were the brethren of S. Augustine's,
Canterbury, who induced the keeper of the altar of the Martyrdom at Christ Church to hand over to them a part of Becket's
skull, promising him as a reward the abbacy of their convent.
The theft and the promise were duly carried out, but as a precaution in the future a watching chamber overlooking the shrine
was occupied day and night by monk-guards, and bandogs were
kept within call during the night. Bedecked with gold and silver
images and precious stones, shrines needed protection from common thieves as well as against envious monks of rival houses. At
S. Albans there still remains a two-storied watching house of timber, on the north side of the shrine of the proto-martyr of England.

The shrine consisted of three parts, the pedestal or 'throne',
the feretrum, and the canopy. The pedestal or base of stone or
marble was architectural in design, enriched with carving or
mosaic and adorned with saintly images of gold or silver. It was
about 6 or 8 feet in height, and in the lower part were a number of
recesses or niches, into which the sick and crippled seeking the
healing virtues of the saint might crouch in hope of a cure. On
the pedestal rested the feretrum, a wooden chest containing the
remains of the saint, and covered with plates of silver or gold, in-
set with rubies, emeralds, and other precious stones. To preserve
the treasures on and around the chest, a wooden box-like canopy
with a gabled roof, and adorned with paintings, was suspended
above the shrine by chains let down from the roof or vaulting. It
was made to work on pulleys, so that it could be readily raised
when the feretrum was to be displayed. In the roof over the site
of the shrine at S. Albans abbey are still to be seen the holes made
by the pulley-fixtures of the canopy.

The majority of pilgrimage churches were served by Benedictine
monks, who built hostels within or without their precincts to
accommodate the crowds of pilgrims who journeyed thither. Fore-

most amongst them were Bury S. Edmunds, Canterbury, Chester (S. Werburgh), Crowland, Durham (S. Cuthbert), Ely (S. Etheldreda), Malmesbury (S. Aldhelm), Rochester (S. William of Perth), S. Albans, Tynemouth, Winchester, Worcester (S. Oswald), and the greatest of all, Westminster abbey, where 'the shrine of the most illustrious King Edward the Confessor was placed on high, so that all who enter the House of the Lord may behold its light' (*Liber Trinitas*).

All sorts of legends and stories of miraculous wonders gathered about the shrines of the saints. An interesting incident that occurred at S. Albans abbey is related by Sir Thomas More. On one occasion Humphrey Duke of Gloucester, son of Henry IV, confronted an imposter in the abbey church, a man who claimed to have been blind from birth and to have received his sight by touching the shrine of S. Alban. The Duke asked the beggar to name the colours of the garments he and his attendants were wearing. Correct answers being made, the impostor was whipped and set in the stocks for his pains. The incident was dramatised by Shakespeare in *Henry VI*, Part II.

Of the many Benedictine shrines that existed before Henry VIII's crusade against relics and his seizure of their treasures, the pedestals of S. Werburgh. S. Etheldreda, S. Alban, and S. Edward the Confessor alone remain, bereft of their mediaeval splendour. Others were dismantled and broken up, leaving no trace of their existence. That of S. Alban suffered a like fate, but in 1872 more than two thousand fragments of the pedestal were found in the retrochoir of the abbey church and were reassembled with amazing skill, presenting us with the form and design of the original (Pl. XXXIII).

Normally the shrine was set up in a bay of the retrochoir behind the High Altar, and was enclosed by screens or by a ring of stately tombs, thus forming a saint's chapel. The provision of such a chapel invariably necessitated the lengthening and remodelling of the eastern arm of a church, the earliest of which was at Christ Church, Canterbury. Other Benedictine houses followed suit, although on different lines. About the year 1200 a big eastern extension was undertaken at Winchester that occupied some thirty-five years (Fig. 8). The old Norman apse of the presbytery was allowed to remain, to the east of which was planned a spacious, squared retrochoir of three bays, with a Lady Chapel farther east flanked by chapels. The central part of the retrochoir was reserved for the saint's chapel in which was placed the shrine of S. Swithun, and the surrounding aisles afforded ample space for processions and pilgrim visitations. Almost a century passed before the Norman

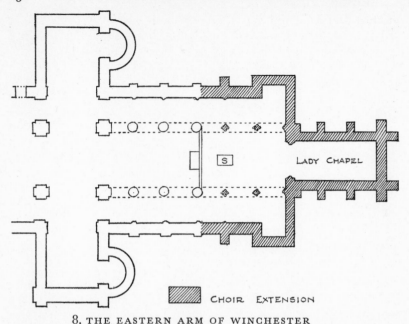

8. THE EASTERN ARM OF WINCHESTER

When the retrochoir was added *c.* 1200, the Norman apsidal presbytery of 1079 remained undisturbed and was not rebuilt until 1320. The Lady Chapel was doubled in length in the fifteenth century.

apse was taken down to permit the rebuilding of the presbytery. In due course the new eastern arm of Winchester served as a model for S. Albans, where a chapel for the shrine was urgently needed. This ambitious scheme was undertaken in 1257 and was more than sixty years in fulfilment owing to lack of funds. Differing entirely from Winchester was the planning of the choir of Henry III's new abbey at Westminster, *par excellence* the ideal for pilgrimage churches (p. 137). Often, Benedictine churches that lacked a shrine, such as Norwich and Peterborough, retained their original Norman choir-arm more or less unaltered through the centuries.

Devotion to the Virgin Mary and the increasing veneration that was paid to the 'Queen of Heaven' as intercessor for the living, gave rise to a cult that was fostered by Pope, bishop, and abbot, and found its material expression in the provision of a chapel specially dedicated to Our Lady, an almost indispensable adjunct of every church of importance from the thirteenth century onwards. By the beginning of the fourteenth century few churches of the Benedictines were without a Lady Chapel. Usually it took the form of an unaisled hall rectangular on plan, which was erected as an eastern annexe of the choir or retrochoir,[1] as at Winchester, S. Albans, Gloucester, and Chester, an addition that elongated still more the eastern extensions of Benedictine and other churches. The new eastern arm of Canterbury, 1175–84, increased the length of the cathedral from 285 to 518 feet, and when the retrochoir and Lady Chapel at S. Albans were completed that great church attained a length of 520 feet.

The thirteenth century was the great period of choir remodelling and extension in Benedictine churches. The earlier Norman choirs were dark and incommodious, more altars and additional space for free movement about the east end were needed. Early in the thirteenth century a modified version of the new retrochoir of Winchester was planned at S. Werburgh's, Chester, although it was not completed for more than a century; and at Malmesbury the Norman apses of the choir were swept away to give place to a retrochoir for the shrine of S. Aldhelm, an ambulatory, and a Lady Chapel (Fig. 9).

No other Benedictine church adopted the form of eastern extension that appeared at Durham, where there was a dearth of altars for the celebration of soul-masses on behalf of benefactors, and where the shrine of S. Cuthbert, most inconveniently situated for pilgrims, stood in the apse behind the High Altar. In 1242 the convent turned their eyes to the unique transept across the east end of the abbey church of Fountains, then on the verge of completion (Fig. 20). This was accordingly copied in the mighty church above the Wear. Athwart the east end was built the wide-spreading transept of the Nine Altars, and on the site of the central apse of the Norman choir was erected a stone platform, 6 feet high, to form an elevated chapel for the shrine (Fig. 20). The new transept, which measured 127 feet from north to south, served as an ambulatory from which the shrine set up on high could be seen to advantage, and at the same time afforded space for nine altars against the east wall. 'Betwixt every altar [was] a very fair and large partition of wainscot, all varnished over, with very fine branches and flowers and other imagery work most finely and artificially pictured and gilded, containing the several lockers or aumbers for the safe keeping of the vestments and ornaments belonging to every altar; with three or four aumbries in the wall pertaining to some of the said altars' (*Rites of Durham*).

[1] There were a few notable exceptions. At Canterbury the whole of the crypt was the Chapel of Our Lady Undercroft, and in the fifteenth century another Lady Chapel was built to the east of the north transept. The five-aisled Lady Chapel at Durham, known as Pudsey's Galilee, stands at the west end of the nave, owing to S. Cuthbert's antipathy to anything feminine. At Ely, Peterborough, and Tynemouth the Chapel of Our Lady was built outside the choir on the north side.

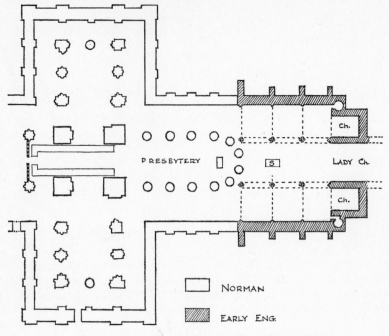

PRESBYTERY

LADY Ch.

Ch.

Ch.

S

☐ NORMAN

▨ EARLY ENG.

9. MALMESBURY ABBEY CHOIR-EXTENSION

A much simpler plan, that can best be described as the aisled rectangle, was favoured by some Benedictine houses intent upon rebuilding their choirs in the thirteenth century. Dispensing with the Lady Chapel as an eastern annexe, the choir and its aisles were continued at unbroken height from east to west. The High Altar was placed against a screen in the second bay from the east, and the altar of Our Lady together with other altars was set up against the eastern wall.

The aisled rectangle was not of Benedictine origin, though it was adopted in many of their choir reconstructions during the thirteenth and fourteenth centuries. Boxgrove priory (Pl. XXIV), the choir of which was laid out in double bays *c.* 1210 (Fig. 10), furnishes an admirable example. Ten years later the monks of Whitby embarked on a complete rebuilding of their church, the work starting at the east. The Norman choir was replaced by one of seven bays with north and south aisles. During the last quarter of the thirteenth century a reconstruction of the abbey church of S. Mary, York, was in progress; the eastern arm, planned as an aisled rectangle eight bays in length, was one of the finest of the

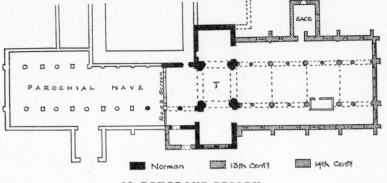

10. BOXGROVE PRIORY

Geometrical period; so magnificent a work that *c.* 1280 the convent at Selby were induced to remodel their choir on similar lines (Fig. 11). It has been suggested that the choir of Selby, seven bays in length, was planned by the master-mason of S. Mary's. It was not finished until *c.* 1375, for the political events of the time seriously interfered with building operations. The monasteries were called upon to supply men and money for the Scottish wars early in the fourteenth century, and the Black Death caused further delay.

The largest and loveliest Benedictine choir of this type now

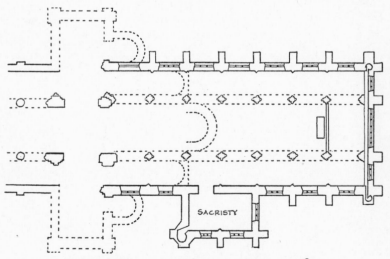

11. THE CHOIR ARM OF SELBY ABBEY, 1280–90

The Norman apses and transepts are in dotted outline.

extant is that of Ely cathedral, commenced in 1235, nine bays in length. The High Altar was set up in the position it now occupies, two bays distant from the east wall; the shrine of S. Etheldreda was erected beyond the High Altar, and the easternmost bay served as an ambulatory. It was completed in 1252, and in October of that year the shrine was installed in the presence of Henry III and a great gathering of ecclesiastics and nobles.

For more than three and a half centuries the conservative monks of Peterborough contented themselves with the three-apsed choir of the twelfth century. The abbey affords a rare instance of a Benedictine church of the first rank and importance that was without a shrine.[1] A saint's chapel not being a necessity, the convent was not burdened with the costly replanning of the choir-arm, which remained undisturbed when the Lady Chapel was built in the thirteenth century outside the choir on the north side. However, during the rule of abbot Ashton, 1438–71, when additional altars were needed, an eastern extension was undertaken, consisting of a square retrochoir equal in width to the choir and its aisles. The Norman lateral apses were pulled down, the aisles were continued eastwards and squared, and the central apse was pierced with arches on the ground level. Completed early in the sixteenth century, the retrochoir provided space for five altars against the east wall.

The last great Benedictine choir to be remodelled was that of Bath abbey, mainly the work of Bishop Oliver King after his translation to the see of Bath and Wells in 1495. The nave and the parallel-apsed choir of the Norman period were removed and a new Perpendicular choir, planned as an aisled rectangle four bays in length, was put up on the site of the eastern half of the old nave, an undertaking that may be said to close the last chapter of mediaeval Gothic.

In a class apart as regards Benedictine planning is the eastern arm of the royal abbey of Westminster, 1245–69. In 1220, in accordance with the fashion of the time, the convent had erected a Lady Chapel at the east end of the church, where Henry VII's chapel now stands. The foundation stone was laid by the young King Henry III on Whitsun eve 1220, an event that may have suggested the rebuilding of the whole abbey to the King. The dedication of S. Chapelle, Paris, at which he was present, and the mighty French cathedrals of Amiens and Rheims, both in course of erection, proved an inspiration to Henry for a new and splendid

[1] The convent possessed relics of S. Kyneburgha, S. Kyneswitha, and S. Oswald, which were probably displayed on altars in the church and attracted pilgrims from all parts.

XVIII. The prior's house, Wenlock.

XIX. The sub-dorter or warming house, Durham.

XX. Ground floor of the domus conversorum, Fountains Abbey.

XXI. The farmery cloister, Gloucester.

XXII. The farmery cloister walk, Canterbury.

XXIII. Interior, Tewkesbury Abbey church.

XXIV. The choir, Boxgrove Priory church.

XXV. Interior, Romsey Abbey church.

XXVI. The nave, Blyth Priory.

XXVII. Towers and nave, Wymondham Abbey church.

XXVIII. The rood screen, Crowland Abbey.

abbey to adjoin his palace at Westminster. Henry III's predilec-
tions being in favour of foreign counsellors and influences, small
wonder that he turned to France for a model for his new abbey
church. The main portion of Westminster abbey is the work of
Henry III's masons. The lay-out of the eastern arm is essentially
French (Fig. 12). The chevet or corona of polygonal chapels was

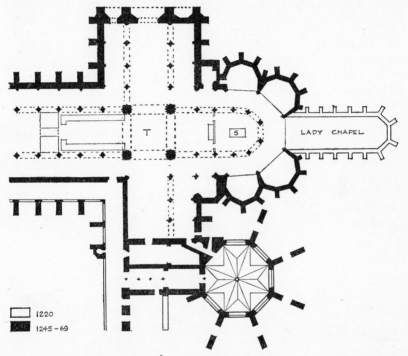

1220
1245 – 69

12. HENRY III'S WESTMINSTER ABBEY

the standard plan for the great churches of the thirteenth century
in the Île de France,[1] and the choir of Westminster was certainly
planned by a master-mason who was well acquainted with the
cathedrals of Amiens and Rheims. It consists of a presbytery of
three bays with a five-sided apse at the east, and opening from the
ambulatory on either side are two polygonal chapels and a small
square chapel to the west. The earlier Lady Chapel was largely
rebuilt in order to bring it into scale with the chevet. In the internal arrangements of the choir, the sanctuary occupied the two

[1] The French chevet plan was the logical development of the apse-and-ambulatory
plan. The one big advantage it possessed concerned the lighting of the chapels off the
ambulatory; for polygonal chapels with three or more straight walls could be opened
up with wide and lofty windows, impossible in the curved walls of apsidal chapels.

western bays, and beyond the High Altar was the chapel for the Confessor's shrine. The ritual choir in which were the stalls of the monks extended into the three eastern bays of the nave where the choristers now seat themselves for the services in the abbey.

Being un-English and alien to our traditions, the chevet of Westminster had little influence on subsequent monastic planning in this country. The square eastern arm for both large and small churches was well established before the choir of Westminster was begun; its construction was a much simpler matter than the complexities of the French plan. The only complete and direct imitations of Westminster were Hayles abbey, a Cistercian foundation commenced in 1271 (p. 171), and Battle abbey, the new choir of which was built early in the fourteenth century. The presbytery of Battle was laid out in six aisled bays, with a polygonal apse and an ambulatory with five radiating chapels.

To some extent the chevet of Westminster influenced the changes that were wrought in the choir of Tewkesbury abbey c. 1390, where five polygonal chapels of varying shapes and sizes and an eastern Lady Chapel were built in place of the three Norman apsidal chapels off the ambulatory (Fig. 13). Except for the Lady Chapel, which has been destroyed, the choir of Tewkesbury, the last of its kind in English Gothic, remains intact (Pl. XXIII).

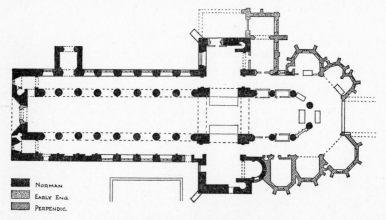

NORMAN
EARLY ENG.
PERPENDIC.

13. TEWKESBURY ABBEY CHURCH

Significant of the wealth and importance of the Benedictines are the outstanding achievements in English architecture that characterised the building of their greater churches in the Middle Ages. No other Order contributed so much to the advance of structural science and to architectural development from the eleventh to the sixteenth century. In the mighty church of the cathedral-priory of Durham, the Norman masons solved the problem of roofing a great building throughout with ribbed vaults of stone, a triumph that embodied the principles that went to the making of Gothic architecture. At Christ Church, Canterbury, the momentous reconstruction of the choir-arm after the fire of 1174 established the saint's chapel as an integral part of great pilgrimage churches, and promoted the choir-extensions that became so general in the thirteenth century. Further, the marble shafting in Canterbury choir set the fashion for the 'Purbeck use'. The rebuilding of the abbey church of Westminster, 1245–69, was the supreme and perfect expression of the finest phase of Gothic; though French in plan and general design, it was English in detail. A rare distinction fell to the masons who transformed the transepts and choir of S. Peter's abbey church (now the cathedral), Gloucester, for their novel re-casing of the Norman work made Gloucester the cradle of Perpendicular Gothic; and when the cloister was rebuilt, the four walks were roofed with fan-vaulting, the earliest in the country. No less remarkable was the 'modernising' of the nave of Winchester in the second half of the fourteenth century. There, the Norman nave was disguised as Perpendicular by William of Wykeham's masons. As at Gloucester the Perpendicular vesture is but skin-deep, and the change, wrought with amazing skill, is one of the marvels of mediaeval masoncraft. To return to Westminster—where the Lady Chapel built by Henry VII seems to close the story of English Gothic on a triumphant note. More elaborate in form and more sumptuous in decoration than anything in England, it was spoken of by Leland as the 'orbis miraculum'; the walls of the chapel are literally glass screens separated by posts of stone, and suspended in mid-air is the miraculous fan-vault, second to none in this country.

Of the monastic churches that escaped destruction at the time of the Dissolution and are still in use wholly or in part, those of the Benedictines are the most numerous. With the exception of Bath and Coventry, all the Benedictine monastic cathedrals were reconstituted as secular cathedrals by Henry VIII, and having suffered little damage other than unsympathetic restoration, they remain outstanding monuments of English mediaeval architecture. In addition a number of other important churches of the Order survive intact, notably Chester, Peterborough, S. Peter's Gloucester, and Westminster,[1] all of which were refounded as cathedrals by Henry VIII; S. Albans, raised to cathedral rank in

[1] Westminster abbey was a cathedral in the diocese of London for ten years only, the see being abolished in 1550.

1877; and Great Malvern, Romsey, Sherborne, S. Helen's Bishops-gate and Tewkesbury, which now serve parochial purposes.

The following is a list of Benedictine churches that have survived only in part and are in use as parish churches. In several instances modern additions have been made to the remains of the monastic church.

A indicates abbey; P, priory

Bath A, Somerset. Choir. Nave completed by Gilbert Scott.

Binham P, Norfolk. Nave.

Blyth P, Notts. Nave and aisles.

Boxgrove P, Sussex. Choir, transepts, and two bays of nave.

Bristol, S. James' P, Gloucs. Nave.

Bromfield P, Salop. Nave and north aisle.

Chepstow P, Monmouth. Nave.

Cranborne P, Dorset. Nave and aisles.

Crowland A, Lincs. North aisle of nave.

Davington P (nuns), Kent. Nave and north aisle.

Deeping S. James P, Lincs. Nave.

Deerhurst P, Gloucs. Nave and aisles.

Dunster P, Somerset. Nave and aisles.

Elstow A (nuns), Beds. Nave and aisles.

Freiston P, Lincs. Nave.

Hatfield Broadoak P, Essex. Nave and aisles.

Hatfield Peveril P, Essex. Nave and north aisle.

Hurley P, Berks. Nave and chancel.

King's Lynn, S. Margaret's P, Norfolk. Chancel.

Lapley P, Staffs. Nave and chancel.

Leominster P, Hereford. Two parallel naves, and north and south aisles.

Little Malvern P, Worcs. Chancel.

Malmesbury A, Wilts. Nave and aisles.

Milton A, Dorset. Choir and transepts.

Minster A (nuns), Sheppey. Nave and north aisle.

Nun Monkton P (nuns), Yorks. Nave.

Pershore A, Worcs. Choir and south transept.

S. Bees P, Cumberland. Nave and one bay of choir.

Shrewsbury A, Salop. Nave.

Thorney A, Cambs. Nave.

Tutbury P, Staffs. Nave and south aisle.

Upholland P, Lancs. Choir.

Wymondham A, Norfolk. Nave and aisles.

York, Holy Trinity P. Nave.

Of very few Benedictine churches that are now in ruins are the remains of any great extent. Invaluable for its Celtic associations and its Norman architecture is the church of Lindisfarne priory, considerable portions of which are *in situ* open to the sky (Pl. XXIX). The short choir, north transept, north nave arcade and aisle, and the west wall of the nave bear witness to the robust quality of post-Conquest building. Of no less importance are the ruins of Whitby abbey, consisting of the shell of the aisled choir, the north transept, and walling of the nave. Even in their forlorn state they afford a noble specimen of English Gothic of the thirteenth and fourteenth centuries. Less abundant are the remains of the great abbey churches of Glastonbury and S. Mary's, York. At Glastonbury the main feature is the roofless Lady Chapel with the Galilee, beyond the west wall of the nave; in the body of the church are the two eastern piers at the crossing together with the arches that opened into the choir aisles, and portions of the south walls of the choir and nave. At S. Mary's, York, which was a splendid example of Geometric Gothic, the scanty remains consist of the north wall of the nave and part of the west front, the north-west pier at the crossing, and fragments of the north transept. Farther north is the ruined church of Tynemouth priory, the portions above ground being chiefly of the walls of the nave, the lower part of the west front, the south and east walls of the presbytery, a portion of the rood screen, and at the extreme east the Percy chantry chapel, the only part of the church that retains its vault and roof.

Practically nothing is left of the famous abbey church of Bury S. Edmunds, and that at Evesham was levelled to the ground, the site being marked by the detached tower at the north.

The only Benedictine cloisters now preserved are those to be seen at Canterbury, Chester, Gloucester, Norwich, Westminster, and Worcester; and in every case the four walks are roofed with the original stone vaulting.[1] Except Norwich all the above-named retain some of their conventual buildings. Those at Chester are the most complete, and include the chapter house and vestibule, the parlour in the sub-dorter, the day-stairs to the dorter, the frater and the cellarium. At Westminster (Fig. 1) the eastern cloistral range is complete, the abbot's house and a long building known as the *calbege* are fairly intact, and there are remains of the farmery cloister, hall, and chapel. At Gloucester, in addition to the chapter house, the library, and the prior's lodging, are the small farmery cloister (Pl. XXI) and a few arches of the farmery hall. The chief

---

[1] The cloister walks at Durham were subjected to drastic alteration in the eighteenth century, and only the timber roofs are mediaeval.

remains at Worcester are the chapter house and frater; and at Christ Church, Canterbury, the chapter house of which is one of the finest extant (Pl. XIV), are the farmery cloister with its water tower, ruins of the farmery hall and chapel, and several buildings in the outer court including the Aula nova, the bakehouse, and brewhouse (Fig. 2).

Although foundations of the conventual buildings of many Benedictine monasteries have been uncovered by excavation, remains existing above ground are scarce compared with those of Cistercian abbeys (p. 173). Unusually extensive are those of Finchale priory, Durham. There, substantial portions are still standing of the walls of the apartments east and south of the cloister, and of the spacious prior's lodging some distance east of the cloistral buildings.

VIII. The Priories of the Cluniac Order

~~~~~~~~~~~~~~~~~~~~~~~~~~~~~~~~~~~~~

An Order of Reformed Benedictines founded at Cluny—The Constitution of the Order—All Priories Subject to the Parent House—La Charité-sur-Loire and S. Martin des Champs, Paris—The Precedence of Lewes in England—The Cluniac Ideal of Splendour—Letter of Protest written by S. Bernard—The Abbey of Cluny—Its Influence on the New Eastern Arm of Lewes—The Parallel-apsed Choirs of Castle Acre and Thetford—Cluniac Churches as Resorts of Pilgrims—The Conventual Buildings—The Love of Ornament and its Influence on Benedictine Architecture—Remains of Cluniac Priories.

~~~~~~~~~~~~~~~~~~~~~~~~~~~~~~~~~~~~~

FOLLOWING HARD ON the heels of the Benedictines who came in the train of the Conqueror were the monks of the Cluniac Order. In the year 817 a great assembly of monastic heads was held at Aix-la-Chapelle and under the guidance of S. Benedict of Aniane, a number of Customs were instituted for the better regulation of the Benedictines, and for welding the scattered units into a religious Order. His death in 823 shelved the reform, but at the abbey of Cluny in Burgundy, founded in 910 by William, Duke of Aquitaine, Berno the abbot and twelve of his brethren founded an Order based on the strict observance of the Benedictine code and on the Customs proposed by Benedict of Aniane.

The Cluniac Order of reformed Benedictines spread widely over Western Europe, and early in the eleventh century Cluniac Customs were introduced into Normandy. After the Norman Conquest William I offered the abbot of Cluny a large sum of money if he would send twelve monks to be abbots in England. The head of Cluny replied that his brethren were not for sale.[1] However, in response to a request from William de Warenne, Earl of Surrey,

[1] Rose Graham, *An Essay on English Monasteries.*

143

who with his lady had visited Cluny and had been admitted into the 'fraternity' of the Order, a number of monks from Cluny came to England and in 1077 settled at Lewes, which became the chief house in this country.

The constitution of the Order differed from that of the Benedictines, for all their houses were founded as priories and were subject to the abbot of Cluny, whereas the Benedictine houses were independent. The ideal of Cluny was the existence of one great central monastery with dependent houses, forming a vast monastic hierarchy. The subordinate priories were dependants in the strictest sense, for the head of every house was to be nominated by the abbot of Cluny, and at first the profession of every member was made by his sanction. The government of the Order was based on this centralised system, with Cluny as the headquarters. Trouble arose on this account at Castle Acre priory, a daughter house of Lewes, in 1283. With the approval of the convent, William de Warenne, the patron, had installed a William de Shoreham as prior of Castle Acre, and all the efforts of the head of Lewes to remove him proved futile. Eventually the abbot of Cluny exercised his authority by appointing Benedict of Cluny in place of the interloper.

The number of priories in Western Europe increased to such an extent that the abbot of Cluny was compelled to delegate his authority in part to other priories, themselves dependent on the parent house. As a result the English houses were made subject either to Cluny itself or to La Charité-sur-Loire or S. Martin des Champs, Paris. Until the Suppression the priory of S. Pancras, Lewes, had precedence over all other English houses of the Order. By the end of the eleventh century three others had been founded, viz. Wenlock c. 1080, and Bermondsey and Castle Acre in 1089. In all there were thirty-two houses of Cluniac monks in the English province, all of which were founded before the end of the twelfth century. In addition to the foregoing, the largest and most wealthy were Lenton, Montacute, Northampton, and Pontefract, and there were many cells of the larger houses. Lewes priory had six off-shoots; Farley, Castle Acre, Monks Horton, Prittlewell, Stanesgate and Tickford. Castle Acre priory in its turn established daughter houses at Bromholm, Normansburgh, Slevesholm, and Mendham. By a Papal bull of 1399 the priory of S. Saviour, Bermondsey, was raised to the status of an abbey, the only instance in England.

To the Cluniacs nothing was too costly or splendid to offer to their Creator, and they therefore made their churches as rich and stately as lay in their power. The arts of sculpture and painting and the craft of the metal-worker were pressed into service to embellish God's house; and their ceremonials and ritualistic observances were lengthy and elaborate. It was the wealth of ornament and decoration lavished upon their churches that roused the ire of the great S. Bernard. In a famous letter written to abbot William de S. Thierry about 1124, S. Bernard, who became abbot of Clairvaux in 1115, protested in vehement terms against Cluniac pomp and luxury. He denounced 'the immense height of their churches, their immoderate length and their superfluous breadth, costly polishing, and the curious carvings which attract the worshipper's gaze and hinder his devotion. . . . We suppose it is done for God's honour, but I as a monk ask "Tell me ye poor, if ye be poor, what doeth this gold in your sanctuary?" . . . We [monks] who have forsaken all precious and beautiful things for Christ's sake, who have counted but dung all things fair to see, soft to the ear, sweet to the smell, pleasant to the touch, whose devotion do we intend to excite by such means? What profit I say do we expect therefrom? The admiration of fools or the oblations of the simple? Doth the root of all this lie in covetousness? Wheresoever [in churches] more abundant wealth is seen, there do men offer more freely. Their eyes are feasted with relics cased in gold, and their purse-strings are loosed. . . . The church is resplendent in her walls, beggarly in her poor: she clothes her stones in gold, and leaves her sons naked. Why lavish bright hues upon that [pavement] which must needs be trodden underfoot? What are such things to do with you poor men, you monks? . . . And in the cloister what profit is there in those ridiculous monsters of deformed comeliness and comely deformity? To what purpose are those unclean apes, those fierce lions, those monstrous centaurs, those half-men, those striped tigers, those fighting knights, those hunters winding their horns? Here is a four-footed beast with a serpent's tail; there a fish with a beast's head. . . . In short so many and so various are the shapes on every hand, that we are more tempted to read in the stonework than in books, and to spend the whole day wondering at these things, rather than in meditating on the law of God. For God's sake, if we are not ashamed of these follies, why do they not shrink from the cost?'

The mighty abbey of Cluny, the third on the site, begun in 1088, was the largest Romanesque church in Christendom. It was 520 feet in length. The sanctuary was encircled by an ambulatory with five radiating chapels; there were eastern as well as main transepts, a tower at each crossing, twin towers at the west, and smaller towers flanking the main transepts. The nave of

K

twelve bays and part of the choir were double-aisled and at the western end of the nave was a narthex of five bays.

But the beginnings of Cluny were humble and arduous, and the brethren were inspired by an intense enthusiasm for spiritual life. Guyot de Provins, a minstrel and later a monk, wrote of the Cluniacs: 'When you wish to sleep they awake you; when you wish to eat they make you fast; the night is passed in praying in the church, the day in working, and there is no repose but in the frater. And what is to be found there? Rotten eggs, beans with all their pods on, and liquor fit for oxen. For the wine is so poor that one might drink of it for a month without intoxication.'

The last Cluniac house to be founded in this country was Slevesholm in 1222. On account of their dependency on Cluny, several were suppressed as alien priories late in the fourteenth century, but a number were allowed to remain as denizen priories free from foreign control (p. 52).

All Cluniac establishments followed the Benedictine Rule, and their first churches in England displayed no marked differences in planning from those of the Black Monks. The choir-arm of Lewes priory, dedicated between 1091 and 1098, was laid out with apse and ambulatory much like that of Battle; but after the rebuilding of the great church at Cluny, 1088–1108, the monks of Lewes set

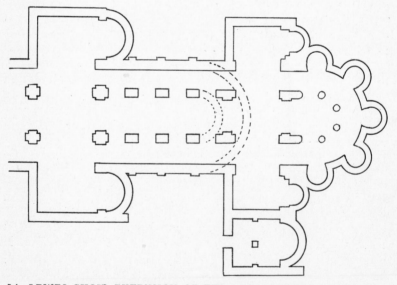

14. LEWES CHOIR-EXTENSION OF THE EARLY TWELFTH CENTURY
The original apsidal termination is shown in dotted lines.

about remodelling the choir of their church on similar lines
(Fig. 14). Doubled in length, the new choir terminated at the east
in an apse and ambulatory with five radiating chapels, and was
remarkable for the choir transepts and the tower at the eastern
crossing.[1] Dedicated after 1142, it increased the length of the
church to 405 feet. The plan seems not to have been adopted for
any other Cluniac church in England. At Castle Acre, 1090–5, the
choir was laid out on the simpler parallel-apsed mode of the Bene-

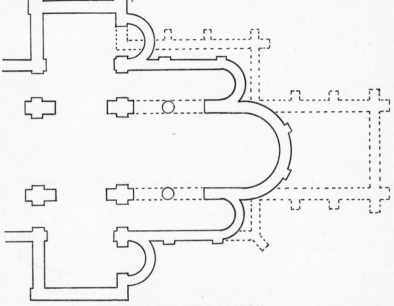

15. CASTLE ACRE PRIORY

The choir-extension of the fourteenth century is shown in dotted outline.

dictines, flanked by a single apsidal chapel to the east of each transept (Fig. 15), and exactly the same plan was employed c. 1104 for
the choir of Thetford priory church. In both cases the parallel
apses were subsequently torn down to make way for more commodious choirs.

The remodelling of the eastern arms of Cluniac churches in the
Gothic centuries was rarely on so big a scale as that of the Benedictines. The choir-extension of Wenlock priory was exceptional.

[1] Lewes was not the first English church in which the choir-transepts of Cluny were
copied. They appeared at Christ Church priory, Canterbury, when the new choir was
commenced by prior Ernulf in 1096. There as at Cluny each transept had a pair of
apsidal chapels at the east. At Lewes there was only a single chapel to each of the
eastern transepts.

There, the Gothic eastern arm was planned in seven bays with north and south aisles, and with a Lady Chapel as an eastern annexe.

Though most Cluniac houses treasured the relics of some saint or a wonder-working image, their churches never rivalled those of the Benedictines as the resorts of pilgrims. In the Lady Chapel of Thetford priory was a miraculous figure of the Virgin Mary, the head of which contained a number of relics. Bromholm priory possessed a famous relic in the form of a patriarchal cross, that an English priest brought from the Holy Land and sold to the convent in 1220. Its miraculous powers made it an object of pilgrimage. In a Papal indulgence of 1401 the church of Castle Acre was described as a repository 'in which are divers relics of saints, and to which a great multitude of people resorts, its high altar and the altar of the said relics, and give alms for the repair or conservation of the church'. The abbey of S. Saviour, Bermondsey, was noted for a miraculous Rood that attracted penitents from all parts.

The disposition of the monastic buildings of Cluniac monasteries was almost identical with that of the Benedictines. The plan of Lewes priory, recovered by excavation, differs little in its main features from that of the contemporary abbey of Battle. The chapter house, parlour, dorter, and frater occupied the same relative position in both houses, the most notable variant at Lewes being the farmery chapel, a detached building north of the farmery hall (p. 73).

The love of ornament and decoration, so favoured by the Cluniac monks, was not without its influence upon the Benedictines. Early in the twelfth century the plain character of Benedictine architecture, hitherto almost devoid of ornament, gave place to sculptured enrichment that was lavished upon doorways, arches, and capitals. It is 'not unreasonable to assign this decorative impulse to some extent to Cluniac example',[1] which persisted increasingly down to the beginnings of Gothic.

Unfortunately no Cluniac church has been preserved for parochial worship. The most important remains of conventual buildings of this Order are those at Castle Acre and Wenlock. Elsewhere the remains are generally of little extent. At Castle Acre the west front of the priory church (Pl. XXX), overlaid with tiers of Norman wall-arcading, is a most striking feature; and on the west side of the cloister garth, adjoining the north-west tower of the church, are the prior's lodging and porch. The two-storied gatehouse of the priory also survives, and there are remains of the cloistral buildings including the chapter house, dorter, and farmery. No

---

[1] A. W. Clapham, *English Romanesque Architecture after the Conquest*, 1934.

less splendid are the remains of Wenlock priory, especially the prior's lodging (p. 74) that formerly adjoined the farmery and is now a residence, in a perfect state of preservation (Pl. XVIII). Parts of the transepts and of the south aisle of the nave are still *in situ*, as also are the walls of the ruined chapter house, faced with intersecting arcading.

IX. The Cistercian Order:
Its Ideals, Abbeys, and Churches

~~~~~~

The Birth of the Cistercian Order—Cîteaux and Stephen Harding—Colonies—The Carta Caritatis—Influence of S. Bernard—Spread of the Order—The General Chapter—Sites of Cistercian Abbeys—The Austere Ideals in the Way of Life and Diet—Exclusion of Women from their Churches—The Crucifix at Meaux Abbey—Conversi or Lay-Brethren and their Duties—Agriculture and Wool-growing—The Horses of Jervaulx Abbey—Smelting Furnaces of Furness—Dialogue of a Cistercian and a Cluniac—Rapid Growth of the Order in England after Waverley—Colonising by the English Houses—The Order of Savigny and its Absorption by the Cistercians—The Founding of Fountains Abbey—Hardships of the Pioneers—Cistercian Ideals embodied in the Architecture of their Abbeys—The Choir of the Conversi—Stone Walls between the Nave and Aisles of their Churches—The Conventual Apartments of the Conversi—The Chapter House—Exceptional Forms at Rievaulx, Abbey Dore, Margam and Whalley—The Novices' House—Warming House, Frater and Kitchen—The Planning of the Frater on a North-to-South Axis—The Western Cloistral Range or Domus Conversorum—The Lane for the Lay-brethren—Their Farmery—The Small Cloister of the Conversi at Tintern—The Capella extra Portas—Absence of Shrines in Cistercian Churches—The Holy Blood of Hayles—Simple Planning of the Early Churches—Waverley and Tintern—The Presbytery and its Lateral Chapels—English Plan compared with Continental Examples—Internal Arrangement of Cistercian Churches—The Western Porch—Simple Planning abandoned in the late Twelfth Century—The Need for more Altars—Changes at Byland and Waverley—The Ambulatory Plan at Abbey Dore—Eastern Transept at Fountains—The Aisled-Rectangle Choirs of Rievaulx and Tintern—The French Chevet at Croxden, Beaulieu, Hayles and Vale Royal—Influence of Cistercians in the Development of Gothic—Transitional Architecture at Fountains, Buildwas and Kirkstall—The Rejection of the Early Austerity in the Design of the Later Churches—Melrose Abbey—Existing Remains of Cistercian Abbeys.

~~~~~~

A REFORM OF far greater consequence and importance to English monasticism than Cluny was that initiated in part by Stephen

Harding, an English monk of Sherborne, at the very end of the eleventh century. On his way back from Rome Harding chanced to stay at the Benedictine abbey of Molesme in Burgundy, where the brethren had fallen into a lax observance of the Rule. The abbot Robert and the prior Alberic together with Stephen Harding made efforts to reform the house but without success; and in 1098 they left Molesme with a few of the monks and sought refuge in a wild wood at Citeaux (Cistercium), and having cleared the site they erected a wooden monastery that was to be the parent house of the famous Cistercian Order. At first they adhered to the strict observance of the Benedictine Rule; the rigid discipline they imposed upon themselves and the untold hardships they endured gained them few adherents or novices. Under Papal direction abbot Robert returned to Molesme, and Alberic became abbot of Citeaux in 1099, succeeded in 1109 by Stephen Harding, the real founder of the Cistercian Order. Although far from flourishing and still in its pioneer stage, Citeaux sent out a number of brethren to colonise a new abbey at La Ferté in 1113, and within three years others were founded at Pontigny, Morimond and Clairvaux. These four together with the mother house became the principal abbeys of the new Order, invested with certain privileges. The special character of the Cistercian Order was due to the constitution, of which Citeaux was the foundation stone, and was formulated in the 'Charter of Charity' (*Carta Caritatis*) drawn up by abbot Stephen and his monks and confirmed by the Pope in 1119.

Four years after Stephen became abbot, the great S. Bernard, 'the last of the Fathers' as he was called, arrived at the abbey with thirty or more novices, and thenceforth the future of the reformed Order was assured. It was said that so great was the eloquence of S. Bernard that 'mothers hid their sons, and wives their husbands, lest they should be persuaded to enter the cloister'. In the year 1115 S. Bernard was sent with twelve monks to establish a Cistercian abbey in the woods at Val d'Absinthe, to which they gave the name Clairvaux. There, 'a cemetery was marked out, an altar set up and some huts erected; before long, permanent buildings began to rise, simple and devoid of ornament. There was nothing on the walls, not even on those of the church, and no lamp hung in the sanctuary. The refectory was unpaved, and narrow windows let in a few rays of light. The dormitory was like a row of coffins, for the beds were mere boxes consisting of four planks. As for the abbot's cell, it was a cupboard under the stairs illuminated by a wretched slit, a hollow in the wall to serve as the seat of government.'[1]

---

[1] H. Daniel-Rops, *Cathedral and Crusade.*

The zeal and energy of S. Stephen and S. Bernard, monastic Puritans, established an Order that was shortly to overthrow the pre-eminence of the powerful and wealthy Benedictines.

The Cistercian Order spread with extraordinary rapidity throughout Western Europe. In 1120 the number of abbeys had grown to twelve, and in 1152 when the General Chapter forbade the founding of further houses, there were 340, of which fifty were in England and Wales. From their habit, a white cassock with a small hood and black scapulary, the Cistercians were styled White Monks.

The *Carta Caritatis* ordained that all Cistercian houses should observe in every respect the way of life kept at Citeaux; and the 'Use of Citeaux' was to be adopted in all their ceremonials and ritual. In order to ensure uniformity in life, discipline, and doctrine, a General Chapter was held at Citeaux every year, which the abbots of all their monasteries were bound to attend. At the General Chapter statutes (*instituta*) were drawn up as occasion required, for the guidance of all concerned. The Order was thus in effect a federation of abbeys, each with its own voice and share in the legislation that governed all, differing in this respect from the Cluniac Order, all of whose priories were dependent on parent houses. Cistercian abbeys were exempt from episcopal visitations, but once a year the abbot of Citeaux was to visit the four daughter houses, and they in their turn were to visit the houses they had colonised. When the number of monks in any one house grew too large, 'Let twelve monks at least with a thirteenth as abbot be sent out to found a new monastery; also let them not be settled there, till the place is so furnished with houses, books, and other necessaries, that they can live and observe the Rule there.'

No Cistercian abbeys were to be built in towns or cities, but in places remote from the conversation of men,[1] and all their churches were to be dedicated in honour of Our Lady. Secluded valleys were favoured as sites, as instanced in the names Valle Crucis, Vale Royal, Vaudey (vallis Dei), and the happy valley of Merivale. 'Our Fathers', said S. Bernard, 'searched out the damp and low-lying valleys wherein to build their monasteries, so the the monks, being often ill in health and having death before their eyes, should not lead a careless life.'

Cistercian churches and buildings were to be of the utmost simplicity; stone bell-towers were forbidden, and wooden towers were not to be 'of immoderate height, unsuited to the simplicity

[1] Exceptional was S. Mary Graces or Eastminster, the last Cistercian abbey to be founded in this country. It occupied the site on which the Royal Mint stands near the Tower of London, and was founded by Edward III in 1350.

of the Order'. The windows were to be filled with plain glass; superfluities and curiosities in carving, paintings, pavements of mosaic or of coloured tiles, and other like things that 'might corrupt the early purity of the Order and are not consistent with our poverty' were banned. Crosses for use in the church were not to be fashioned of gold or silver but of painted wood; their one candlestick was to be of iron, and the censers of copper or iron. Copes and dalmatics were forbidden, and the chasubles, vestments and altar-cloths were to be of plain material without gold or silver embroidery. The Cistercians vowed 'to remove from their lowly chapels everything which might flatter curious eyes and charm weak souls'. The uniformity in the planning and character of their churches was attained by sending out from their mother houses experienced monks to direct the building operations of new foundations. Thus, Geoffrey of Ainai was sent by S. Bernard from Clairvaux to Fountains c. 1135.

In the early days simplicity and restraint governed all the details of Cistercian life; their buildings, dress, food, and the ornaments for their ritual. Flesh was strictly forbidden as an article of diet except for the inmates of the infirmary. Their strictness in this respect is well illustrated by an incident that occurred at Beaulieu abbey in 1246. On the occasion of the dedication of the church in June of that year, Henry III and his Queen together with a large company of magnates of the realm were feasted by the convent; but at the next Visitation by a Cistercian superior the prior and the cellarer were deposed from their office, because they had broken the Rule by serving their guests with flesh in the frater. Early in the fifteenth century, however, authority to dispense from this Rule was granted the heads of Cistercian houses, and in 1485 the brethren were allowed to eat meat on Sundays, Tuesdays, and Thursdays, provided it was served in the misericord or flesh-frater.

Women were forbidden to enter a Cistercian church after the Octave of the dedication. An exception occurred at Meaux abbey, Yorkshire, during the rule of abbot Hugh, 1339–49. A wooden crucifix had been made for the choir of the lay-brothers, by a sculptor who worked with a naked man before him as a model. Miracles were said to be wrought by the crucifix, and the abbot was granted a dispensation to admit men and women to behold the wondrous image. 'We thought that if women might have access to this crucifix, common devotion would be increased, and it would redound to the great profit of our monastery. Therefore we petitioned the abbot of our mother house at Citeaux, who granted us special licence to admit men and women of good repute to the aforesaid crucifix, provided only that they should not enter through our cloister or dormitory or other domestic buildings, save only our patron or his wife or daughter; yet even these might not spend the night within the abbey precincts, nor enter before prime, nor stay beyond compline; if this rule were broken the licence should be null and void henceforth and forever. Under pretext of this licence women flock frequently to the aforesaid crucifix, yet only to our own damage, since their devotion is but cold, and they do but come to gaze at our church, and increase our expenses by claiming hospitality.'[1]

A notable peculiarity of Cistercian monasticism was the division of the brethren in each abbey into monks and lay-brothers, or *conversi*. From the first the reformers of Citeaux attached more importance to manual labour than to literary pursuits. Learning was accounted little; their motto was 'Labour is prayer', the work of the hands being held as acceptable an offering to God as the recitation of the offices in the church. The conversi were as truly monks as the brethren who could read and write; but a conversus, precluded from such learning, was a manual labourer who worked on the abbey lands, in the fields, in the workshops and mills, and in the outlying granges under the control of the cellarer. The Statutes of 1256 decreed that no conversus was to have a book, but was to learn the Paternoster, the Creed, the Miserere, and prayers by rote. He dwelt in the monastery unless he was working on some far-distant grange, and he was required to take the vows of poverty, chastity, and obedience, and to subject himself to the same rules of silence and abstinence as the choir-monks. The conversi had their own choir and altar in the abbey church, and their own dorter, frater, and farmery. Thus Cistercian houses were more self-contained than the Benedictines, who hired outside labourers and servants for the manual and menial tasks. In most houses the conversi outnumbered the choir-monks. At Waverley towards the end of the twelfth century there were 70 monks and 120 lay-brethren, and at Louth Park the number of monks was 66 and of conversi 150. During the rule of abbot Aelred, 1147–66, there were said to be 140 monks and 600 lay-brothers at Rievaulx, 'so that the church swarmed with them like a hive with bees.'

But conversi were not everything to be desired, and often became unruly and defiant. Early in the fourteenth century an insubordinate lay-brother of Whalley was sent by his abbot to another house for correction. 'The bearer of this letter', wrote the abbot, 'a very strong wheelwright and a subtle lay-brother of our house, we have thought good to send to you Father, with plenty of clothes, begging you earnestly to keep him and deal with him

[1] *Chronica de Melsa.* R.S. III.

according to the discipline of our Order; that every Friday he is to have bread and water and he is to be beaten at every chapter meeting at which he is present until Easter; and for a year he is to eat no meat.'[1]

In course of time the number of lay-brethren in Cistercian houses declined. From the Statutes of 1256 it is evident that some abbeys were then without conversi, and after the Black Death, 1349, they were practically non-existent.

With such ample labour at their command the Cistercians reclaimed worthless tracts of desolate moorland; they drained swamps and converted barren lands into pastures, plantations, and tillage. They became the farmer-monks, the cattle-breeders and wool-growers. In fact they laid the foundation of England's agricultural prosperity. An indication of the chief source of wealth in their houses is afforded by the fact that in 1193 the Cistercian monasteries of this country were compelled to give up the whole of their wool for the year towards the ransom of Richard I from imprisonment in Germany where he was held by Emperor Henry VI. The White Monks were again fleeced of their wool by Richard I in the following year.

The monks of Jervaulx were noted for their famous breed of horses. In a letter to Thomas Cromwell, Sir Arthur Dacey wrote of the abbey he was commissioned to destroy: 'I think that at Jervaulx and the granges incident, the King's highness should have there the most best race that should be in England, hard and sound of kind, for surely the breed of Gervais for horses was the tried breed in the North.' The brethren of Furness abbey were pioneers in an entirely different industry. In the thirteenth century they were working the iron ore that was mined in the district; they possessed smelting furnaces on Walney Island opposite Barrow, and they had their own trading vessels for exporting the iron they produced. In 1292 a large part of their income was derived from their smelting-works. It was these Cistercian pioneers that made Barrow in Furness what it is.

In the *Dialogue of a Cistercian and a Cluniac*, written in the second half of the twelfth century by a Cistercian monk, the difference between the ideals of the two Orders is well defined.

> 'CLUN: Although we labour neither in the garden nor in the field, yet we are not utterly idle. Some read, some work with their hands.
> CIS: I know those idle works of yours.
> CLUN: Why do you call them idle?

[1] F. Crossley, *The English Abbey*, Batsford, 1937.

CIS: Even as those words which do not edify are idle, so
        those works which pertain not to necessary uses are
        rightly called idle. I will say no more of the others,
        but will ask, Is it not useless and idle work to grind
        gold to powder, and therewith to paint great capital
        letters?

CLUN: You reproach us with our handiwork, calling it idle
        and useless, as if your own were very laborious and
        very useful.

CIS: We devote ourselves to the field-work which God
        created; we all work together, we and our [lay] breth-
        ren and our hirelings, each according to his ability;
        and all in common we live on our labour.'[1]

Cistercian monks made their first appearance in England at
Waverley in 1128, a house that was colonised by the abbey of
L'Aumone in Normandy. Waverley was followed by Rievaulx in
1131 and by Fountains in 1132. Many of the fifty abbeys that
sprang up by the middle of the twelfth century were daughter
houses of these first arrivals. Thus, Rievaulx founded Warden,
Dundrennan, Revesby, and Rufford; and Fountains sent forth
brethren to establish colonies at Newminster, Louth Park, Wo-
burn, and a foreign house at Lysa in Norway, all of which were
founded by 1146. So popular were the White Monks that in 1147
they absorbed the thirteen Savigniac monasteries then existing in
England and Wales.[2]

On account of the abundant water supply and the remote sites,
Yorkshire was greatly favoured by the Cistercian settlers. Many
were the trials and hardships they suffered in establishing themselves in what was then wild and uninhabited country. The story
of the founding of Fountains abbey borders on the heroic. In the
year 1132 the prior and twelve other monks of the Benedictine
abbey of S. Mary, York, dissatisfied with the laxity of living there,
left the convent with the intention of embracing the Cistercian

---

[1] Martène, *Thesaurus*, V.

[2] Foremost amongst the Savigniac abbeys were Furness, founded in 1127, and
Buildwas, *c.* 1135. After their transfer to the Cistercians both of these houses retained
certain rights they possessed over houses that were formerly their dependencies. When
Savigny submitted to the Cistercians, the abbot Peter of Furness, who resisted the
change, journeyed to Rome and obtained from Pope Eugenius III a pronouncement
that Furness should remain in the Order in which it had been founded; but on his
way back from Rome the abbot was invited to Savigny, and the convent there induced
him to resign his abbacy and adopt the Cistercian Rule. Ultimately he was made the
abbot of Quarr in the Isle of Wight, and one of the monks of Savigny was sent to
Furness to win over the convent to the new Order. Furness subsequently founded a
number of abbeys in Ireland, including Fermoy, and Holy Cross in the diocese of
Cashell.

Rule. Taking them under his protection Archbishop Thurstan of York assigned them 'a place remote from all the world, uninhabited, set with thorns, and among the hollows of mountains and prominent rocks on every side more fit as it seemed for the dens of wild beasts than for the uses of mankind. And the name of this spot is Skelldale, a valley of the stream flowing in the same place.' Here they laboured in extreme poverty, their only shelter being a thatched hut beneath a great elm tree, and at one time they were reduced to feeding on herbs and boiled leaves, so that 'the elm under which they abode conferred a double benefit on them, being a shelter in winter and food in summer'. A monk was despatched by S. Bernard of Clairvaux to instruct them in the Cistercian Rule, to which they were in due course admitted. Despite their hard living they were joined by the dean and a few canons of York, and thenceforth the community at Fountains increased in wealth and importance and their future was assured. When the monks of Byland settled on waste land given them by Roger de Mowbray in 1177 'they began manfully to root out the woods, and by long and wide ditches to draw off water from the marshes; and when pry land appeared they prepared for themselves an ample fitting and worthy site . . . where they built their fair and great church, as it now appears. May the All Highest perfect it and preserve it for evermore'.

The abbeys of Rievaulx, Byland, Fountains, Jervaulx, Roche, Kirkstall, Meaux, and Sawley, all in the county of Yorkshire, embodied Cistercian ideals in their architecture and marked noble stages in the development of English Gothic. At the time of the Dissolution there were about a hundred Cistercian abbeys in England, in addition to many small dependencies. Three quarters of them were founded in the twelfth century, the remainder in the thirteenth, with the exception of S. Mary Graces, London.

The church and the cloistral buildings of Cistercian abbeys differed in several respects from those of the Benedictine and other Orders, for provision had to be made for the housing of the conversi and for their religious offices in the church. On account of their heavy labours, the conversi rose at a later hour than the monks except on Sundays and non-working Feast days. The canonical hours they kept in the church were modified; instead of the lengthy Psalms and lessons, they recited the Paternoster and Gloria Patri alternately several times, and after prime they began the tasks of the day.

The choir of the conversi (*chorus conversorum*) occupied the greater part of the nave of Cistercian churches. Two or three eastern bays that formed the western part of the monks' choir were shut off from the rest of the nave by the rood screen, against which was placed the lay-brothers' altar. Peculiar to Cistercian churches were the solid walls of stone, about 2 feet thick and 6 feet high, that divided the nave from the aisles (Figs. 16, 17). At Tintern they were bonded into the nave piers, and were surmounted by a gabled coping, traces of which are still to be seen; at Strata

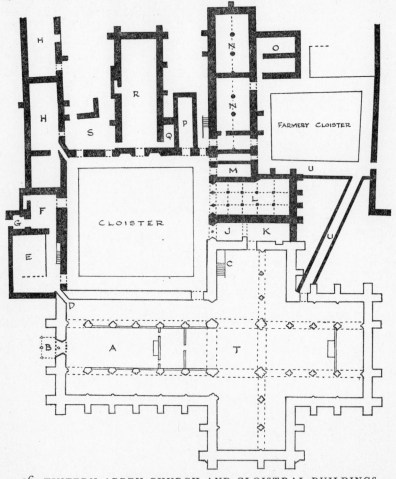

16. TINTERN ABBEY CHURCH AND CLOISTRAL BUILDINGS

A. Choir of conversi. B. Porch. C. Night-stairs. D. Passage to lay-brothers' cloister, E. F. Outer parlour. G. Porch. H. Domus conversorum. J. Book closet. K. Sacristy. L. Chapter house. M. Parlour. N. Monks' dorter (novices' lodging below). O. Rere-dorter. L. Calefactorium. Q. Larder. R. Monks' frater, S. Kitchen. T. Tower. U. Passage to farmery cloister.

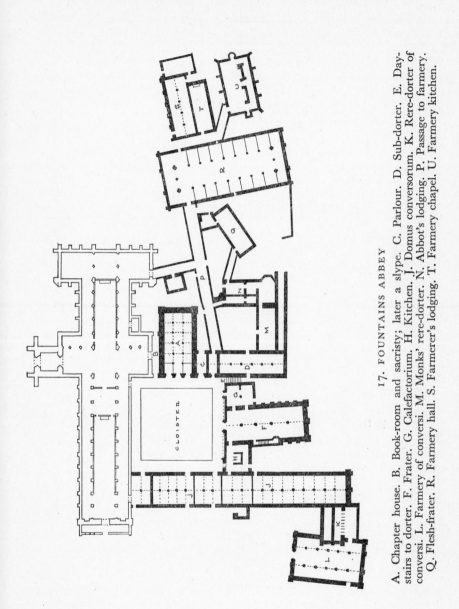

17. FOUNTAINS ABBEY

A. Chapter house. B. Book-room and sacristy; later a slype. C. Parlour. D. Sub-dorter. E. Day-stairs to dorter. F. Frater. G. Calefactorium. H. Kitchen. J. Domus conversorum. K. Rere-dorter of conversi. L. Farmery of conversi. M. Monks' rere-dorter. N. Abbot's lodging. P. Passage to farmery. Q. Flesh-frater. R. Farmery hall. S. Farmerer's lodging. T. Farmery chapel. U. Farmery kitchen.

Florida, Cardigan, the piers of the nave stood on the screen-walls. In the westernmost bay of the nave the walling stopped short, so that the conversi could enter their choir by the night-stairs from their dorter on the west side of the cloister (Fig. 17). The purpose of the screen-walls was to serve as a backing for the wooden stalls of the conversi. At Tintern, where the cloister lay to the north of the nave, the western bay on each side was unwalled (Fig. 16). The presbytery or monks' choir was similarly enclosed from the aisles by stone screens that were built flush with the faces of the piers.

The chapter house in the eastern range of cloistral buildings was invariably rectangular in Cistercian abbeys, and was divided into three vaulted aisles by two rows of columns, as at Netley, Byland, Tintern, and Fountains (Fig. 17). At Roche abbey it was two-aisled, and at Croxden the chapter house was square on plan, divided by four columns into nine vaulted bays. That at Rievaulx was planned like an apsidal church with an encircling ambulatory (Fig. 21), the aisles and vestibule being vaulted, but the central area covered with a flat timber roof. In the fifteenth century, however, the encircling aisle was pulled down and the arcade of the apse walled up. Quite exceptional were the chapter houses of Abbey Dore and Margam, which were polygonal buildings of twelve sides, and that at Whalley was octagonal on plan.

At Furness and Fountains the westernmost bay flanking the entrance of the chapter house was walled off from the others, and fitted up as a book closet.

The sub-vault of the eastern range of cloistral buildings, which in Benedictine houses was the warming-house, was assigned to the novices and was probably divided into a dorter and a common room; at Jervaulx and Croxden the southern part was opened up with arches, for what purpose is not known.

The range of buildings opposite the church, south or north of the cloister as the case might be, comprised the warming-house at the east, the kitchen at the west, and between them the frater. The warming house was a square or oblong apartment with a fireplace in one of the walls; at Tintern abbey the fireplace was in the middle.

The Cistercian frater was planned with its main axis at right angles to the cloister-walk and not parallel as in houses of other Orders. This was done to provide for a large kitchen at the west that would serve the lay-brothers' frater as well as that of the choir-monks; and to the east was the calefactorium, which in Benedictine abbeys was in the sub-dorter. The warming-house at Fountains was a lofty and spacious room with two enormous fireplaces (Fig. 17). The late Sir Harold Brakespear was of opinion that the Cistercian practice of planning the frater north-to-south was not generally adopted until about 1150. There are indications that at Kirkstall, Tintern, and Fountains the frater was originally set out on an east-to-west axis; and such was the arrangement at Waverley, *c.* 1130, at Sibton in Suffolk, and in the Savigniac houses before they adopted the Cistercian Rule. When Furness was transferred to the Cistercian Order, the frater was rebuilt on a north-to-south axis and its lengthening in the thirteenth century was therefore a simple matter. At Whalley, a new site to which the Cistercians of Stanlaw migrated early in the fourteenth century, the cloistral buildings were not erected until *c.* 1425, and as there were then no conversi amongst the inmates, the frater was built on the east-to-west plan, as also was the case when the monks of Cleeve rebuilt their frater in the fifteenth century.

At Rievaulx abbey the frater, 124 feet in length, was raised upon a vaulted basement that may have been used as a flesh-frater; and that at Fountains was unusual, being divided internally into two aisles by a range of four columns (Fig. 17).

Entered by a doorway in the cloister-walk, the kitchen was so arranged that it communicated directly with the monks' frater at the east and that of the conversi on the west. There were service-hatches and turn-tables in the walls between the kitchen and each frater. The fireplaces in the kitchen were usually against the walls but at Fountains and Kirkstall they stood back to back in the middle of the room.

In all Cistercian abbeys the western cloistral range, two stories in height, was allotted to the lay-brothers and was known as the *domus conversorum.* The ground floor was partitioned into a number of apartments, including the frater, the outer parlour, and several cellars; and above was the lay-brothers' dorter, at the northern end of which were the night-stairs to the church. No finer example of a domus conversorum exists than that at Fountains (Pl. XX), the sub-vault of which is 300 feet in length and is divided into twenty-two bays, with a central row of columns (Fig. 17). It is vaulted from end to end; the dorter above was covered with a flat timber roof. The lay-brothers' block at Byland abbey, 275 feet long, was similarly vaulted in two spans. More often the ground floor was narrow and unaisled as at Netley and Rievaulx.

In some Cistercian abbeys, as for instance Beaulieu, Byland, and Kirkstall, a broad passage known as 'the Lane' intervened between the west walk of the cloister and the lay-brothers' range, a feature that was apparently borrowed from Citeaux or Clairvaux. Its purpose has never been satisfactorily determined, though it led to the western processional doorway of the church. In the east wall of the Lane at Byland are thirty-five recesses that were used for seats, which

L

seem to indicate that the passage served as a walk for the conversi.

At that end of the domus conversorum remote from the church was usually the rere-dorter or necessarium for the lay-brothers, and not far distant lay their farmery. The farmery at Fountains (Fig. 17) was a spacious hall 90 feet in length, divided into a nave and aisles by arcades of five bays.

At Tintern, where the cloister lay to the north of the nave, the southern end of the western block was occupied by the outer parlour entered at the west by a porch. Between the outer parlour and the church was the lay-brothers' small cloister, with narrow walks on the east and south, from which the church could be entered by a skew-passage in its north-west angle (Fig. 16).

After the Black Death, when lay-brothers formed no part of personnel of Cistercian establishments, the western cloistral range was put to other uses. No doubt the cellarer claimed some of the apartments for use as storehouses and cellars. Late in the fourteenth century the chorus conversorum in the abbey church of Rievaulx was dismantled, and the eastern bays of the aisles were fitted up as chapels and fenced with timber screens.

In keeping with the austerity of the Rule, the early Cistercian churches were planned on very simple lines. Far removed from populous places, they were built solely to accommodate the brethren and the conversi for the recitation of the Divine offices. No provision was made for parochial worship, although a small chapel (*capella extra portas*) was often built near the gatehouse of a Cistercian abbey or within the outer court, where persons not allowed within the precinct might worship, as for example at Coggleshall, Merivale, and Rievaulx. The last-named was subsequently enlarged and became parochial.

Nor were Cistercian churches the objects of pilgrimage. Wonder-working shrines and relics were eschewed, lest pilgrims should invade the precinct.[1] From the first, the elaborate planning of the choir-arm, with saint's chapel and ambulatory, so favoured by the Benedictines, was rejected by the Cistercian monks. For the same reason their churches were not built over tombs of the saints, and this may account for the absence of crypts in their churches.

The Burgundian monks who settled in England in the second quarter of the twelfth century imported a plan peculiarly their

[1] Hayles abbey in the Cotswolds and Rievaulx afford exceptions. At Hayles a relic of the Holy Blood, presented to the convent in 1270 by Edward, Earl of Cornwall, was enclosed in a shrine behind the High Altar. At Rievaulx are the remains of a thirteenth-century stone shrine that once contained the relics of S. William, the first abbot of the house and at one time secretary to S. Bernard. The reliquary itself was displayed beneath the canopy of the upper stage, but the shrine was not installed in the church and stood in one of the openings in the west wall of the chapter house.

own, which subsequently influenced the whole trend of the planning of the greater churches of this country throughout the Middle Ages. From the first the Cistercians rejected the apse as the eastern termination of the choir, and planned their churches with a rectangular presbytery. In its simplicity the plan of Waverley, founded in 1128, embodied the Cistercian ideal of the period (Fig. 18). Having a total length of about 180 feet, it consisted of an unaisled nave, a short rectangular presbytery, and shallow transepts each with a square eastern chapel.[1]

Excavations undertaken by Sir Harold Brakespear at Tintern, also a colony of Aumone, 1131, revealed the plan of the first church there (Fig. 18), modelled on that of Waverley, but with two chapels to the east of each transept; and when Roche abbey was founded in 1147, the transept and choir-arm followed the Tintern plan, though the nave of eight bays was flanked by north and south aisles.

Shortly after the transfer of Furness abbey to the Cistercian Rule, the convent set about the reconstruction of the eastern arm of their church on Cistercian lines, c. 1150. Here three transeptal chapels flank the presbytery, and when Kirkstall was founded shortly afterwards, the same plan was adopted (Fig. 18).

In all such churches the presbytery walls rose to the full height of the nave and transepts, but the lateral chapels were roofed at a lower level and were separated from one another by solid walls. Other notable examples of this plan in England included the first church at Fountains, 1132; Calder, 1134; Buildwas, 1148; Abbey Dore, 1148; Bindon, 1172; Cleeve, 1188; and Valle Crucis, 1200, all of which had two chapels to the east of each transept. At Quarr, Isle of Wight, 1131, Louth Park, 1139, and Strata Florida, 1166, the same form of plan was adopted, but the presbytery was flanked by three chapels on either side. This was the common lay-out for Cistercian churches throughout Christendom in the twelfth century. It occurred at Fontenay and Clermont in France, at Maulbronn in Germany, Cappel in Switzerland, Fossanova in Italy, Santa Creuz in Spain, Alvastra in Sweden, and Boyle in Roscommon, to name but a few.[2]

[1] The plan of Lysa, the first Cistercian house in Norway and colonised by Fountains in 1146, was very similar to that of Waverley.

[2] Fontenay, the oldest surviving church of the Cistercian Order in France and intimately connected with S. Bernard, was founded in 1119 and affords an excellent example of the normal type in its primal simplicity (Fig. 18). The presbytery with two lateral chapels on either side may have been the model for Buildwas, and like Kirkstall the aisled nave is eight bays in length. This Cistercian plan was adopted by the Augustinian canons at Lesnes abbey, Kent, founded in 1178. The rectangular presbytery flanked by three square chapels on either side was much like the east end of Kirkstall, and remained so until 1370, when the southern chapels were swept away to make room for a Lady Chapel.

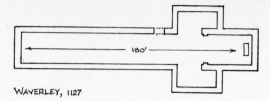

WAVERLEY, 1127

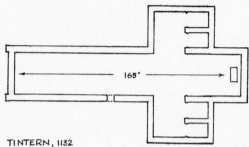

TINTERN, 1132

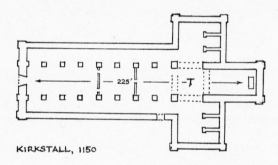

KIRKSTALL, 1150

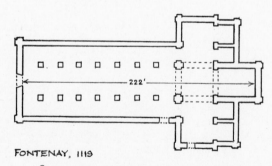

FONTENAY, 1119

18. EARLY CISTERCIAN CHURCHES

In the internal arrangements the High Altar stood in the presbytery or sanctuary, and the monks' stalls occupied the crossing
and one or two bays of the nave, the ritual choir being closed at
the west by the pulpitum, which had a central doorway with an
altar on either side. One bay farther west stood the rood screen,
having an altar for the conversi against its western face (Figs.
16, 17). The space between the pulpitum and the rood screen was
known as the retrochoir. The monks' choir was entered by doorways (ostia chori) in the screen walls that ran across the transepts.
Minor altars were placed in the chapels flanking the presbytery.

A feature peculiar to Cistercian churches was the low porch
attached to the west front. Deriving from Clairvaux and Pontigny
and fairly common in Burgundy, it appeared at Fountains, Rievaulx, Byland, Tintern, and Newminster. At Fountains (Fig. 17)
the front of the porch was opened up with a small arcade carried
by coupled shafts standing on a low wall, a part of which remains,
and in the centre was originally a wide entrance arch (Pl.
XXXVII). It was a favourite burial place for the monks of Fountains. At Byland, where the porch was spoken of as the Galilee,
the corbels of the lean-to roof remain below the western window
of the nave. The porch at Tintern, an addition of the fifteenth century, had an upper chapel dedicated to Our Lady, and was mentioned in an indulgence of 1414 that was granted to the faithful who
visited the chapel and contributed alms.

The planning of the early Cistercian churches was as incon-
venient for processional purposes as the parallel-apsed plan of the
Benedictines, and within fifty years of their advent in this country,
nothing loth to abandon the simple planning of their first churches,
the Cistercians adopted what was in reality a squared version of
the apse-and-ambulatory choir. In this new plan the presbytery
had full-length aisles on either side, and beyond its high eastern
wall were built a number of low square chapels all of equal depth.
The eastern wall of the sanctuary below the window was opened up
with three arches, and the easternmost bay of the choir gave access
to the chapels and at the same time served as a processional path,
the High Altar being set up in the second bay from the east. This
was the plan of Byland after 1177 (Fig. 19), and it was employed
again at Waverley c. 1203, when the convent undertook the rebuilding of their church on a grand scale. In both cases three low
chapels were built beyond the sanctuary, and provision was made
for still more altars in the transepts of these churches; at Byland
there were two eastern chapels to each transept,[1] and three at

[1] Byland also had western aisles to both transepts, unusual in Cistercian churches;
at Beaulieu the north transept alone had an aisle at the west (Fig. 22).

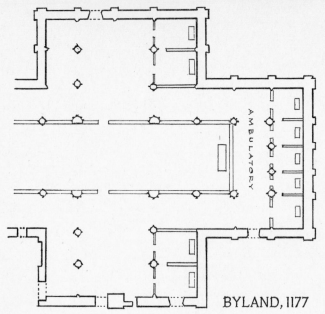

BYLAND, 1177

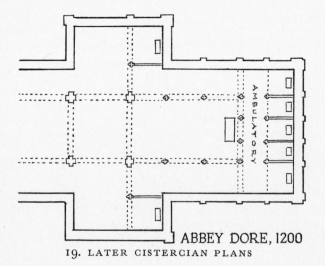

ABBEY DORE, 1200

19. LATER CISTERCIAN PLANS

Waverley, where the new church, planned with an aisled nave of ten bays, covered an area about five times as large as the church of 1128.

Still further was the Byland plan developed at Abbey Dore, c. 1200 (Fig. 19).[1] There, both ambulatory and eastern chapels (in a state of perfect preservation to-day) (Pl. XL) are roofed at a low level east of the sanctuary, forming as it were a double aisle, the inner being the ambulatory, and the outer and eastern aisle divided into five chapels by perpeyn walls about five feet high.

The problem of providing more altars was solved in a remarkable and unique fashion at Fountains abbey early in the thirteenth century, during the rule of three abbots all of whom bore the name of John. The choir was too small to accommodate the ever-increasing number of monks, nor were there sufficient altars for the masses. Abbot John I, 1203–11, set to work enlarging the eastern arm of the church; he pulled down the old short and square-ended presbytery and lengthened it by three bays, and his successor between 1211 and 1219 started the great eastern transept, which was completed by John III, 1220–47. This great transept set athwart the east end of the choir provided a large hall that served as an ambulatory, and a range of seven chapels (Fig. 20). In length from north to south it measured 132 feet, and was divided into three sections, the central narrower than the lateral, by arcades of two arches springing from clustered piers. This special glory of Fountains abbey, one of the loveliest of Gothic creations, was soon afterwards imitated at Durham (Fig. 20).

In the interesting sketchbook of the thirteenth-century French master-mason, Villard de Honnecourt, is a rough plan of a church beneath which is inscribed 'Plan of a square church designed for the Cistercian Order'. Whether the church was actually built is not known; none has been identified in France, but the plan of Byland bears a great resemblance to Honnecourt's sketch.

The final and definitive method employed in planning the choir-arm of churches of this Order, though not peculiarly Cistercian, was the aisled-rectangle, a lay-out that characterised the vast choirs of the cathedrals of Ely, Lincoln, and York. Low eastern chapels were dispensed with, the aisles were carried the full length of the choir, so that the eastern arm of the church was of one height from the crossing to the east wall. Notable Cistercian examples of the aisled-rectangle were Rievaulx, Jervaulx, and Tintern (Fig. 16), The two last-named were four bays in length, but Rievaulx was laid out in seven bays (Fig. 21), and was 144 feet in

---

[1] The original eastern arm of Abbey Dore, c. 1147, was planned like that of Tintern, 1132.

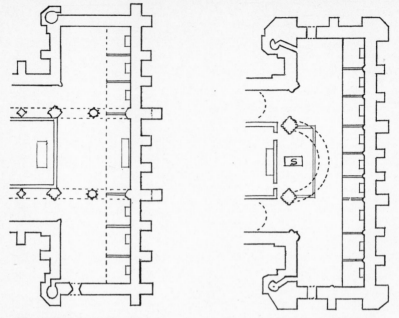

20. THE EASTERN TRANSEPTS OF FOUNTAINS AND DURHAM

length. So long an eastern arm made it unnecessary to extend the ritual choir into the crossing and the nave. The pulpitum was therefore erected between the eastern piers at the crossing, and the monks' stalls occupied two western bays of the new choir. The rood screen spanned the nave at the second bay.

In choirs of this type the easternmost bay was occupied by four or five altars divided by timber screens and it also served as an ambulatory. The High Altar stood in the next bay to the west.

The Cistercian impress of the square choir-arm in one form or another diverted English church-planning from the methods employed on the Continent. In France the apse-and-ambulatory type developed into the chevet, which being foreign to English tradition was rarely adopted in this land. Croxden, Beaulieu, Hayles, and Vale Royal afford the only Cistercian examples.

Founded in 1176, Croxden abbey was colonised by monks from Aunay in Normandy. The church was planned with a nave of eight bays, transepts each with two square chapels at the east, and a short choir laid out with a chevet of five chapels off the ambulatory (Fig. 22). The chevet was a copy of that at Aunay. By 1181 enough of the choir had been built for the monks to perform the Divine offices therein, but the whole church was not

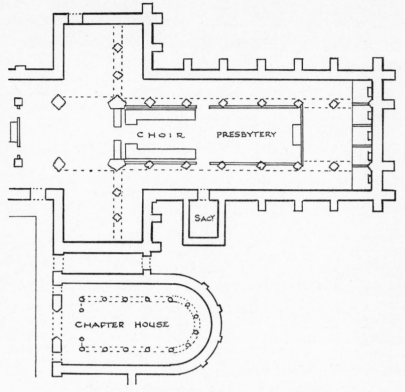

21. THE CHOIR-ARM OF RIEVAULX, 1230

completed and dedicated until 1254. Beaulieu abbey was founded in 1204 by King John in expiation of his persecution of the Cistercians, and he ordered all the abbots of that Order to contribute to the building of Beaulieu. The church that was reared between 1221 and 1245 was almost an exact copy of the abbey church of Clairvaux that had been entirely reconstructed on a new plan in 1175. The choir terminated in an apse, encircled by an ambulatory around which was a ring of ten low chapels, divided by walls and beneath a common roof (Fig. 22). Ample provision was made at Beaulieu for masses at lesser altars, for in addition to the ten chapels off the ambulatory there were three in each transept. The abbey church was erected under the supervision of a French master-mason named Durandus who hailed from Rouen. On the occasion of the dedication of Beaulieu in 1246 in the presence of Henry III and his Queen, the King's brother, Richard, Earl of Cornwall, in fulfilment of a vow made on escaping shipwreck, induced the

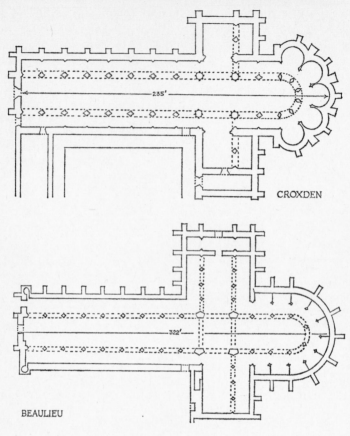

CROXDEN

BEAULIEU

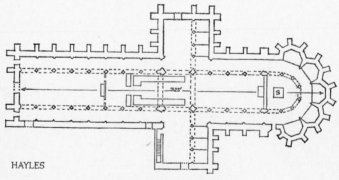

HAYLES

22. CISTERCIAN PLANS

abbot to send forth monks to found a daughter house at Hayles, Gloucestershire. As originally planned the choir of Hayles was square-ended with a low range of chapels and an ambulatory, similar to that of Abby Dore. In 1270 Richard's son Edmund presented the convent with a reliquary containing the Holy Blood, the authenticity of which was vouched for by the Patriarch of Jerusalem, afterwards Pope Urban V. The following year the east end of the choir of Hayles was destroyed by fire, a disaster that gave the convent an opportunity to plan a new choir, with a chapel beyond the High Altar for housing the treasured relic. Accordingly the new east end was laid out with a five-sided apse and ambulatory, with five polygonal chapels, a typical French chevet (Fig. 22). Probably the Hayles chevet was modelled on that of Westminster abbey, and as it was built at the cost of the Earl of Cornwall the plan may have been drafted by one of the royal master-masons of Westminster.

In 1958, excavations undertaken at Vale Royal brought to light the foundations of the east end of the abbey church that was rebuilt in 1359 at the instance of the Black Prince. The abbey was founded by Edward I in 1277 in pursuance of a vow made during a stormy passage at sea. The new fourteenth-century choir of Vale Royal was planned as a chevet similar to that then in course of erection at Hayles, but on more elaborate lines, for there were seven polygonal chapels off the ambulatory.[1]

The influence of the Cistercians, Burgundian in its origin, was of great importance in the development of English mediaeval architecture, for their churches and monasteries were being built at the very outset of the so-called Transitional period, when new forms were being evolved and structural progress was effecting the change from round-arched Norman to the pointed style known as Gothic. The progressive character of much Cistercian building in the twelfth century hastened the Transition. There was never an architectural style peculiar to the Cistercians, but certain distinctive features characterised their manner of building in the early days. In the planning and the internal arrangement of their churches and monasteries as well as in the restraint enjoined by the Rule, they display a strong family likeness. This restraint is at once apparent in the bay design of the interiors of Cistercian churches. In Benedictine and Augustinian churches of any size, the internal elevation was of three stages, the triforium stage between the nave arcade and the clerestory usually being a considerable feature; but in accordance with their ideal of simplicity, the

[1] The author is indebted to F. H. Thompson of the Grosvenor Museum, Chester, for this information.

Cistercians at first dispensed with that useless stage in bay design. At Buildwas, where the nave is 36 feet high, a three-storied design could not be expected, but at Fountains (Pl. XXXVIII) and Kirkstall (Pl. XXXIX), the naves of which are 55 feet in height, a well-defined bay-design of three stages like that of the Augustinian church of Christ Church, Hampshire, 58 feet high, would have been possible. Instead a bold course divides the elevation into a nave arcade and clerestory.

In the earliest Cistercian churches of this country, the arches in the nave arcades were pointed, a form that had for some time been employed by the Cistercian builders of Burgundy. The pointed arch used in conjunction with the semi-circular arch for windows and doorways is common in the early Cistercian churches, and is a marked feature of Transitional architecture. Except for the pointed arcades, the naves of Fountains (Pl. XXXVIII) and Buildwas (Pl. XXXVI), with their cylindrical piers, scalloped capitals, and square bases, are pure Norman in style. A Burgundian importation was the pointed barrel vaulting of the aisles of Fountains nave and of the eastern chapels at Kirkstall, an un-English feature that was not adopted elsewhere. The naves were covered with timber roofs, but at Kirkstall the presbytery has a ribbed vault, the diagonals of which are pointed arches, as important a step in the advance of Gothic as was the high vault at Durham cathedral some years before.

The Statutes of the General Chapters of Cîteaux, put together and completed in 1152, forbade the use of sculpture and painting for decorative purposes in churches or monastic buildings, 'because while attention is paid to such things, the profit of godly meditation or the discipline of religious gravity is often neglected'.

As a result, their early buildings are direct and plain if not severe in design; the absence of carved decoration and of rich mouldings affording a striking contrast to the redundant ornament, the surface decoration, and the wall-arcadings so loved by the Benedictines.

The primal austerity of the Cistercians, however, lasted for less than a century. The acquisition of wealth and of broad acres resulted in a falling away from the ideals of S. Bernard, and in general the Rule became less rigorously observed. The architectural expression of Cistercianism lost its simplicity and asceticism, as is evident in the planning and the interior design of such churches as Byland, Abbey Dore, Rievaulx, and Tintern. At Fountains and Kirkstall provision was made for a central tower, and abbot Huby of Fountains, 1496–1526, built a stone tower of four stories and

170 feet in height adjoining the north transept to supersede that at the crossing. The rejection of the primal simplicity is also apparent in the bay design. When the abbeys of Roche, Furness, and Byland were built late in the twelfth century, the triforium appeared as a feature of the interior design, as in the greater Benedictine churches. Further, carved stonework, mural paintings, and stained glass made their appearance in Cistercian churches; at Byland the church was paved throughout with coloured tiles of geometric pattern, the floor of the chapels in the south transept retaining much of this decorative treatment to this day; and on the wall of the north aisle of the nave are the remains of a large painting of the Pieta, probably of the fourteenth century. The architecture of Melrose abbey, a famous Cistercian house beyond the Border, rebuilt after its destruction by fire in 1385, is remarkable for the total disregard of Cistercian restraint; it exhibits a display of decorative exuberance, the masonry being fretted with exquisite carving and intricate tracery, glittering with crocketed pinnacles and canopied niches.

No Cistercian church in this country has survived in its entirety. Prior to the Suppression the laity possessed no parochial rights in churches of this Order, and the King's wreckers therefore had a free hand in their task of destruction, which was so drastically carried out that only four Cistercian churches in part are in use for public worship. Second to none is Abbey Dore, the choir and transepts of which, restored in the seventeenth century, afford an admirable example of Early English Gothic. At Swine priory, a house of Cistercian nuns in the East Riding, the nave and transepts have disappeared but the aisled chancel is parochial; and the naves of Hulme Cultram and Margam serve the same purpose. A unique survival is the frater of Beaulieu abbey, now the parish church (Pl. XVI).

Despite their ruined condition, the remains of the abbey churches of Fountains (Pl. XXXVIII), Furness, Kirkstall (Pl. XXXIX), and Tintern (Pl. XLIII) are fairly complete, and at Rievaulx the splendid choir and transepts are *in situ* (Pl. XLII). So extensive are the ruins of cloistral and other buildings at the above-named (Pls. X, XVII, XX), that the complete Cistercian plan can easily be determined; and at Cleeve abbey, though the church and the cloister-walks have been swept away, the buildings about the cloister are roofed and are in a remarkable state of preservation (Pl. XI). At the east are the sacristy, the chapter house, the parlour and day-stairs to the dorter that extends over the eastern range; on the south is the frater and at the west the sub-vault of the domus conversorum.

The most notable remains of other Cistercian abbeys are as follows:

Bindon, Dorset. Foundations of the church, and parts of the east and south cloistral buildings.

Buildwas, Salop. Most of the church; the chapter house.

Byland, Yorks. Walls of the church.

Calder, Cumberland. Church and chapter house.

Croxden, Staffs. South wall of church; eastern cloistral buildings.

Hayles, Gloucs. Walls of cloistral buildings.

Jervaulx, Yorks. Conventual buildings.

Netley, Hants. Parts of the church; cloistral buildings.

Quarr, Isle of Wight. Ruins of cloistral buildings.

Roche, Yorks. Transepts.

Valle Crucis, Denbigh. Much of the church; complete chapter house (Pl. XII), dorter.

Whalley, Lancs. Abbot's lodging and domus conversorum.

X. The Houses of Regular Canons

IN THE EARLY centuries of the Christian faith there were in existence small groups of priests or seculars attached to particular churches and living in common, though not bound by the observance of any Rule. From the first most cathedral churches were served by clergy of this kind, and in the eighth century Bishop Chrodegang of Metz, 742–66, introduced a rule of life or *canon* amongst the priests of his cathedral, who came to be known as *canonici*. Their corporate existence as chapters subsequently led to the founding of the Augustinian Order of Regular Canons, whose Rule was based on a letter of S. Augustine of Hippo. The secular chapters, however, were clergy who lived in the world, whereas the Regular canons were priests who had taken monastic vows and led the normal life of monks or regulars, except that they were ordained.[1]

In Saxon England there were many churches to which a community of clergy were attached, constituting a *collegium*, as for example Beverley and Wimborne, the members of which probably ministered in the parish churches of the district. But in many cases the want of a Rule and the general insecurity of the times led to a laxity in their way of life. After the Norman Conquest, therefore, some were suppressed and others were established as houses of Augustinian canons. The necessity for such changes is clearly indicated in the foundation charter of Waltham Holy Cross, where the pre-Conquest college survived until 1177, when Henry II converted it into an Augustinian foundation. 'And especially, inasmuch as secular canons had lived there in a very irreligious and carnal life, so that the ill-repute of their conversation, passing measure, had been a stumbling block to many, it seemed to our archbishops and bishops and other men of religion that it was a work of piety to remove those who were stained by the mark of ill fame, and to put in their place men of holy conversation and of praiseworthy reputation; so that at one and the same time the purpose of the King's highness might obtain its holy effect, and a shameful example might be removed from a place of high renown.'[2]

The Augustinian Rule was of such brevity that most houses supplemented it by Customaries or Observances which laid out in greater detail the regulations governing the every-day life, and the conduct and activities of the canons. The *Observances of Barnwell priory*, near Cambridge[3] reveal how closely their life resembled that of other monks. The round of offices in the church from matins to compline, the duties of the canons and of the obedientiaries are specified in detail. 'Clothes are only to be washed as the superior decides . . . and when a bath is ordered, it is to be taken without grumbling. When a brother says he is in pain, he is to be believed, but for his treatment a physician is to be consulted.'

---

[1] After the year 1311 all regulars were under the obligation of taking Holy Orders.
[2] Sir William Dugdale, *Monasticon Anglicanum*.
[3] Edited by J. W. Clark, 1897.

Augustinian canons were not bound to manual labour, but they ministered in the parish churches that had been appropriated to them. Guyot de Provins, a minstrel and later a monk, wrote of them in the thirteenth century: 'Among them one is well shod, well clothed and well fed. They go out when they like, mix with the world and talk at table.' The Augustinians were known as B ack canons from their habit, which consisted of a long black cassock and hood. They also wore a black biretta, which distinguished them from monks, who adopted the tonsure.

Augustinian canons were introduced to this country by Archbishop Anselm, the earliest foundation being the priory of S. Botolph at Colchester c. 1100. In recognition Pope Paschal II issued a bull in 1116 vesting the canons of Colchester with authority over all other English houses of the Order. 'We decree that, even as you have been the first to do battle in England in this Order, so shall you also for ever be held first in rank of the same; so that wheresoever throughout the houses of canons in England, there is, by the carelessness of the brethren, a hint of weakness, your authority may come to the aid with the power given by us.'

During the twelfth century houses of Augustinian canons to the number of 140 sprang up in England and Wales, mostly in the Midlands and East Anglia. In all there were at one time and another 212 of their foundations, of which about 170 were in existence at the Dissolution. The majority were designated priories, being presided over by a prior, i.e. the first amongst the brethren. Twenty-five attained the dignity of an abbey,[1] thirteen of which were either founded by the Crown or were of royal patronage. The abbots of Waltham and Cirencester had seats in the House of Lords.

Few Augustinian establishments ranked in size or wealth with the greater abbeys of the Benedictine Order, and as a rule their revenues were quite modest. Within twenty years of the founding of S. Botolph, Colchester, thirty more or less important houses of the Augustinian Order came into being, including Walsingham and Worksop in 1105, S. Mary Overie, Southwark, in 1106, Holy Trinity, Aldgate, and Llanthony in 1108, Leeds in Kent, 1110, Barnwell in 1112, Merton and Cirencester in 1117, S. Osyth in 1118, and Bolton in 1120.

---

[1] Waltham and S. Osyth's, in Essex; Keynsham and S. Augustine's, Bristol, in Somerset; Haughmond and Lilleshall, in Shropshire; Dorchester and Oseney, in Oxfordshire; Missenden and Nutley, in Buckinghamshire; Bourne, Thornton, and Wellow, in Lincolnshire; Leicester and Owston, in Leicestershire; Cirencester, Gloucestershire; Kenilworth in Warwickshire; Lacock (nunnery) in Wiltshire; Lesnes, in Kent; Darley in Derbyshire; Hartland in Devon; Rocester in Staffordshire; Wigmore, Herefordshire; S. James's, Northampton; and Creake in Norfolk.

M

Like the abbeys of the Benedictine Order, Augustinian houses were independent communities, although, with the exception of S. Botolph, Colchester, and Waltham which came under Papal jurisdiction, they were all subject to episcopal visitation. The rapid growth of the Order in England made it impossible for the prior and convent of Colchester to exercise control over all the houses in this country, and in the thirteenth century General Chapters of the province were convened every four years or as occasion arose. They were held at various places; at S. Bartholomew's, Smithfield in 1231, at Huntingdon in 1328, and three years later in the parish church of Cheshunt 'for the good cause, in the Octave of Holy Trinity'. The General Chapters were attended by the heads of all Augustinian convents.

Like the Benedictine and Cistercian communities, though to a less extent, the Augustinians sent out brethren to found daughter houses. Exceptional in this respect was Nostell priory, Yorkshire, that colonised no fewer than six cells, of which Bamburgh, Northumberland, was probably the most important. Unlike the Benedictines, in general they made no bid for pilgrims, for only a few of their churches housed a shrine or possessed relics that made them popular resorts of the faithful. In the priory church of S. Frideswide, Oxford (now the cathedral) is preserved the stone pedestal that was once the base of the shrine of S. Frideswide; and at Dorchester abbey, a shrine containing the remains of S. Birinus formerly stood in a chapel south of the choir, specially built for the purpose in the late thirteenth century. At Walsingham priory was the miraculous image of the Virgin Mary, that proved a great attraction to pilgrims who flocked from all parts of Western Christendom. Foreigners of all nations, kings and queens amongst them, journeyed to Walsingham to behold the image; Henry VIII presented a costly necklace to adorn it, and the canons had little difficulty in convincing credulous pilgrims that the Milky Way in the heavens was a heaven-sent indication of the road to the priory, whence it came to be called the 'Walsingham Way'.

At Bridlington priory, the shrine of S. John of Bridlington was housed in an elevated chapel beyond the lofty reredos of the High Altar. The vandals who swept away the choir at the Dissolution wrote: 'Between the same [reredos] and the east window is the shrine . . . in a fair chapel on high, having on either side a stair of stone for to go and come by. Underneath the said shrine be five chapels with five altars and small tables of alabaster and images.'

In many Augustinian churches the nave or one of the aisles was granted to the laity for parochial worship. It is not easy to say to what extent the canons took part in parochial ministrations or were responsible for the cure of souls in the Middle Ages. Many abbeys and priories of this Order were endowed with large gifts of churches, and in some instances the terms of the foundation charter seem to imply that the founder took for granted that the priory would become a centre for the administration of the parish churches of the endowment. In 1398 Papal licence was granted for three vicarages belonging to Launceston priory to be served by canons of the house.

Nevertheless, the prime duty of the canons was the recitation of masses and the observance of the canonical hours in their own church; if, as frequently happened, an appropriated church was far distant from the priory, the canon who served the parish would necessarily be an absentee from the conventual church. In the cathedral churches it was the custom for the canons to appoint vicars to churches on their prebendal estates, and most likely this practice became general in Augustinian establishments.

The great London hospitals of S. Thomas and S. Bartholomew bear witness to the part played by regular canons in ministering to the physical needs of the destitute and diseased in the metropolis of the Middle Ages. Both of them, founded in the early twelfth century, were associated with Augustinian priories. In the year 1106 the church of S. Mary Overie, Southwark, that had been collegiate since the ninth century, was made Augustinian, and a century later, after a disastrous fire had ruined the church and devastated the surrounding area, the canons founded a hospital close by for relieving the distress and disease that were the aftermath. About the year 1228 the hospital was removed to a more healthy site in the neighbourhood, and was dedicated to S. Thomas of Canterbury.[1]

S. Bartholomew's priory and hospital in Smithfield were founded in 1123 in pursuance of a vow made by a royal jester named Rahere, who had fallen a victim to malaria whilst on a pilgrimage to Rome. On his return he was granted a piece of marshy land in Smoothfield by Henry I as a site for the priory and hospital. The latter was dedicated to S. Bartholomew and 'in honour of the Exaltation of the Holy Cross', and was built to the south-west of the priory and planned to accommodate a master, eight brothers, and four sisters, who were to tend the patients. The charter of 1147 defined the purpose as being 'to do all that could be done for the needy, for orphans, for outcasts, for the poor of the district, for

---

[1] In 1540 the dedication was changed to S. Thomas-the-Apostle, and that of the church to S. Saviour. The hospital was transferred to the Albert Embankment in 1871, and the church was elevated to cathedral rank in 1905.

every kind of sick person and for homeless wanderers'. A considerable portion of the priory church commenced by Rahere is still standing and the hospital, entirely rebuilt and enlarged, is now one of London's greatest healing institutions.

A third great Augustinian priory in London of which a hospital formed an integral part was S. Mary Spital, Bishopsgate, founded in 1197. At the Dissolution the hospital had a hundred beds. All traces of the priory disappeared after 1540, but in 1937 parts of the walls of the church and bases of the piers were brought to light during excavations at the south-east corner of Spital Square. The church seems to have been second only in size to that of S. Bartholomew the Great, Smithfield.

In the early part of the twelfth century a reformed branch of Augustinian canons came into being at the abbey of Arrouaise in Picardy, to which a few English houses were affiliated and designated abbeys. Amongst them were the cathedral-priory of Carlisle, and the abbeys of Dorchester, Lilleshall, and Lesnes. The heads of all Arrouaisian houses were required to attend a yearly chapter at Arrouaise. A few other Augustinian convents belonged to the little-known Order of S. Victor of Paris.

No particular form of plan was evolved by the Augustinian canons for their churches, nor was the arrangement of their conventual buildings marked by any features peculiar to the Order. In the disposition of the cloistral apartments there was little to distinguish Augustinian houses from those of Benedictine monks. Nothing differentiated the priory and church of S. Bartholomew, Smithfield, from those of a Benedictine abbey of the same size and period. Normally the Augustinian cloister was situated to the south of the nave, the canons' apartments being ranged about it on the Benedictine model. Bolton priory, Yorkshire, furnishes a typical instance (Fig. 23). On the east side was the two-storied dorter block, between which and the south transept was the vestibule of the octagonal chapter house, an uncommon form in houses of regular canons. To the south lay the frater and kitchen, and west of the cloister was the cellarer's building, with the outer parlour at its northern end. The ground floor of the cellarium, used for storage, was divided into two aisles, and the floor above was probably the guest-house.

In general, Augustinian churches were on a smaller scale than those of the Benedictines, though important houses such as Bristol, Oxford, Southwark, and Christ Church, Hampshire, had a fully developed plan and approximated in size to the cathedrals and greater churches of the Middle Ages. By far the larger number were originally unaisled, but were planned with two or more chapels

east of the transepts, as at Bolton, Lanercost, Lilleshall, and Newstead. In its complete form the great abbey church of Waltham
must have been one of the largest and most splendid in the land.

Unfortunately the church of the first Augustinian foundation,
S. Botolph's, Colchester, has, with the exception of the nave, been
utterly demolished, and no excavations have been undertaken to

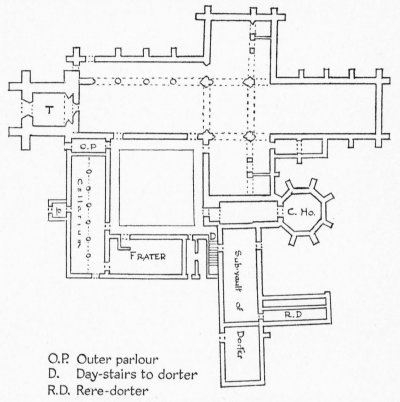

O.P. Outer parlour
D.   Day-stairs to dorter
R.D. Rere-dorter

23. BOLTON PRIORY, YORKSHIRE

reveal the plan of the eastern arm and transepts. The remains of
the nave indicate that the church was laid out on a big scale. It
had a total length of 245 feet, and it is reasonable to assume that
the choir-arm was of the apse-and-ambulatory type.

The priory of S. Bartholomew the Great, Smithfield (Fig. 24)
illustrates how closely the Augustinians adhered to the Benedictine model. Commenced in 1123 or shortly afterwards, the priory
church was a cruciform building, with an aisled nave of ten bays,
an apsidal choir of four bays with an ambulatory and three

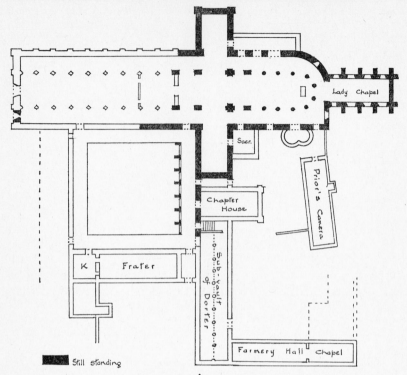

Lady Chapel

Sacr.

Prior's Camera

Chapter House

Sub-vault of Dorter

K   Frater

■■■ Still standing

Farmery Hall Chapel

24. S. BARTHOLOMEW'S PRIORY, SMITHFIELD

radiating chapels (Pl. XLI). and north and south transepts. The easternmost chapel off the ambulatory terminated in an eastern apse, but was pulled down in the fourteenth century to make way for the larger Lady Chapel that now occupies the site; and the lateral chapels were doubly-segmental on plan like those of Norwich cathedral. The ritual choir extended beyond the crossing into one bay of the nave. The cloister lay to the south of the nave, and the arrangement of the canons' apartments was exactly that of Benedictine houses (Fig. 24). In the eastern cloistral range was the rectangular chapter house, separated from the south transept by a slype. The canons' dorter extended southwards, with the calefactorium beneath. To the south of the cloister were the frater, with the misericord or flesh-frater at the east and the kitchen at the west. On the west side of the cloister was a two-storied building, the ground floor being the cellarer's quarters with the guest-hall above. East of the dorter block were the farmery buildings, and early in the sixteenth century a lodging for the prior was built between the farmery and the choir. A passage from the upper floor of the lodging led into the triforium chamber on the south side of the choir, and there still remains the three-sided oriel window built by prior Bolton *c.* 1517 in the triforium opening, whence he could watch the proceedings in the sanctuary during the Divine offices.

Of this fine twelfth-century church the eastern arm, together with the Lady Chapel, the transepts in part, and one bay of the nave, now serve as a parish church. The choir with its massive cylindrical piers, the triforium, and the aisles and ambulatory roofed with groined vaulting present an invaluable specimen of Norman architecture. The Lady Chapel, completed in 1335, is 60 feet in length and beneath the eastern end is a vaulted crypt or charnel house. The priory buildings have disappeared, but six bays of the east cloister-walk were restored early in the present century.

Not all Augustinian churches were planned on so elaborate and ample a scale as Smithfield. The simple parallel-apsed choir of the Benedictines was not favoured by regular canons, although at Holy Trinity priory, Aldgate, *c.* 1108, the aisles of the choir terminated in apses. Most of their churches were cruciform on plan and in the early days were unaisled, as at Haverfordwest in Pembroke, Dorchester, and Kirkham, *c.* 1125 (Fig. 25). With the exception of those built in towns and populous places or of royal or wealthy patronage, Augustinian churches were laid out on simple lines and were little more ambitious than the parish church of the period.

The rectangular presbytery flanked by lateral chapels in the manner of early Cistercian planning (p. 164), was the form adopted for the priory churches of Lilleshall and Haughmond, in both of which the nave was originally without aisles. In course of time, however, when the enlargement of such churches was taken in hand, the existence of the cloister on the south restricted the widening of the nave to an aisle on the side remote from the cloister. This accounts for the lopsidedness of the naves of Lanercost (Fig. 25), Bolton (Fig. 23), Haughmond, Brinkburn, and Ulverscroft to name a few. On the other hand the aisling of the choir presented no such difficulty. Indeed the whole eastern arm of the church could be torn down for a complete remodelling, as was the case at Kirkham, where a new choir of eight bays with north and south aisles was commenced *c.* 1230. A happy variant of the Cistercian choir-plan occurs at Lanercost, Léez, Repton, and Carmel, where the walls of the chapels flanking the presbytery, instead of being solid as at Lilleshall, were opened up with arcades. At Léez in Essex the two chapels on the north were taken down in

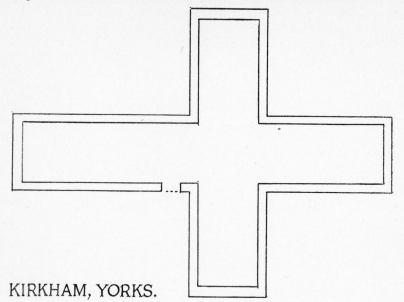

KIRKHAM, YORKS.

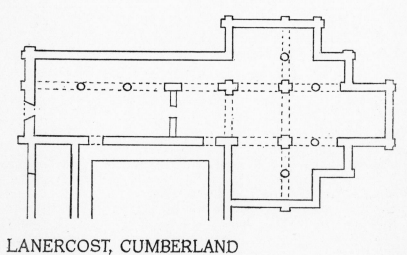

LANERCOST, CUMBERLAND

25. AUGUSTINIAN PLANS

1300, and in their place was built a Lady Chapel, 79 feet long, that extended eastwards beyond the presbytery. Of the same type but rather more advanced was the eastern arm of S. Frideswide priory, Oxford, a splendid piece of late Norman building, commenced *c.* 1158 and finished after 1180. There, the choir of four bays was flanked with aisles, and at the extreme east was a short square sanctuary. Subsequent additions have obliterated the original arrangement on the north side of the choir. The church had its full complement of aisles; the nave, curtailed to four bays when Wolsey was building Cardinal College, was aisled north and south, and both transepts originally had aisles at the east and west.[1]

The larger churches of Augustinian canons that were built or rebuilt in the Gothic centuries were modelled more or less on those of the Benedictine Order, though as a rule they were of smaller dimensions. A modified version of the eastern arm of Winchester (p. 132) was adopted when the choir of Dunstable priory was rebuilt *c.* 1220. It was five bays in length with aisles, and beyond the High Altar was a squared ambulatory that led to the Lady Chapel, built as an eastern annexe. It has long since vanished, but seven bays of the aisled Norman nave though robbed of the clerestory stage are in parochial use. Very similar to the choir-arm of Dunstable was that of Thornton abbey church that was remodelled about thirty years later. Here again an aisled choir of six bays was squared at the east, with an ambulatory and Lady Chapel beyond. It was about 180 feet long, including the Lady Chapel.

Amongst the many choir-extensions that characterised monastic building in the early thirteenth century that of S. Mary Overie, Southwark, is of special interest, being a further development of the Cistercian method employed at Waverley and Abbey Dore. After the fire of 1212 the eastern arm of Southwark was rebuilt with a choir of five bays flanked by aisles, that leads to the noble retrochoir, a low annexe three bays deep from west to east, and divided by slender Early English piers into four aisles from north to south. The retrochoir is roofed with quadripartite vaults, and formerly the 'Little Chapel of Our Lady' (now destroyed) extended farther eastwards.

In the reconstruction of the eastern arms of S. Augustine's,

---

[1] Of unique interest is the bay design of S. Frideswide's, an architectural eccentricity indulged in by the masons to ensure an effect of height in a church that was abnormally low. Unwilling to dispense with the triforium, the builders carried the cylindrical and octagonal piers of the choir and nave up to the triforium level, and heavily-moulded arches were made to spring from the capitals. Beneath is the triforium stage, that is really carried by the nave arcade, whose arches spring from corbels attached to the piers. So relatively unimportant are the lower arches that the bay design appears to embrace only a lofty nave arcade and a clerestory.

Bristol, during the fourteenth century, and of Christ Church priory, Hampshire, in the fifteenth, the Benedictine method of choir-planning was employed. In both instances the aisles are carried eastwards of the High Altar, with a square processional path that gives access to the Lady Chapel at the extreme east.

The choir of Bristol, begun in 1298, is characterised by structural innovations that are a measure of the ingenuity of the master-mason employed by the canons. The traditional bay-design of three stages was abandoned; the triforium and clerestory were dispensed with, the arches of the choir arcade being carried up the full height of the interior. The aisles were built to the same height and the Lady Chapel roofed at the same level. The underlying motive of the design was the provision of side-lighting in preference to top-lighting. The lierne vaulting of the choir with its kite-shaped cells was the earliest of its kind; and the vaulting of the aisles, consisting of ribbed conoids perched on horizontal stone girders, is a peculiarity that appears in no other mediaeval building. The canons of S. Augustine's were hard pressed to raise the money for these masterly experiments, for a chronicler wrote: 'They were in such want that when the hour of dinner came, they were compelled to send to the burgery of Bristol asking for necessary victuals as a loan or gift'.

The church of Christ Church priory, Hampshire, presents a fully-developed plan that might well be that of a Benedictine abbey of the first rank (Fig. 26). The establishment had been

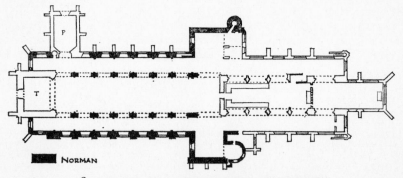

26. CHRIST CHURCH PRIORY, HAMPSHIRE

founded before the Conquest as a collegiate church, and in 1150 was converted into a house of Augustinian canons. The aisled nave of eight bays with its three-storied bay-design, the north and south transepts, and the crypts beneath the choir and transepts are Norman work of the first half of the twelfth century (Pl. XLIV); and the whole of the choir-arm, which is Perpendicular in character, is

a reconstruction that began with the building of the Lady Chapel
c. 1390 and was not completed before the early years of the sixteenth century. The eastern arm is a smaller and modified version
of that at Winchester or S. Albans. As there was no shrine at
Christ Church, a saint's chapel was not needed, but beyond the
High Altar is a spacious retrochoir and Lady Chapel.

Very few Augustinian churches of the twelfth century were not
subjected to some alterations in course of time. The church of
Dorchester abbey was transformed out of all recognition. An important and imposing church might be looked for there. In the
year 634 Dorchester was made the seat of the first bishop of the
West Saxons and later it was the cathedral of the diocese of Lincoln, until the Norman prelate Remigius transferred the see to
Lincoln. In 1140 Dorchester was converted into an Augustinian
house. The church of the twelfth century was an unaisled cruciform building about 175 feet in length (Fig. 27). About the year

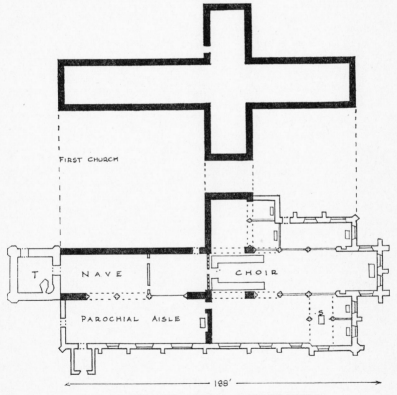

27. DORCHESTER ABBEY, OXFORDSHIRE

1225 an aisle was added to the north side of the choir, and a square chapel thrown out to the east of the north transept. Fifty years later, when the canons desired a housing for the shrine of S. Birinus, a saint's chapel divided into two aisles was erected south of the sanctuary (Fig. 27). This was followed shortly afterwards by a westward extension, into which the south transept was incorporated by the removal of its eastern wall. In 1335 a southern aisle was added to the nave, of the same width as the new choir-aisle. This aisle was provided for parochial worship, the canons' cloister being north of the church. The east end of the parochial aisle was built over a charnel house, in which were deposited bones from the graves that had occupied the site. Finally a short square sanctuary was added to the presbytery, and a porch built at the south-west of the nave. The addition of aisles to the original choir and nave entailed the destruction of the outer walls and the erection of arcades in their place. The whole of the church to the east of the nave was reserved for the canons, the pulpitum stood at the east end of the nave, and the rood screen 10 or 12 feet to the west.

One of the greatest ecclesiastical buildings of the Middle Ages, ranking in size and importance with Peterborough or Ely, was the abbey of Waltham Holy Cross, Essex, a Saxon collegiate foundation which Henry II reconstituted as a priory of Augustinian canons in 1177. An immense scheme of reconstruction was put in hand almost immediately after. Excavations made in 1938 on the land to the east of the present church brought to light the foundations, in part, of a church, the total length of which was about 480 feet. For the ambitious undertaking of the late twelfth century, the old Norman choir was swept away; the nave, transepts and central tower were allowed to remain, and a complete cruciform church was built east of the transepts (Fig. 28). By the middle of the thirteenth century a vast and unique building had arisen on the site.

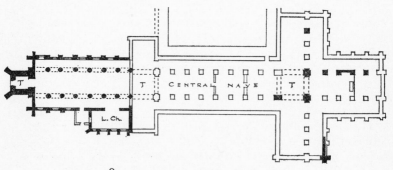

28. WALTHAM ABBEY CHURCH

To the east of the Norman transepts was an aisled nave of eight bays and 160 feet long, and farther east were large north and south transepts with eastern aisles. A lofty tower rose at the crossing of the new transepts, and farther east was built an aisled presbytery of five bays. The cost of this big reconstruction must have been enormous, for the expenditure as recorded in the Rolls of the Exchequer between 1177 and 1183 exceeded £1,400, equal to more than £80,000 to-day, a vast sum when the wage of the ordinary labourer was 1d. a day and that of the master-mason not more than 1s. In the internal arrangements of this great church, the western nave and transepts being parochial were shut off from the central nave by a screen beneath the western arch of the western crossing. The ritual choir undoubtedly extended two or more bays into the central nave, and was enclosed at the west by a pulpitum. Spanning the nave farther west stood the rood screen. The High Altar was set up against a screen two bays from the east wall of the presbytery, and in the retrochoir was installed the tomb or shrine of Harold, the last of the Saxon kings. The deep transepts of the new eastern arm afforded space for six altars in all. Early in the fourteenth century the canons provided themselves with a Lady Chapel which, owing to the restricted space at the east end of the church, was built in the angle of the south-west transept and the western nave. Begun in the year 1316 the Lady Chapel is a remarkably spacious building, beneath which is a vaulted undercroft or crypt that was used as a chapel.

The western nave of Waltham, now in use as a parish church, was about one quarter of the whole abbey church in length. The cloister and conventual buildings were situated to the north of the central nave, and were bounded at the east and west by the canons' and the parochial transepts. The main entrance to the abbey precinct was the gatehouse, of which only a fragment remains about 200 yards north-west of the church. To the west of the precinct is a large open square now used as a market, that was known as Romeland, so named from the dues that were appropriated to the Holy See in the Middle Ages. Henry III granted the canons the privilege of holding fairs on certain days, in requital of their hospitality on which he made many demands.

Many churches of Augustinian canons are in use today for Christian worship. S. Augustine's Bristol, Carlisle, and Oxford were reconstituted as cathedrals of the New Foundation by Henry VIII, and Southwark and Portsmouth have been elevated to cathedral rank in recent times. Christ Church cathedral, Oxford, has lost three western bays of the nave but otherwise remains as it was before the priory of S. Frideswide was suppressed; and the nave of Carlisle was shortened by five bays during the Civil War. The naves of Bristol, Southwark, and Portsmouth are modern.

Important Augustinian churches that survive in their entirety and serve parochial purposes are Brinkburn, Cartmel, Dorchester, and Christ Church, Hampshire. A number of other churches of the Order, existing only in part, are now parochial, the most noteworthy being the following:

A indicates abbey; P, priory

Bolton P, Yorks. Nave and north aisle.

Bourne P, Lincs. Nave.

Breedon P, Leics. Choir.

Bridlington P, Yorks. Nave.

Chetwode P, Bucks. Choir and north chapel.

Dunstable P, Beds. Nave and aisles.

Goring P, Oxon. Nave and north aisle.

Hexham P, Northumberland. Choir and transepts.

Lanercost P, Cumberland. Nave and north aisle.

Letheringham P, Suffolk. Nave.

Little Dunmow P, Essex, South choir aisle.

Porchester P, Hants. Nave and north transept.

S. Bartholomew's P, Smithfield. Choir, Lady Chapel and transepts.

S. German's P, Cornwall. Nave and aisles.

Thurgarton P, Notts. Nave.

Waltham A, Essex. Nave, aisles and Lady Chapel.

Worksop P, Notts. Nave and aisles.

Amongst the Augustinian churches now in ruins the remains of Lilleshall, Llanthony, and S. Botolph's, Colchester are the most complete. Although the ruins of Lesnes abbey are somewhat scanty, excavations made in 1909–13 and in 1938–9 have revealed almost entirely the plan of the church, cloister, and conventual buildings. The only surviving cloister-walks of Augustinian establishments are those at Lacock (p. 230), and Christ Church, Oxford, and many of the apartments about the cloister at Lacock remain fairly intact.

In addition to the Augustinians there were two other Orders of Regular canons viz., the Premonstratensians and Gilbertines, though the houses were comparatively few in number and of less importance.

The Premonstratensian Order was founded in 1120 by S. Norbert, a man of noble extraction born at Xanten in the Duchy of Cleves in 1080. His mother was a cousin of the Emperor Henry IV. At an early age he became a canon in his native place, and in 1118 he embraced a life of utter poverty in order that he might devote himself to ministering to the poor. He became a wandering preacher in Flanders and in 1119 settled at Prémontré, a marshy valley in the vicinity of Laon, and there the bishop of Laon built a house for S. Norbert where he established an Order that was marked by a singular asceticism and rigour. The Rule was based on that of the Augustinian canons, though the constitution was framed on Cistercian lines. On Christmas Day 1121 forty of his followers received the habit of regular canons, and four years later the Premonstratensian Order was formally approved by Pope Honorius I. Premonstratensians were spoken of as White canons from their habit, that consisted of a long white cloak and hood, over a white cassock, and a white cap.

The Premonstratensians were the Puritans amongst regular canons, as the Cistercians were amongst monks. Conversi formed part of the personnel in each house. The abbot of Prémontré was the abbot-general of the whole Order, and to preserve uniformity in their observances and way of life, an annual chapter of all the abbots was convened at Prémontré on the Feast of Dionysius, 9th October. Of the English houses the abbot-general demanded three things: regular attendance of all the heads at the annual General Chapter; the appointment of a *visitor* to examine and report on the state of English houses; and the right to tax affiliated abbeys for the benefit of the Order. This last demand placed the abbots in a difficult position. In 1302 Edward I's Parliament passed an Act that forbade the heads of religious houses to pay subsidies or taxes imposed upon them by foreign superiors. As defaulters the Premonstratensian abbots were summoned to the General Chapter. A royal prohibition precluded their attendance, but two of their number were deputed to cross the Channel and state their case. The matter was finally settled amicably by some sort of compromise.

Towards the end of the fifteenth century Richard Redman, Bishop of S. Asaph and formerly abbot of Shap, Westmorland, was made the commissary-general of English houses, but Prémontré maintained authority over them all until 1512, when a bull of Pope Julius II conferred the jurisdiction of English houses upon the abbot of Welbeck, who was made superior of all Premonstratensian convents in England and Wales.

Their abbeys were usually built in places remote from towns and cities, and were generaly dedicated to Our Lady. From the parent house bodies of canons were sent out to colonise other houses. Bayham and Bradsole were the only English houses that were colonised direct from Prémontré. They borrowed much from Cistercian customs; manual labour was obligatory, but none was admitted as a canon who was not a Latin scholar. Insistence was laid on courtesy and good manners and on a scrupulous ceremonial.

Like the Augustinians the Premonstratensian canons were often responsible for the cure of souls in parish churches. In 1476 six of the canons of Welbeck were acting in this capacity.

The earliest abbey of this Order in England, founded in 1143, was Newhouse, Lincolnshire, the canons of which came from Lisques near Calais. In the course of seventy years Newhouse sent out colonies to eleven other abbeys. The first daughter house was Alnwick in Northumberland, 1147, which in turn founded Dryburgh, the earliest of six houses in Scotland. The abbey of Welbeck, colonised by Newhouse in 1153, was responsible for seven more. In all there were thirty-one Premonstratensian establishments in England and Wales.

Being allied in customs with the Cistercians, it follows that the planning of their churches approximated to that of the White monks. In none of them was provision made for parochial worship, and this may account for the aisleness naves of most of their churches.

Originally the churches of this Order were mostly cruciform buildings without aisles, the planning of the eastern arm resembling that of the early Cistercian churches. Flanking the rectangular presbytery were two or more chapels that projected from the transepts and were separated in the Cistercian manner by solid walls as at Bayham (Fig. 29), or less often by arcades or screens, as at Cockersand and Easby. The church of Torre abbey, a daughter house of Welbeck and one of the largest of the Order,

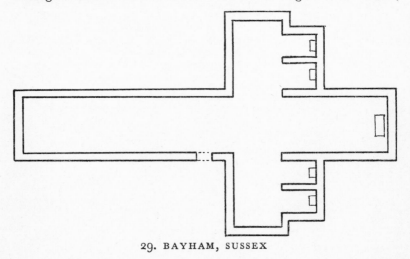

29. BAYHAM, SUSSEX

was almost an exact copy of the first church of Tintern (Fig. 18), having two chapels on either side of the presbytery, and an un-aisled nave. Similarly, the church of Talley abbey, the only Pre-monstratensian house in Wales, might have been a copy of Kirk-stall (Fig. 18), though on a smaller scale and half a century later. In both churches the presbytery had three chapels on either side, and a tower at the crossing. The aisled nave of Talley would have been eight bays long, like that of Kirkstall, had not the house been so impoverished by costly litigation that work on the nave was abandoned in the thirteenth century, when only part of the south aisle had been erected.

As a rule the presbytery was more elongated than in Cistercian churches. At S. Agatha's, Easby, it was approximately the same length as the nave, which had north and south aisles; and the choir of Bradsole was of such length that the eastern half beyond the high Altar was used as a Lady Chapel (Fig. 30). The pulpitum at Bradsole spanned the east end of the nave, the canon's stalls

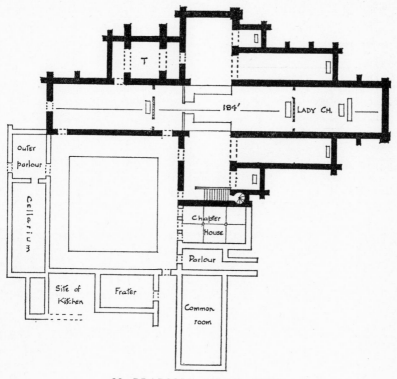

30. BRADSOLE ABBEY, KENT

occupied the area at the crossing, and the High Altar was set about half-way up the eastern arm and was backed by a screen-reredos, in which doors on each side of the altar opened into the Lady Chapel. An abnormal feature of Bradsole was the tower, which stood on the north side of the nave and was flanked by wings, the purpose of which it is not easy to say.

When the nave of a Premonstratensian church had originally been laid out without aisles, enlargement was only possible by building an aisle on the side remote from the cloister. The abbey church of West Langdon (Fig. 31) furnishes a good example of

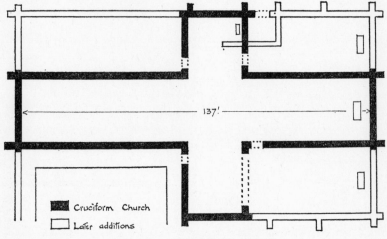

137'

Cruciform Church

Later additions

31. WEST LANGDON, KENT

such treatment. Not only was a north aisle added to the nave of this cruciform church, but an aisle was built on each side of the presbytery, of the same length and width. Further, the new choir-aisles absorbed the transepts, the eastern walls of which were taken down to permit this. As at Bayham, the presbytery walls of West Langdon were solid. At Langley, however, arcades of three arches divided the presbytery from its flanking aisles, the northern of which served as the Lady Chapel. Both aisles were of the same length as the presbytery.

The planning of the monastic buildings in Premonstratensian abbeys followed more or less the arrangement in Cistercian houses, with variations occasioned by the site and other considerations. Their chapter houses were invariably rectangular on plan, and were divided into two aisles, as at Bradsole, Beeleigh, and Shap; but at Cockersand there still remains a small octagonal chapter house, and that at Alnwick was circular. As will be seen in the plan of Bradsole (Fig. 30), the eastern block of the cloistral buildings followed the normal lay-out. In addition to the chapter house were the dorter, the sub-dorter or common room, and the canons' parlour. The western range was the cellarium, and the frater running east-west was the main apartment south of the cloister.

The only Premonstratensian church now in use is Blanchland in Northumberland, the present building consisting of the choir and north transept of the abbey church.

The most attractive Premonstratensian ruins are those of Easby abbey, Yorkshire. Less survives of the church than of the conventual buildings, which are of special interest on account of the irregular lay-out of the cloister and the apartments about it, occasioned by the peculiarities of the site. Further, for reasons of drainage, the canons' dorter and the guest-house were built on the west side of the cloister; and the large farmery with the abbot's lodging attached are situated north of the church and were entered by a passage from the north transept.

The following is a list of the chief remains of other Premonstratensian establishments, some of which are incorporated in farmhouses or residences.

Bayham, Sussex. Ruins of church and gatehouse.

Beeleigh, Essex. Chapter house.

Coverham, Yorks. Parts of the nave and north transept.

Egglestone, Yorks. Portions of the ruined church.

Halesowen, Worcs. Walling of choir and transept, parts of frater and sub-vault.

Leiston, Suffolk. Ruins of choir, transept, and frater.

Shap, Westmorland. Tower.

Titchfield, Hants. Parts of nave and chapter house.

Torre, Devon. Portions of transepts and chapter house; and sub-vault of frater.

Of English origin was the Gilbertine Order of Regular Canons, founded c. 1131 by S. Gilbert, the rector of Sempringham, Lincolnshire. His ideal was that of dual houses, of nuns and canons. At Sempringham, which became the parent house of several priories, S. Gilbert founded a house of nuns who at first observed the Cistercian Rule, but failing to obtain recognition by Citeaux, the sisters adopted the Benedictine Rule. Primarily attached to a Gilbertine priory for the administration of the sacraments to the nuns, the canons lived under the Augustine Rule. Conversi and conversae formed part of the double establishments, and were admitted as novices 'ready to labour in poor dress, content with the food of the poor'. No meat was to be taken by the nuns or canons except in the case of sickness; nor was it to be served in the guest-house save for a bishop or a Papal legate, and then it was not to be prepared by any of the canons or conversi, but by the prelate's own attendants. Further, the canons were forbidden to eat or drink with a guest unless he were an archbishop or bishop, and then only if invited to do so. The Statutes of the Order also laid down that 'for the avoiding of scandal, if the nuns having no beer, are obliged to drink water, the masters of the house who provide the supplies shall share in their deprivation'.

The Gilbertine canons wore a black habit with a white cloak and a hood lined with lamb's wool; the women had a black cloak, hood and tunic.

All Gilbertine priories were under the control of the Master of Sempringham, and were free from episcopal jurisdiction. Strict provisions were made in the Statutes to ensure the seclusion of the nuns and canons respectively in buildings about their own cloisters. Eleven of the twenty-seven houses were double, but those founded after the death of S. Gilbert were chiefly for canons only.

Paper restoration of the plan of Watton priory, Yorkshire, by the late W. St. John Hope and Harold Brakespear after excavations, indicates the infinite care with which the nuns' and canons' buildings were separately laid out. To the north of the church was a cloister which was 'to be better built and more beautiful and honourable than those of the canons' and about which were grouped the nuns' apartments. In the eastern range were a rectangular chapter house, a parlour, and a warming-house, with the dorter over; the northern block consisted of the nuns' frater and kitchen, and the two-storied western range was the lodging and dorter of the lay-sisters, or conversae. To the east of the nunnery lay the cemetery, and some distance farther east were the canons' cloister and buildings, with a chapel on the south, the chapter house and dorter at the east, the frater on the north, and a hall at the west. The prior's lodging, consisting of a hall and other chambers, stood to the south-west of the canons' chapel.

The church of Watton priory, about 280 feet in length, was a cruciform building, with a square presbytery, a north transept having two eastern chapels, a south transept, a tower at the crossing, and a wide western arm or double nave (Fig. 32). The Statutes decreed that the churches of double houses should be divided throughout their entire length by a partition-wall, the northern and larger half being for the nuns and the southern for the canons. The wall was to be 'high enough to prevent the canons and nuns from seeing each other, but not so high that the nuns could not hear the celebration of masses at the canons' altar'. On

the dividing wall stood an arcade, and in the presbytery the wall
was pierced by a doorway that was used for processional purposes.
In both halves of the church the western part served as the choir
of the lay-brethren.

In Gilbertine priories that were served only by canons, the
church and the cloistral buildings were planned on the Augustinian model. At Old Malton, Yorkshire (Fig. 32), the church,
dating *c.* 1150, was a cruciform structure, with a square presbytery
flanked by short aisles, north and south transepts each having an
eastern chapel, an aisled nave of eight bays, a central tower, and
twin towers at the west. The cloister, which lacked a northern
walk, occupied the normal position south of the nave.

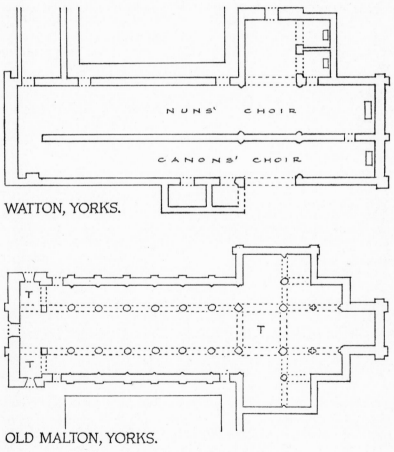

WATTON, YORKS.

OLD MALTON, YORKS.

32. PLANS OF GILBERTINE CHURCHES

XI. The Knightly Orders and their Churches

THE MILITARY Orders of Knights Templars and Knights Hospitallers, bound like the religious of other Orders by vows of poverty, chastity, and obedience, were founded after the First Crusade. In the year 1076 the Holy City had fallen into the hands of the Saracens, and the ill-treatment of pilgrims on their way to visit the church of the Holy Sepulchre in Jerusalem incited Pope Urban II and Peter the Hermit to preach the Crusades. 'I would rather risk my life to deliver the Holy Places than govern the universe' were the words of Urban's predecessor Gregory VII, on the eve of his death in 1085.

The Knights Templars were founded by Hugh de Payens and nine knights in 1118 for the protection of pilgrims *en route* to the Holy Land. Their headquarters were in the palace of Baldwin II, King of Jerusalem, that stood on the site of Solomon's temple; hence their name. The great S. Bernard took the Templars under his wing, and in response to a request at the Council of Troyes in 1128, he provided a Rule and statutes for the 'Order of the Poor Fellow Soldiers of Jesus Christ, and of the temple of Solomon'. Of extreme severity and asceticism, the Rule forbade all luxury and display; it enjoined constant devotional exercises, fasting, self-mortification, and the regular observance of the canonical hours. The Templars were governed by a Grand Master who had his seat first at Jerusalem, and later at Antioch, Acre, and Limasol in Cyprus, successively. The personnel of their houses, or *preceptories*, consisted of knights and chaplains, and of sergeant-commoners or servants. All professed knights were to wear white cloaks adorned with a red cross and their retainers were to wear black. They dined in common in the frater, where they made known their wants by signs 'in a gentle and private way'. Never was an idle word or immoderate laughter to go unpunished. Soothsayers, jesters and story-tellers, ribald songs and stage-plays were to be eschewed as insane follies. No brother was allowed to hawk, to shoot in the woods with crossbow, to halloo to dogs, or to spur a horse in the pursuit of game. When travelling abroad, Templars were to lodge with men of good repute, and were to keep a light burning at night 'lest the dark enemy, from whom God preserve us, should find some opportunity'. They were to shun 'feminine kisses', whether of mother, sister, aunt, or any other woman. No brother was permitted to despatch or receive letters without permission of the master of his house. No gold or silver was to be used in bridles, breast-plates, or spears; and if ever such trappings were given them in charity, they were to be discoloured to avoid an appearance of arrogance.

In its early days the Order of Templars consisted entirely of lay members, priests being employed to celebrate the Divine offices in their churches, and for other spiritual ministrations. In 1162, however, Pope Alexander III issued a bull sanctioning the admission of clergy to the Order.

During the twelfth century the Templars spread rapidly throughout Eastern and Western Christendom, and became organised into provinces. In the East were the provinces of Palestine, Antioch, and Tripoli, and the nine in the West embraced Italy, Greece, Germany, Spain and Portugal, Hungary, France and the Low Countries, and England. The Order was under the jurisdiction of the Grand Master in Jerusalem until the year 1187, when the Holy City was captured by Saladin, and Acre then became the headquarters. All the preceptories in England were subject to the Temple in London. In 1172 Pope Alexander III issued a bull conferring special privileges on the English Templars, including the right of sanctuary in their houses, exemption from tithes and taxes, and immunity from episcopal jurisdiction, the Pope himself being the immediate bishop of the Order. In such esteem were the Templars held that Innocent III, one of the greatest of the Popes, 1198–1216, chose to be admitted to the Order.

Knights Templars were introduced to England in 1128 by Hugh de Payens, Master of the Order, and they first settled on the south side of Holborn in London. When the Crusades were at an end and Acre was re-taken by the Saracens in 1291, the Templars lost their *raison d'être*. During their two centuries' existence they had grown proud and arrogant; they had amassed enormous wealth and had become the international bankers of Western Christendom. Their fall was brought about by the greed of Philip the Fair, King of France, who coveted their possessions. Monstrous and ill-founded charges were levelled against them, particularly in France, where their fall was accompanied by acts of incredible barbarity. In this country the Templars were brought to judgment at S. Martin's church, Ludgate, strange charges being preferred against them. It was claimed that on admission to the Order, a novice was required amongst other things to deny the Crucifixion, to spit upon the Cross, and to denounce the Sacraments.

Finally the Order was abolished by Pope Clement V in 1312. Of the twenty or more houses in England, eighteen were made over to the Hospitallers. In all there were some twenty-three preceptories connected with the London Temple, one of which, Ferriby in Yorkshire, was refounded as an Augustinian priory.

The first house occupied the site of the present Southampton Buildings at the northern end of Chancery Lane, London, but early in the reign of Henry II the Templars purchased land bounded on the north by the Strand and on the south by the Thames, where the Inner Temple now stands.

The churches of the Knights Templars differed in one important respect from those of other monastic Orders in having a circular nave, or round, attached to the choir, a form that was adopted in imitation of the church of the Holy Sepulchre at Jerusalem containing the tomb of Our Lord. To the east of the round was usually an unaisled choir terminating at the east in an apse.

The finest remaining example in England is the Temple church, London (Fig. 33), which was consecrated in February 1185 by Heraclius, the patriarch of Jerusalem, in the presence of Henry II. An inscription over the western portal states that the church was dedicated in honour of the Blessed Mary. Internally the central area of the nave is divided from an encircling aisle by six clustered piers of Purbeck marble that carry the clerestory wall (frontispiece). The entrance at the west is enclosed by a porch with three open sides, erected in 1195. The Temple round affords a fine example of Transitional building, and is noteworthy for the eight Purbeck marble effigies of knights on grave-slabs in the pavement,

XXIX. The Priory church, Lindisfarne.

XXX. The west front, Castle Acre Priory.

XXXV. Bronze sanctuary knocker, Durham.

XXXIV. The pilgrims' door, S. Albans.

About fifty years after the dedication of the church, the twelfth-century choir was pulled down and in its place was built a rectangular choir, five bays in length with wide north and south aisles that are of the same height as the choir. The quadripartite vaulting throughout springs from the capitals of the clustered piers, the whole presenting a choice and unusual specimen of Early English Gothic, despite drastic restorations of the nineteenth century. Originally a small rectangular chapel dedicated to S. Anne stood at the junction of the round and the south-western end of the choir; it was taken down in 1825, and the crypt on which it was raised was brought to light about a century ago. The new

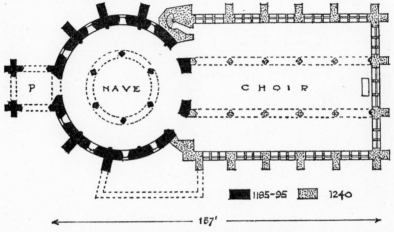

33. TEMPLE CHURCH, LONDON

Early English choir, 88 feet long, was consecrated in 1240 in the presence of Henry III and many nobles and ecclesiastics.

Complementary to the Templars were the Knights Hospitallers of the Order of S. John of Jerusalem, whose purpose was to succour sick and needy pilgrims and to tend wounded Crusaders. The real founder of the Order was Gerard de Martigues who, before the First Crusade, had established hospices in Jerusalem for the care of pilgrims. About the year 1120 Raymond de Puy, a French nobleman, re-organised the foundation into the Order of Knights of S. John, pre-eminently military in its character and completely autonomous, being exempt from tithes and episcopal jurisdiction. The Rule of the Hospitallers, drawn up by Raymond and confirmed by Pope Boniface, was based on the Augustinian Rule, and the personnel, like that of the Templars, was constituted in three grades—knights, chaplains, and serving brethren—all of whom took monastic vows and wore a black robe with a white eight-starred cross on the left breast. 'We place this cross on your breast my brother', ran the ritual of admission 'that you may love it with all your heart; and may your right hand ever fight in its defence and for its preservation. Should it ever happen that, in combating against the enemies of the Faith, you should retreat and desert the standard of the Cross and take flight, you will be stripped of the truly Holy Sign, according to the customs and statutes of the Order, and you will be cut off from our body as an unsound and corrupt member.'

The head of the Order was the rector or Grand Master. None was admitted into the Hospitallers unless he were of blameless life and character, and of noble and legitimate birth, exception being made in favour of natural sons of kings and princes. They were to eat but twice on Wednesdays and Saturdays, and no flesh was to be taken from Septuagesima to Easter except by the aged and infirm. If two brothers were found quarrelling they were to eat only bread and water on Wednesdays and Fridays, and to dine off the bare ground for seven days. They were forbidden to talk at meals and after retiring to the dorter, and nothing was to be drunk after compline. When soliciting alms they were to carry candles with them, and to wear no skins of wild beasts, or garments degrading to the Order.

Both of the Knightly Orders possessed many strong castles in Syria, and founded priories in all parts of Western Europe. The establishments of the Templars were in the nature of military barracks with exercising grounds where they practised the art of warfare. The houses of the Hospitallers were, as the name implies, hospitals for sick and wounded Crusaders. Unfortunately nothing is known of the arrangement of the conventual buildings of the English priories of the Knightly Orders.

The Hospitallers became a very wealthy Order; according to Weever, they owned no fewer than nineteen thousand lordships and manors in Christendom in 1240. Their churches, like those of the Templars, were planned with a circular nave, or round, to the west of the choir. The headquarters of the English Hospitallers was the priory of S. John, Clerkenwell, founded c. 1150, to which were attached fifty or more cells, or commanderies. The head of Clerkenwell was the Grand Prior of England; he ranked as the first baron and took precedence of all the temporal peers of the realm.

The church of S. John's priory consisted of a round nave, 65 feet in diameter, with a western porch, and a short unaisled choir having an apse at the east and a crypt beneath (Fig. 34). The site of the round is marked in the roadway to the west of the present church. The western part of the crypt with its late Norman quadripartite vaulting remains in a fine state of preservation. In the last quarter of the twelfth century the small choir was demolished and a new three-aisled choir, four bays in length, was erected, and was consecrated by the patriarch Heraclius in the same year that he performed a like ceremony at the Temple. The aisles of the new choir were raised on vaulted crypts, the character of which shows the advance made in the architecture of the late twelfth century.

During the Wat Tyler revolt of 1381 the priory was attacked, the prior slain, and the rebels 'set fire to this house causing it to

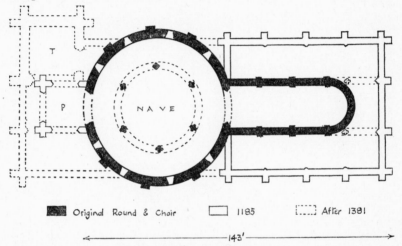

Original Round & Choir   ☐ 1185   After 1381

←——————— 143' ———————→

34. S. JOHN'S CLERKENWELL

burn by the space of seven days together, not suffering any to quench it'. The church was entirely rebuilt and in place of the round a nave of six bays with north and south aisles and a massive tower at the north-west were erected. Of the original choir, parts of the outer walls and bases of the piers of the arcades alone remain. After the Suppression the nave and the tower were blown up by gunpowder in Edward VI's reign, and the stone was carted away to be used for the building of the Protector's house (Old Somerset House) in the Strand. In Mary's reign a west front was added to the old choir, which underwent many alterations and restorations in the eighteenth and nineteenth centuries. The conventual buildings covered a considerable area, mainly to the north of the church. Some distance to the south, in S. John's Lane, is to be seen the great gatehouse of the precinct erected by prior Docwra in 1504.

S. John's priory was the wealthiest monastic establishment in London and the immediate suburbs, the revenue amounting to the huge sum of £2,385 at the time of the Dissolution. In the year 1211 Lady Joan Grey left her manor of Hampton Court covering several thousand acres to the priory. It was on this estate, leased to Cardinal Wolsey in 1515 for ninety-nine years at £50 per annum, that the ambitious legate reared the magnificent palace of which a great part is yet *in situ*.

The priory was the resort of royalty at various times. In 1212 King John spent a whole month there, and after a banquet on Easter Sunday he knighted Alexander, son of the King of Scotland. Henry III's son, Edward, and his bride, Eleanor of Castile, passed their honeymoon there in 1266; and in 1399 Henry IV was entertained at the priory for five days before his coronation. Henry V was 'lyvinge at Sent Jones' in 1413; and just before Easter 1485 the wily monarch Richard III summoned a meeting of the civic authorities of London in the great hall of the priory, and there and then disavowed his intention of marrying his niece, Elizabeth of York.

Of the many commanderies that were subject to S. John's, that of Little Maplestead, Essex, with its round nave, is the only one of any importance that has survived.

XII. The Carthusian Houses

THE MOST RIGOROUS and exacting of all the religious Orders of the Middle Ages was the Carthusian, of which there were only nine houses in England. The Order was founded in 1084 by S. Bruno, a native of Cologne and a canon of Rheims, whose love of silence and solitude led him to withdraw with six followers to the Chartreuse, a wild place in the Alps of Dauphiné. There he drew up a Rule and established the parent house, La Grand Chartreuse, whence the Order derived its name.

The Carthusian fathers were eremitical, their ideal being not merely isolation from the world but from one another. They aimed at the life of the solitary; each father led his life alone, perpetual silence being broken only by short periods of recreation, and during a weekly walk. Instead of dining in a frater and sleeping in a common dorter, each dwelt alone in his own small house of three or four rooms, standing in its own tiny walled garden off the cloister. Their meals were brought from the conventual kitchen and placed in an L-shaped hatch in the front wall of their 'cell'. Only on Sundays and festivals did the fathers dine together in the frater and once a week they were allowed to walk and talk together. The work of the house and garden was done by the inmate, for nobody was admitted but the prior. When two of the brethren met in the cloister, they neither looked at each other nor spoke, but drew the hood of their cowls over their faces. They never touched meat, poultry, or game, and took fish when it was given them in charity. Their food consisted mainly of eggs, pulses, and bread and water, but on one day in the week they fasted.

The Statutes of 1259 prescribed that for clothing, each father was to be provided with two hair-shirts, two tunics, two pilches, two cowls, three pairs of boots, four pairs of socks, a cap, night shoes and day shoes, and a girdle, all of canvas, 'for among all monks, and especially among us, it is ordered that meanness and coarseness of clothes and everything else we use, worthlessness, poverty, and self-abasement belong'.

Amongst the Lansdowne MSS. in the British Museum is a fifteenth-century manuscript of the Rule of the Carthusian priory of Sheen in Surrey, founded by Henry V in 1414. It gives in some detail the procedure in chapter when postulants sought admission to the house. After certain preliminaries, the candidate was addressed by the prior to 'set before your eyes the strictures and austoritie' of the Rule, and 'the length and prolixitie' of the day and night offices in the church. 'For your cloathing and lodging after you have received the habitt, you can make no further use of lynen except handkerchers, towels and the like, but for your body you are to weare a shirte of heare and a cord about your loynes and a wolen shirte. You are to lie upon strawe or a bed of chaffe with a blanket betweene. For your diet it is a perpetuall abstinence from flesh insomuch that in the greatest or most dangerous sickness, you can expect no dispensation therein. Also a good parte of the yeare we abstaine from all whitmeates, as in Advent, Lent, and all other Fridayes of the yeare, besides many other fasts of the Church and of our Order. Likewise from the Exaltation of the Holie Crosse until Easter wee fast with one meall a day, except some few days of recreation before Advent and Lent. For silence and solitude it ought to be perpetuall, except when our Statutes give licence, or that you ask leave. These be the general observances . . . common to seniours as to juniours. But there are some particular[ly] ordained and appointed for novices or newly professed, for theire soner attaining of humility and solid vertue, as in the dressing up of alters, sweeping of churches and chappels, making cleane of candlestickes, serving of others and suchlike. Which workes by how much they are more vile and contemptible in the eyes of the world, by so much they are more precious and meritorious in the sight of Almighty God. . . . These according to our Statutes and the Custome of our house I have layed unto you. *Putasne ista posse performare?'*

The Carthusian Order was the Order of buried talent. It produced nothing characteristic in art, philosophy, or literature; but the fathers were noted for their skill in gardening. It was said that wherever they settled 'they made the desert blossom as the rose', and amid the barren heights of Chartreuse they converted the stony waste into a garden.

Owing to the extreme asceticism and hardship of Carthusian life, the Order never became popular amongst those who chose to enter the cloister. In all there were only 150 of their houses in Christendom. The first in this country was founded in 1181 at Witham in Somerset, and for more than a century and a half, no other priory was established here except Hinton, also in Somerset, 1227. The remaining seven houses were founded after 1343; Beauvale, Nottinghamshire in 1343; the London Charterhouse in 1371; Hull, 1378; Coventry, 1381; Epworth, Lincolnshire, 1395; Mount Grace, Yorkshire, 1397; and Sheen in 1414.

The ideals of the Carthusians differing entirely from those of other religious Orders, their conventual buildings were necessarily arranged in accordance with the isolated existence they led. The small houses in which they lived alone were built on the four sides of a large cloister-court, the doors opening directly on to the walks. There was no infirmary in Carthusian priories, a sick father being nursed in his own cell where there was ample room for an attendant.

The church was invariably planned on simple lines and was of modest dimensions. Nothing remains of the priories of Witham, Hull, Epworth, or Sheen, and comparatively little of Hinton, Beauvale, and Coventry. The best-preserved Charterhouse is the priory of Mount Grace, Yorkshire, or, to give it the correct name, the House of the Assumption of the Most Blessed Virgin in Mount Grace. Its extensive remains afford an almost complete example of the planning and arrangement peculiar to Carthusian establishments. Excavations carried out in 1896, 1898, and 1900 revealed almost in its entirety the lay-out of the conventual buildings which were ranged round two irregular four-sided courts, divided from each other by the priory church and the frater (Fig. 35). About the northern or cloister-court, that had covered walks on four sides, are fifteen houses or cells each with its little garden. The other court, lying to the south of the church, is bounded on the west and south by ranges of buildings including stables, barns, and guest-houses, and on the east by a lofty wall. The original church, dating c. 1400 and about eighty-eight feet in length, stood to the south of a wall dividing the two courts, and was an unaisled structure consisting of a choir and nave. The latter served as the choir of the lay-brothers whose altar stood against the pulpitum at the west end of the monks' choir. A covered way from the south walk of the cloister led to a doorway in the north wall of the church, by which the fathers entered the nave from their cells. There was

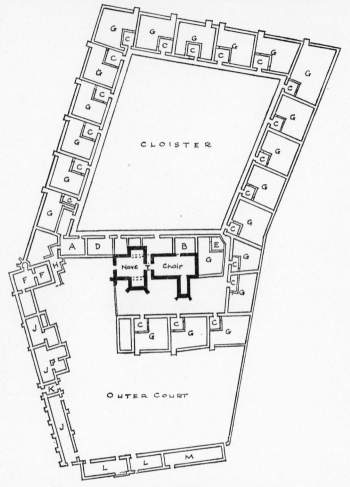

35. MOUNT GRACE PRIORY, YORKSHIRE

A. Frater. B. Chapter house. C. Cell with garden, G. D. Prior's cell. E. Sacrist's cell. F. Brewhouse and bakehouse. H. Kitchen. J. Guest-houses. K. Gatehouse. L. Stables. M. Barn.

another portal in the western wall of the church. The choir was extended eastwards in the fifteenth century by about twenty feet, to provide a sanctuary, which flanked the chapter house on the north. At the same time chapels or quasi-transepts were built on either side of the nave, and a square tower was raised on two parallel walls between the nave and choir. Save for the roof and the internal flooring the tower is in an almost perfect state of preservation. About the middle of the fifteenth century a vestry was added to the chapel south of the nave, and a chapel was built south of the new sanctuary. The chapter house was a small apartment about 28 feet square, and, as was usual in Carthusian priories, there was an altar against the east wall.[1] The sacrist's cell and garden adjoined the chapter house and sanctuary on the east. To the north-west of the church were the prior's lodging and the frater, and between them was an entry from the cloister.

Off each of the eastern, northern, and western walks of the cloister were five cells, each with its own garden. Here the fathers spent most of their time. These little dwellings were about 27 feet square and were of two stories, and were supplied with water for domestic purposes by lead pipes from a conduit in the middle of the cloister-court. In the wall by the entrance to each cell was a rectangular opening about a foot square that served as the hatch through which the inmate's food and drink were passed, so contrived that neither he nor the server saw each other. Internally the ground floor of each dwelling was divided by timber partitions into a lobby, a large living-room, and two smaller apartments, one of which was a bedroom and the other a study. The lobby was a narrow passage in the front of the house; at one end of it was a wooden staircase to the upper floor, and at the other a door to the garden. The upper floor was one large apartment that was used as a workshop. From the back of the house a pentise led to the garde-robe built against the outer wall of the garden.

In 1421 Henry V granted the convent of Mount Grace a number of alien priories that had been suppressed, and as a result cells for five more fathers were built round the open area to the south of the church. On the western side of the outer court was a range of two-storied buildings about 275 feet in length, comprising the bakehouse and brewery at the northern end, and two guest-houses divided by the gatehouse. The upper floor of the southern guest-house was used for the storage of grain. South of the outer court was another two-storied block that consisted of stables and barns (Fig. 35).

Although the greater part of the mediaeval London Charterhouse has been destroyed, in particular the great quadrangular cloister and its twenty-four cells, it had been possible to determine the general plan of the priory.[2] The dwellings and gardens

[1] In the chapter house of the London Charterhouse there was 'an altar wyth a table [reredos] of alabaster, wythe the seven joies of Owr Ladye', and traces of an altar are visible in the chapter house at Hinton.

[2] W. H. Godfrey, *History of Architecture in London*. The Charterhouse suffered damage from enemy bombing during the Second World War, and excavations subsequently undertaken by Prof. W. F. Grimes revealed the original plan of the buildings.

O

resembled in every respect those of Mount Grace priory, and in the centre of the great cloister was an octagonal conduit that was supplied with water brought across the fields from Islington. From the conduit-house water was conveyed to the kitchen and the cells. The chapel (remodelled in the seventeenth century) together with the chapter house and the frater occupied the same relative position as at Mount Grace, and to the south-west was a small court surrounded by houses and a hall that were used for the accommodation of guests.

XIII. The Mendicants and their Friaries

S. Francis and the Order of Friars Minor—The Ideals of the Mendicants, and their Way of Life—The Order of Poor Clares—Dominicans
and Carmelites—Division of the English Province of Franciscans into
Seven Custodies—The Distinctions of the Carmelites—Pope Innocent IV's
Pronouncement on Mendicants' Property—The Numbers of Friaries at the
Dissolution—Austin Friars, London—The Minoresses—The Patronage
of Royalty and the Nobility—Mendicant Churches as Burial Places of
the Nobility—Lesser Orders of Friars—The Friars Observants—The
Preaching Naves of the Churches—The Cross-Aisle between the Nave and
Choir—The Bell-Tower—Open-Air Pulpit—The Dominican Church
at Norwich—Grey Friars, Newgate Street—The Cloister and Conventual
Buildings—The Church and Buildings of Black Friars, London.

'GO AND SELL that thou hast and give to the poor . . . and come
and follow me' (Matthew XIX. 21). 'Take nothing for your journey,
neither staves nor scrip, neither bread, neither money, neither
have two coats apiece' (Luke IX. 3). These words were quoted by
Francis Bernardone, the son of a wealthy wool merchant of
Assissi, when with twelve companions he was received in audience
by Pope Innocent III in the year 1210 to explain the mission
to which the Master had called him. Six years later these few
'penitents of Assissi' became established as the Order of Friars
Minor, the first of the Mendicants. But friars were not monks;
their ideal was not retirement *from* the world, but service *in* the
world. Clad in peasant garb, and professing utter poverty, S.
Francis and his adherents travelled the countryside and the towns
of Italy, preaching and teaching, and ministering to the poor. With
no fixed dwelling place they begged their daily bread and lived on
the alms men gave them. Of them Matthew Paris the chronicler
of S. Albans wrote: 'Wherever men are most wretched, stricken
down by the most loathsome diseases, starved by famine, or trodden down by the great, there went the Grey Friars of S. Francis.'

Their self-sacrifice and renunciation of all worldly goods endeared them to all. Their habit consisted of a grey cloak with hood of coarse material, and a grey cassock; they girded themselves with a knotted cord and went barefooted.

The increase of commerce in the thirteenth century resulted in the rapid growth of towns and cities, in the poorer quarters of which dwelt crowds of the uncared-for, the plague-ridden and lepers, to whom the Franciscans ministered unceasingly. In 1219 they numbered some five thousand, and by 1224 the Order of Friars Minor had spread throughout Western Christendom.

An offshoot of the Franciscans was the Order of Poor Clares for women (*Dominarum Pauperum*), so named from the foundress S. Clare, a beautiful lady of noble birth who abandoned the world after hearing S. Francis preach in Assissi cathedral in 1221. At the bidding of S. Francis, S. Clare and her associates lived at first under the Rule of S. Benedict; hence Franciscan nunneries were called abbeys and the superior was the mother-abbess. In the year 1224 at the desire of the foundress, the Order of Dominarum Pauperum was given a Rule by S. Francis, more austere than that of the Friars Minor.

Side by side with the Grey Friars there grew up other Orders of Mendicants, notably the Dominicans or Black Friars, the Carmelites, and the Augustinians. The Dominicans, who earned the title 'Friars Preachers', owed their origin to Dominic the Spaniard, an Augustinian canon and an itinerant preacher, and in 1217 they were formally instituted by Papal decree. The Order was to consist of preachers and scholars who, like the Franciscans, were bound to absolute poverty. A General Chapter held at Bologna in 1222 forbade them to own churches, convents, or any kind of property. Their preaching was addressed to the more literate classes, and the Order attracted some of the most learned men of the time. Many of the high administrative offices in the Church came to be filled by learned brethren of the Mendicant Orders. Dominicans twice occupied the Papal throne, eight became cardinals, and no less than four hundred and fifty bishops.[1] In the last quarter of the thirteenth century the arch-see of Canterbury was held by a learned Dominican, Robert Kilwardy, 1273–8, and his immediate successor was John Peckham, a Franciscan. The dress of the Dominicans was a black cloak and hood, over a white tunic, and a square black cap.

The Carmelites or White Friars sprang from a community of hermits who lives in the caverns of Mount Carmel, and upon them the patriarch Albert of Jerusalem imposed a rigorous Rule in

[1] H. Daniel-Rops, *Cathedral and Crusade*.

1209. Twenty years later they emigrated to Europe, where they spent their lives preaching in the Mendicant manner.

About the middle of the thirteenth century an Order known as the 'Hermits of S. Augustine' came into being, composed of three small bodies of hermits who had been living under the Rule of S. Augustine. They were brought under one obedience by Pope Alexander IV in 1256, and were known as Augustinian or Austin Friars. They wore a long black gown and hood over a white cassock.

From the first the Franciscans, Dominicans, and Carmelites were distinguished for their ardent devotion to the Mother of Christ. Pope Honorius III directed that they should be styled 'The Family of the Most Blessed Virgin Mary'.

The first Mendicants to arrive in this country were the Dominicans, a small band of whom settled at Oxford in 1221, and three years afterwards a party of Franciscan pioneers, nine in number and armed with recommendations from the Pope, landed at Dover and made their way to Canterbury, where they were received and entertained somewhat ungraciously by the monks of Christ Church priory. Despite their poverty, their foreign tongue, and the ridicule that was poured upon them on their arrival, the Franciscans multiplied rapidly in England. By the middle of the thirteenth century they had established forty-nine priories in populous cities such as London, York, Bristol, and Norwich, and the Franciscan province in England was divided into seven manageable areas or *custodies*, for purposes of administration, the centres being Cambridge, London, Newcastle, Oxford, Salisbury, Worcester, and York.

In 1240 the Carmelites founded houses in London, and at Aylesford and Hulne, and the province was divided into four custodies or *distinctions* with centres in London, Norwich, Oxford, and York. In all there were about fifty Carmelite friaries in this country.

Forbidden by their Rule to own or accept property or land, the Mendicants were in their early days without churches or conventual buildings; but when they were permanently settled in London and other populous places where the environment and the climate were not favourable to open-air preaching, spacious churches were built to accommodate large crowds of worshippers, and attached to the churches were friary buildings grouped about a cloister. In 1245 Pope Innocent IV solved the problem of ownership by declaring that all the property of the Mendicants was to be vested in the Holy See, and in England the church and the buildings of a friary were held in trust by the bishop of the diocese or by the town corporation.

At the Dissolution there were about sixty-eight Franciscan establishments throughout the land, fifty-four houses of the Dominican Order, thirty-six Augustinian friaries, and forty of the Carmelites. As far as can be ascertained the total number of Mendicants was about eighteen hundred.

There were large foundations of the preaching friars in London. The Grey Friars were in Newgate Street, where they were succeeded by the famous Christ's Hospital; of the Black Friars and the Carmelites only the names remain, but the Austin Friars are in better case, for there still stands the nave of their fine church off Broad Street, gutted during the second world war but since restored (Pl. XLV). Remarkable for its spaciousness and lofty proportions, the church of Austin Friars is typical of the preaching churches of the Mendicant Orders.

Nuns of the Franciscan Order of S. Clare, or *minoresses* as they were called in England, came to these shores about 1290, and were represented in London by the house of The Grace of the Blessed Mary that stood in the Minories between Tower Hill and Aldgate. The abbey was founded by Edward I's brother, Edmund, Earl of Lancaster, whose wife, Blanche of Navarre, brought nuns from Spain or France for the convent. The foundation was confirmed by Edward I in 1293. Of the Order of Poor Clares there were twelve houses in the English province in 1316.

Royalty and noble families held the Mendicants in high esteem, and favoured them with benefactions and endowments. When Grey Friars, Newgate, was rebuilt early in the fourteenth century, Queen Margaret, the second wife of Edward I, bestowed money and lands on the house, and on her death her remains were buried before the High Altar of the new choir. Generous gifts were also bestowed upon Grey Friars by Isabella, Edward II's Queen, and by Queen Philippa, wife of Edward III. The Dominican friaries also attracted royal favour. In the year 1308 Edward II founded the priory of King's Langley, Hertfordshire as a house of prayer, for the souls of his Plantagenet ancestors, and according to tradition the church was built by the King as a burial chapel for his favourite, Piers Gaveston. Edward endowed the priory with 500 marks a year for the support of a hundred friars, who were to recite daily masses for the soul of his lamented minion. Edward III made generous gifts to King's Langley, and there the remains of Richard II after his death at Pontefract were taken for burial.

Nobles who were slain in battle or who perished on the scaffold were buried in one or other of the Mendicant churches of London. The lord-barons who fell at the battle of Barnet were taken to Austin Friars, where also was buried Edward, Duke of Buckingham, executed on Tower Hill in 1541. In the church of Grey Friars, Newgate, that became as popular as Westminster abbey as a burial place, was a proud array of tombs. The London historian Stow gives the names of upwards of a hundred and twenty 'defaced monuments in this church, a remarkable list of queens, dukes and duchesses, earls and countesses, barons, etc., . . . where were nine tombs of alabaster and marble environed with strikes [grilles] of iron in the choir, and one tomb in the body [nave] of the church, also coped with iron—all pulled down, besides seven score gravestones of marble'.

There were lesser Orders of Mendicants, viz., the Friars of the Holy Cross (*Fratres Crucifixi*), of which there were a dozen houses in England; the Friars of the Sack, or of the Penance of Jesus Christ; the Trinitarians, and the Friars Observants. The Fratres Crucifixi first settled at Reigate in 1245, and founded a house in London in 1249, memorialised in the street bearing the name Crutched Friars in Aldgate. They carried a cross upon their staves and wore a red cross on their habit. The seventeen English houses of the Order of the Sack were suppressed in 1317, following the abolition of the Order at a General Council at Lyons.

In their origin the Trinitarians or Maturins were associated with the Crusades as one of the redemptive Orders whose purpose was to rescue Christian captives held by the Moslems, and to assist poor travellers. The Order was founded in 1198 by S. John of Matha, and they came to be known as Maturins or *Donkey-Brothers*, from the humble method of their travelling. They observed the Rule of S. Augustine and wore a white habit with a red and blue cross. Each of the ten English houses consisted of a prior and six inmates, of whom three were lay-brothers. The earliest was Hounslow, Middlesex, founded *c.* 1200.

Of greater importance were the Friars Observants, an Order that was founded early in the fourteenth century by an Italian, Paoluccio de Trinci, whose ideal was a rigid observance of the Franciscan Rule. The great patron of the Observants was S. Bernardo of Sienna who re-constituted the Order about 1400 and thereby saved it from extinction. The Observants came to this country at the invitation of Edward IV, but it was not until 1482 that their first house was established at Greenwich, which Pope Sixtus IV gave the friars 'leave to accept'. Their friaries were said to be 'of the foundation of Henry VII'. Of the five English houses those at Canterbury, Newcastle and Southampton were originally Franciscan, and were made Observants by the first of the Tudors. All the English houses were suppressed in 1534 owing to their refusal to acknowledge Henry VIII's supremacy of the Church and to their condemnation of the King's divorce.

The fashion of making pecuniary bequests to the Mendicants grew to a marked degree in the fourteenth century. In their preaching the friars poured forth warnings of the terrors of purgatory, and the wealthy opened their purses and made bequests to build and furnish their churches, to found chantries and make provision for soul-masses at the altars. To be numbered amongst the 'familiares' of the Mendicants was a privilege no less valued than that of spiritual fraternity with the convents of other religious Orders.

As regards planning, the churches of the Mendicants differed characteristically from those of other Orders. The main feature was a spacious and well-lighted 'preaching nave', capable of accommodating large crowds of worshippers. 'The friars were trained preachers who quickly attracted large audiences. Racy, provocative, entertaining and informative, their sermons were packed with illustrations and stories from their own experiences, and from the books of *exempla* which were compiled for their use.'[1]

To the east of the preaching nave but of smaller proportions lay the choir, usually unaisled and reserved solely for the Divine Offices of the brethren, their stalls being ranged on either side at the western end. The Carmelite Church of Hulne, Northumberland, dating *c*. 1240, was planned with both nave and choir unaisled. At Winchelsea the unaisled choir, which is all that remains of the Grey Friars' church, terminates at the east in a three-sided apse.

Between the nave and the choir ran a cross-aisle or passage that effectively divided the two halves of the church, and gave access to the cloister and the priory buildings from the outside (Fig. 36). From the centre of the cross-aisle rose a bell-tower, the upper stages of which were generally octagonal in form. At King's Lynn is still to be seen the octagonal tower of brick and stone that formerly rose from the centre of the Grey Friars church; and at Richmond, Yorkshire, the bell-tower of the Grey Friars is square on plan and is similar in design to many a parish church tower of the Perpendicular period. Each of the walls of the cross-aisle was pierced by two arches that opened respectively into the nave and the choir. Transepts very rarely formed part of a Mendicant church, and as shrines were never set up in the choir, no provision was made for a saint's chapel.

According to the exigencies of the site, the cloister and the friary buildings were planned to the south or north of the nave,

[1] J. R. H. Moorman, *History of the Church in England*, Black, 1954.

the dorter, chapter house, and frater occupying the same relative position as in monastic houses. Where the site was not restricted, the cloister was often divided from the church by a narrow passage or lane, a distinctive feature of Mendicant planning, as in the Franciscan priory of Walsingham.[1]

In the open area on that side of the church remote from the cloistral buildings was often an open-air pulpit, from which sermons were preached when weather permitted. At Hereford there still remains the pulpit-cross that formerly stood to the west of the Dominican priory church. It is an octagonal structure of stone, each side being opened up with a pointed arch, and within was the pulpit. Above rose a slender spire surmounted by a cross.

No complete example of a Mendicant church survives in this country, but that of the Dominicans at Norwich, now S. Andrew's Hall, remains in great part. Built between 1440 and 1470 it consists of an unaisled choir of seven bays and 100 feet long, and an aisled nave of seven bays, together with the cross-passage that was originally surmounted by an octagonal tower. In the larger churches such as those of Grey Friars and Austin Friars, London, both the nave and the choir had north and south aisles, the eastern ends of the choir aisles serving as chapels (Fig. 36).

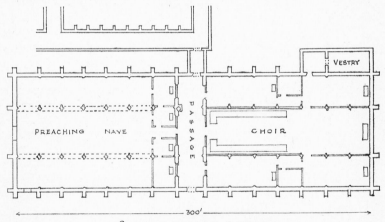

36. GREY FRIARS, LONDON

The church of Grey Friars, Newgate, was probably the largest Mendicant church in England. It was commenced in 1306 and was consecrated in 1325; from east to west it measured 300 feet and had a total width of 89 feet. A cross-passage divided the friar's choir from the preaching nave, both of which were seven bays in

[1] R. Gilyard-Beer, *Abbeys.*

length and were flanked with wide aisles. The aisles of the eastern half were subdivided by timber screens into chapels; on the north were the chapels of S. Mary and All Hallows, and in the south aisles were chapels dedicated to the Holy Apostles and to S. Francis. Against the eastern wall of the nave were four altars. The choir stalls were erected at a cost of 350 marks, the gift of Margaret Segrave, Countess of Norfolk. In his *Survey of London*, Stow gives full details of the gifts of royal and noble benefactors towards the building and furnishing of Grey Friars, in which mention occurs of the chapter house, the dorter and refectory, the infirmitory, the study, and the library. The cloister and the friary buildings lay to the north of the nave. Characteristic were the slender piers that would not obstruct the view of the preacher, the large windows that flooded the interior with light, and the general spaciousness of the great nave.

On a smaller scale was the London house of Black Friars, not a vestige of which remains, but which has been reconstructed on paper by the late Sir Alfred Clapham[1] (Fig. 37). The priory was founded in 1221 on a site near Holborn, and in 1274 the Black Friars removed to land that had been given them on the north bank of the Thames near Ludgate. The church differed from that of Grey Friars, the choir-arm being unaisled. The nave of seven bays, 114 feet in length, had north and south aisles, and flanking the western half of the northern aisle was a Lady Chapel. Between the nave and the choir was an octagonal bell-tower with a spire. South of the nave was the cloister, around which were ranged extensive conventual apartments that stretched considerably to the south and east. The eastern block, in the middle of which was the chapter house, was a two-storied building, the upper floor being the friars' dorter. To the south-east lay the farmery cloister. The chief apartment of the southern cloistral block was the frater, at the west of which stood the kitchen and buttery. A two-storied building on the west side of the cloister was the guest-house, with a great hall on the upper floor. Further south were a chapel dedicated to S. Anne and a large building spoken of as the upper frater or Parliament House, the exact purpose of which is not known, though it was doubtless the scene of the trial for the divorce of Katherine of Aragon and Henry VIII.

[1] A. W. Clapham and W. H. Godfrey, *Some Famous Buildings and their Story.*

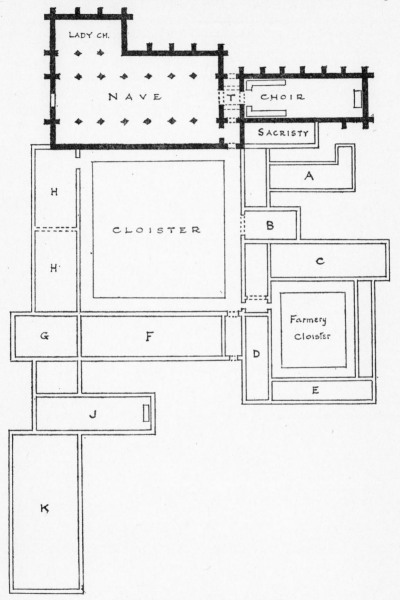

LADY CH.

NAVE

CHOIR

T

SACRISTY

A

B

C

CLOISTER

Farmery
Cloister

H

H

G

F

D

E

J

K

37. BLACK FRIARS, LONDON

A. Prior's lodging. B. Chapter house. C. Dorter (over). D. Farmery hall. E. Farmery bakehouse and brewhouse. F. Frater. G. Kitchen. H. Guest-house. J. S. Anne's chapel. K. Parliament house.

XIV. Mediaeval Nunneries

CENTURIES BEFORE THE Norman Conquest, Saxon ladies of noble blood and high estate, daughters of kings and chieftains, chose to abjure the world and adopt the monastic life. In Kent there were the Saints Eadburg, Eanswith, and Mildred; in East Anglia, Etheldreda of Ely, and Wendreda; in Mercia, Kyneburga, Kyens- with, and Werburga; amongst the East Saxons, Osyth and Ethel- burga of Barking; in Wessex, Frideswide, Sidwell, and Cuthburga; and in Northumbria, Ebba and Hilda, to name a few. In 657 Hilda became abbess of Whitby, one of the most famous monasteries of Saxon England. Around the wooden church at Whitby dwelt the nuns and monks of the community that did much to Christianise the North. The Saxon religious houses were often double establish- ments following the Irish tradition, and were modelled on Whitby. Such were Barking, founded in 666, and Wimborne, *c.* 705. Not only were these early houses important missionary centres, but they became seminaries of learning. One of the servants of Whitby, afterwards a monk, was Caedmon, the sacred poet; and a greater than Caedmon and the most learned man of his age was the Venerable Bede, 673–735, 'a servant of God and priest of the monastery of the blessed Apostles Peter and Paul' at Jarrow by the Tyne, that had been founded mainly by Benedict Biscop, 628–89.

Between the years 867 and 870 all the religious houses of Northumbria and Mercia were ravaged and sacked by the Danes, and under Viking rule Christianity was almost entirely stamped out in the North, the Midlands, and the East. During the monastic revival of the tenth century that was largely inspired by the great S. Dunstan, a few of the Saxon nunneries were refounded, only to disappear in the clean sweep that was made of Saxon abbeys and cathedrals by the Norman ecclesiastics who swarmed into the country after the Conqueror's victory at Hastings. Nothing remains therefore of the nunneries of pre-Conquest days, and little is known of their churches or conventual buildings.

Of the 140 that existed at the time of the Dissolution, more than half were of the Benedictine Order; there were twenty-five Cistercian nunneries and about eighteen establishments of Augustinian canonesses. The majority were priories, and the nineteen that attained the status of an abbey were mostly Benedictine.

Nunneries were most numerous in the North and the East Midlands, but with the exception of Barking and Syon the most wealthy were to be found in the counties south of the Thames. Few if any ranked in importance with monasteries and in general were poorly endowed and were often reduced to such straits that they were unable to provide the stipend for a priest to celebrate masses in their church.[1] Attached to the larger nunneries such as Romsey and Shaftesbury were chaplains who had a stall in the nuns' choir and held prebends on the conventual estates. The richest English nunnery was Syon abbey, Middlesex, founded in 1414 by Henry V, the annual revenue of which, derived from lands and properties in a dozen counties, amounted to £1,945 at the Dissolution.

In general the personnel was small in numbers. At the end of the fifteenth century there were sixty houses with fewer than ten sisters, the average being about fourteen. Syon abbey, a double convent, was exceptional, being served by an abbess and fifty-one nuns, thirteen chaplains, eight lay-brothers, and four deacons.

[1] Such was the case at the little Benedictine Nunnery of S. Sepulchre, Canterbury. To meet the situation Robert Vyntier of Maidstone founded a chantry in the nun's church in 1369, thus providing the sisters with their daily mass, from which the founder himself derived spiritual benefit.

'Mediaeval nunneries were recruited almost entirely from the upper classes.'[1] As a rule it was only ladies of noble or gentle birth who were received as nuns. The abbess or prioress was always a person of some social standing or of a wealthy family, and when the business of her house necessitated a journey, her retinue was often that of a nobleman. Amongst the distinguished abbesses of Barking were three queens and two princesses, and the names of others, De la Pole, De Vere, Montacute, and Becket (a sister of the martyred archbishop) indicate their social status. Several abbesses of Romsey also were of royal or noble parentage. In 1086 the convent was ruled by Christina, the daughter of Edgar Atheling, and under her care Henry I's wife had been educated.[2]

Of the rank and file in nunneries, great numbers were gently-nurtured ladies who took the veil from the desire for a life of spiritual devotion; and there were others, unwanted daughters of the country gentry and wealthy families, who were foisted upon the nunneries as an alternative to marriage. After a visitation of Romsey in 1327, Bishop Stratford of Winchester wrote: 'It is notorious that their house was burdened with ladies beyond the established number which used to be kept, and he heard that they are being forced to receive more damoyseles as nuns.' Notwithstanding, six years later there were no fewer than ninety-one nuns in the convent, after which the numbers declined, and when Romsey was surrendered to the Crown in 1540 there were the abbess and twenty-five nuns.

Other female encumbrances who were sometimes consigned to the cloister were those of illegitimate birth. At the time of the Suppression a natural daughter of the great Cardinal Wolsey was an unprofessed nun at Shaftesbury abbey, Dorset, on behalf of whom John Clansey wrote a letter to Thomas Cromwell in which he stated that Wolsey 'wold hur to be namyd my doythter; and the troyth ys she was his dowyther; and now by your visitacyon she hathe commawynment to departe', a reference to an injunction that the profession of a nun by a maid under the age of 24 was invalid, and those thus committed were to be expelled.[3]

---

[1] Eileen Power, *English Nunneries*.

[2] Another famous abbess of Romsey was Mary, the youngest daughter of King Stephen, who had spent her childhood in the nunnery of Stratford-le-Bow. In 1160 she became the abbess of Romsey, but the following year she ran away to marry Matthew, Count of Flanders. After ten years Mary and her husband separated and she ended her days in a convent at Montreuil in France.

[3] Five under-age nuns who had been dismissed from the House of the Blessed Mary in the Minories, Aldgate, wrote to Cromwell: 'May we come again into our religion, or have licence to be in the cloister till we are twenty-four, and then to be professed again if God shall call us?'

With the rise of the merchant classes in England in the fourteenth and fifteenth centuries, unmarriageable daughters of the nouveaux-riches found their way into nunneries, sums of money or 'dowries' being paid and often expected on their admission, a practice that was contrary to monastic purpose.

Any woman or virgin could be professed after a year's probation by an abbot or a Visitor of the house, usually at the age of sixteen; but the elaborate ceremony of *consecration* could be performed only by a bishop, and not until the sister was 25, and was reserved for virgin nuns only. 'After the beginning of Mass and before the reading of the Epistle, [she] came before the altar robed in white, carrying the religious habit in her right hand and an unlighted taper in her left. The habit she laid before the altar at the bishop's feet, and held the taper in her hand. The bishop then consecrated the habit and gave it to her, the veil excepted, saying "Take girl the robe, which you shall wear in innocence", upon which she went into the re-vestry, put it on and returned with a lighted taper in her hand, singing "I love Christ. . . ." Then after the Epistle, the Gospel and Creed, the bishop said "Come! come! daughters, I will teach you the fear of the Lord", upon which the nun came before the altar singing "And now we follow with our whole hearts." A litany was then said by the clerks, and seven psalms by the bishop, after which the bishop arose and began the *Veni Creator*; then the nun rose and came before the altar, when the bishop put the veil on her head as she stooped. She then made her profession, placed a cross on the altar and said three times "Receive me O Lord", after which she lay prostrate before the altar while certain psalms were sung.'[1]

The spiritual side of life in mediaeval nunneries differed little from that observed in houses of monks. The canonical hours, fasts and festivals, processions, and the community life in general were much the same for nuns as for monks. But on the temporal side the administration of lands and properties, that were usually leased to tenants at annual rents, was entrusted to paid officials. An abbess or prioress was vested with all the authority and powers of an abbot; she was the landlord of estates and properties belonging to the convent; she took tithes from the appropriated churches, to which she appointed vicars for the cure of souls. It was not an easy matter for an abbess or any of her obedientiaries to manage distant estates without ignoring the rule respecting enclosure, and it therefore became the custom for the convent to appoint a layman as *custos* or warden to administer the properties and attend to their finances. At S. Helen's priory, Bishopsgate, the steward who

---

[1] T. D. Fosbroke, *British Monachism*.

collected the rents and was responsible for the external business of the convent lived within the precinct, probably in a chamber over the gate-house. He was paid £12 a year with an additional 20s. for his livery and food and drink; and he received two cart-loads of fuel and ten quarters of charcoal every year. Here and there the head of a nunnery was a capable business woman, who did not neglect the material aspect of religious life. In the Chartulary of the Benedictine nunnery of Wherwell, Hampshire, is an account of the activities of abbess Euphemia, 1226–57, under whose rule great improvements were made in the sanitation and drainage of the conventual buildings. 'The court of the abbey manor, owing to the useless mass of squalid buildings, and the nearness of the kitchen to the granary and old hall, was in much danger of fire; whilst the confined area and the amount of animal refuse was a cause of offence both to the feet and nostrils of those who had occasion to pass through.... Realising that the Lord had called her to the Rule, not that she might live at ease, but that she might, with due care and despatch, uproot and destroy and dissipate all that was noxious, and establish and erect that which would be useful [she caused to be] demolished the whole of these buildings, levelled the court, and erected a new hall of suitable size and height. She also built a new mill some distance from the hall, and constructed it with great care, in order that more work than formerly might be done therein for the service of the house. She surrounded the court with a wall and the necessary buildings, and round it she made gardens and vineyards and shrubberies in places that were formerly useless and barren, and which now became both serviceable and pleasant.'

All English nunneries including those of the Cistercian Order were subject to episcopal visitation, the records of which reveal that worldliness and its temptations could not be wholly excluded from the cloistered life. Time and again bishops issued injunctions to enforce the rule, more honoured in the breach than the observance, against nuns wandering beyond the precincts of their houses without good reason. In the second half of the thirteenth century the Cardinal Legate Ottobon on the occasion of a visit to this country enjoined the bishops to enforce the enclosure of nuns, and c. 1299 Pope Boniface VIII issued a bull known as *Periculoso*, which ordained that 'all and sundry nuns to whatever Order they belong and in whatever part of the world shall remain profitably enclosed within their monasteries; so that no nun ... shall henceforth have or be able to have the power of going out of those monasteries ... unless perchance any be found manifestly suffering from a disease so great and of such a nature that she cannot, without grave danger or scandal, live with the others'.[1] But bulls and injunctions respecting the claustration of nuns proved of little avail, as is evident from the records of visitations in the episcopal Registers of subsequent centuries.

When the vicar-general of Archbishop Morton made a visitation of Romsey abbey in 1492, the prioress deposed that the nuns went into town and frequented taverns there, and another sister complained of the unseemly noise in the choir, and of the poor beer served at meals. At another visitation two years afterwards it was revealed that the abbess had allowed the roofs of the choir and dorter to fall into disrepair, 'so that if it happened to rain, the nuns were unable to remain in the choir in the time of divine service, or in their beds. And the funds that the abbess ought to have expended on those matters have been squandered on Master Bryce [the vicar]; and there was a grave scandal about these two.' On such findings the abbess resigned, but strange to say she was re-elected by the nuns in chapter. In 1397 the prioress of Nunmonkton, Yorkshire, was brought to book by the Archdeacon of Richmond for wearing furs and silken veils. The keeping of animal pets such as dogs, rabbits, and monkeys, a practice indulged in by many nuns, was frowned on by bishops and their deputies. Visitations revealed that the nuns in some houses took little puppies with them into choir during the canonical hours. In the *Ancren Riwle*, a treatise compiled in the thirteenth century for the use of anchoresses but applicable to the inmates of nunneries, occurs the injunction 'Ye shall not possess any beasts, my dear sisters, only a cat'.

The severity of the penance or punishment imposed upon defaulting nuns by the visitor depended upon the nature of the offence. When the vicar-general of the Bishop of Lincoln visited the Cistercian nunnery of Greenfield in 1525, two of the sisters were found guilty of grave moral lapses, and for penance they were required 'to lie prone at the door of the chapter house, for the nuns to walk over them as they entered, every Wednesday and Friday' for specified periods.[2] For less serious offences, penance took such forms as fasting on certain days of the week, or loss of seniority and therefore taking a lower place in choir and chapter.

In the later Middle Ages the nunneries were taking in daughters of the local gentry as paying guests, who led a far more genteel life there than in their own households, and received some sort of education. When Cromwell's Commissioners visited the nunnery

---

[1] Eileen Power, *English Nunneries*.
[2] *Visitations of the Diocese of Norwich, 1492–1532*. Edited for the Camden Society by A. Jessopp, 1858.
P

of S. Mary, Winchester, in May 1536, they found there twenty-six girl boarders, 'chyldren of lordys, knyghttes, and gentylmen brought up yn the said monastery'. The list of these girls included 'Bryget Plantagenet, dowghter unto the Lord Vycounte Lysley', and members of the Titchborne, Copley, Tyrrell and Dingley families. John Aubrey, writing in the seventeenth century of ladies boarded in the Wiltshire nunneries, observed that 'young maids were brought up . . . at nunneries, where they had examples of piety and humility, modesty and obedience to imitate and to practice. Here they learned needlework, the art of confectionery, surgery, physic, writing, drawing, etc. . . . This was a fine way of breeding up young women who are led more by example than precept; and a good retirement for widows and grave single women to a civil, virtuous and holy life.'

Long before the Dissolution a great number of nunneries had sadly declined; they were saddled with debt and the inmates were few in number. Under some pretext or other, bishops found little difficulty in procuring Papal sanction and royal licence for suppressing certain decayed houses, the revenues of which were to be devoted to the founding or the endowment of colleges (p. 53); and the twenty-five monasteries that were swept into Cardinal Wolsey's net of confiscation for the founding of his colleges at Oxford and Ipswich included the Benedictine nunneries of Littlemore, De la Pré, and Wix.

In general, nuns' churches were planned on simple lines and were of modest dimensions. The elaborate lay-out of the larger Benedictine churches, with saint's chapel, retrochoir, and ambulatory, was extremely rare. Exceptional was the abbey church of Barking, which was planned on an ample scale, larger than Rochester cathedral. As a rule the unaisled rectangle consisting of a choir and nave sufficed, the High Altar being all that was needed for the nuns' offices. As there was no resident body of priests each under the obligation of reciting a daily mass, additional altars were not required. The church of Lacock abbey, a house of Augustinian canonesses, founded in 1232, may be regarded as typical (Fig. 41). Having a total length of 165 feet and a width of 28 feet, it was divided into seven bays, but there was no arch or structural division between the nave and the choir. The latter was enclosed at the west by the pulpitum near the eastern door into the cloister. The westernmost bay of the nave was screened off to form a vestibule. The only addition to the thirteenth-century church was a Lady Chapel of three bays, built c. 1315–20 to the south of the choir.

The Benedictine nunnery of S. Helen, Bishopsgate, was somewhat unique, for when the priory was founded in 1210 the site was partly occupied by the parish church. The nuns' church, rectangular on plan, was therefore attached to it on the north (Fig. 38), together with the cloister and conventual buildings. The parallel churches were separated by a solid wall, except at the extreme east, where the wall was opened up with an arch. In the last quarter of the fifteenth century, however, the wall was replaced by the present lofty arcade of four arches, and screens or

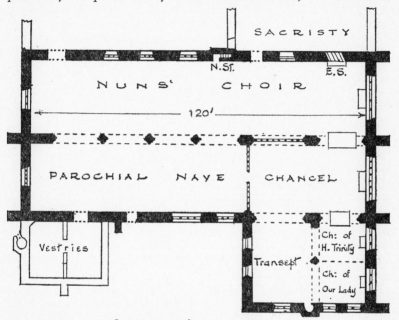

38. S. HELEN'S, BISHOPSGATE

low walls were built from pier to pier to ensure privacy for the nuns when they were in their choir. In the north wall of the sanctuary is a canopied tomb-like structure of the Perpendicular period that was probably used as the Easter Sepulchre. The lower part is pierced with a series of vertical squints that commanded a view of the High Altar from the adjoining sacristy on the north. An arrangement of parallel churches that served nuns and parishioners, similar to that at S. Helen's, occurs at Minster, Sheppey, a house of Benedictine nuns, where the northern nave of the twelfth century (now an aisle), was the nuns' chapel, and the southern nave, of the thirteenth century, was parochial.[1]

[1] The church was served by two priest-monks of S. Augustine's abbey, Canterbury, one of whom acted as chaplain and confessor for the nunnery, and the other as vicar of the parish church. They occupied chambers in the gatehouse to the west of the church.

The largest and most splendid nuns' church in mediaeval England was that of Barking abbey in Essex. Rebuilt early in the twelfth century it was a cruciform building, with a parallel-apsed choir five bays in length, shallow transepts each having an eastern apsidal chapel, a nave of ten bays flanked by aisles, and towers at the crossing and the west. At the beginning of the thirteenth century, important extensions were made at the east, undoubtedly to provide an ambulatory and a saint's chapel to house the shrine of S. Ethelburga. The three Norman apses of the choir were taken down, and beyond the High Altar was built a square retrochoir, three bays long and divided into three aisles (Fig. 39). The shrine was installed in the central aisle, and farther east was erected a narrow Lady Chapel. The new extension gave ample space for free movement about the shrine. Thus completed, this great church was 337 feet from east to west. The dedication of the new choir-arm took place in 1240. The lay-out of the abbey church is marked out in the turf of the recreation ground that now covers the site.

Although not comparable in size with Barking, of equal interest as regards its planning is the abbey church of Romsey, the finest mediaeval nuns' church now existing in England. Its planning and sumptuous Norman architecture place it almost in the front rank of the greater churches. According to tradition the abbey was founded for Benedictine nuns in the year 907, though the present church was commenced in 1120.[1] On plan it consists of an aisled nave of seven bays, north and south transepts with apsidal chapels at the east, a tower at the crossing, and a square choir-arm of three bays (Fig. 40). The aisles of the choir lead to a square ambulatory, and internally the wall at the east end is hollowed out into apses, each of which contained an altar. Formerly a rectangular Lady Chapel extended eastwards beyond the ambulatory. The eastern arm of Romsey was in effect a squared version of the Benedictine apse-and-ambulatory plan, and was perhaps the earliest of its kind. Architecturally the massive compound piers, the large triforium with two sub-arches, the fine clerestory, and the rich Norman work render the interior of Romsey one of the outstanding examples of Anglo-Romanesque building in the south of England. Being a nunnery church, there was no western door for the laity, but the north aisle of the nave and the north transept were assigned to the parishioners for their worship.

The laity being excluded from the precincts of Cistercian abbeys, whether of monks or nuns, no provision was made for parochial

---

[1] In 1900 the foundations of an earlier Norman church, completed c. 1090, were brought to light beneath the pavement of the crossing. It was a small cruciform building without aisles, terminating at the east in an apse, and was about 100 feet long.

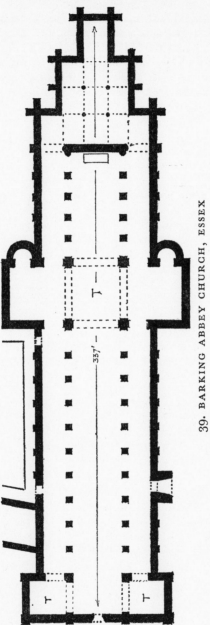

39. BARKING ABBEY CHURCH, ESSEX

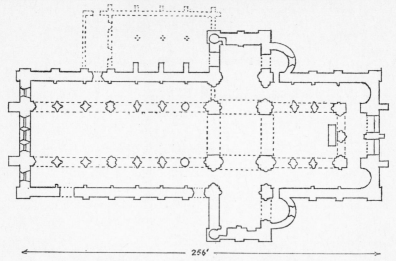

256'

40. ROMSEY ABBEY CHURCH, HAMPSHIRE

worship in their churches. A rare exception was the church of
Swine priory in the East Riding, a house of Cistercian nuns, where
the nave and transepts were used by the convent and the chancel
was parochial.

Contrary to the normal arrangement in monastic houses, the
cloisters and conventual buildings of nunneries were more often
built on the north side of the church, as was the case at Barking,
Lacock, and S. Helen's Bishopsgate. The apartments grouped
about the cloister usually occupied the same relative position as
in the houses of monks. Thus at Lacock (Fig. 41), where the cloister
is 80 feet square, most of the conventual buildings remain *in situ*.
The cloister was remodelled and widened in the fifteenth century,
and the western walk was subsequently taken down. The three
remaining walks are lighted by Perpendicular windows of four
lights and are roofed with lierne vaults enriched with many
carved bosses. The eastern cloistral range, two stories high, consists of the dorter and chapter house (Pl. XIII); the nuns' frater
occupies most of the northern block, and the building at the west
was mainly the abbess's lodging.

Adjoining the nun's choir is a two-aisled chamber that once
had two altars against the eastern wall, the western part being the
sacristy; and in the thickness of the western wall is a stone stairway that leads up to the dorter. North of the sacristy is the rectangular chapter house, divided into two aisles and vaulted, and
beyond is the slype that led to the farmery. The warming-house,

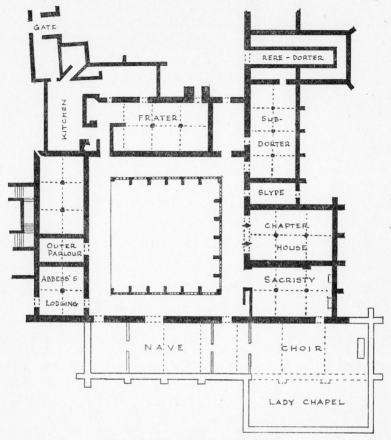

41. LACOCK ABBEY, WILTSHIRE

also two-aisled and vaulted, occupies the rest of the sub-dorter, at right angles to which at the northern end stood the rere-dorter.

The nuns' frater, raised upon a sub-vault or cellar, is flanked on the east by the nuns' parlour and on the west by the kitchen. The western range is two-storied, the upper floor being post-Suppression. On the ground floor are three chambers, the central one being the outer parlour, and above was the abbess's hall. Over the west end of the south cloister-walk was the abbess's chapel, and a gallery that communicated with the nun's dorter. Of the farmery that stood to the east of the dorter there are no remains.

Except for the western block, the conventual buildings at Barking abbey were planned on the same lines. There, a long building measuring 166 feet by 24 feet stood on the western side of the

cloister, the first floor of which was the nuns' dorter, an arrangement that is also found at the cathedral-priory of Durham. The
sub-vault was probably used as the cellarium, and attached to it
on the west was the rere-dorter.

XV. The Building of
Mediaeval Monasteries

~~~~~~

Abbots credited with Building Projects—Prior Walsingham and the Octagon at Ely—Prior Chillenden's Nave at Canterbury—The Master-mason and the part taken by Abbots and Monks in Building Operations—Burgundian Masons and the Early Cistercian Abbeys—Anglo-Norman Monasteries the work of Imported Craftsmen—Native Masons in the Gothic Centuries—Procedure when a Building Scheme was to be Undertaken—Master-masons Summoned by the Convent—William de Sens and William the Englishman at Christ Church Priory, Canterbury—Eyewitness Account by the Monk Gervase—Activities of William de Sens—The Cementarius—Masons Depicted in Carvings and Manuscript—The Master-carpenter—The Various Grades of Artificers—Freemasons and Banker Marks—Journeymen working for a Weekly Wage—Task Work of Sculptors—Social Status of the Master-mason—Furred Robes and Gloves as Symbols of his Office—The Making of Roads and Bridges to facilitate Transport of Stone from distant Quarries—Preparation for the Building of the Octagon at Ely—The Master-carpenter and his many Duties—Huts built to House the Workers—Lodges for the Masons and Woodworkers—The Tracing House for the Master-mason—Platts and Rough Sketches—The Custos Operis or Clerk of the Works—Fabric Rolls—Records of the Building of Westminster Abbey by Henry III—The Roll of 1253 and its Details of Wages paid and Materials purchased—Later Computus Roll of Westminster Abbey—The Building of Vale Royal Abbey—Men, Materials, and Tools in 1278–80—The Contract of 1359 for Reconstructing the Choir of Vale Royal—Fabric Rolls of Syon Abbey, 1479–80—Wages of the Craftsmen Employed—The Levelling of the Site of an Abbey—Laying Out the Plan—The Progress of Building from East to West—Foundations—Method of Remodelling the Choir-arm of a Monastic Church.

~~~~~~

IN THE ANCIENT records of the building or enlargement of a mediaeval monastery, the abbot or prior during whose rule the work was undertaken is invariably credited with the project. Such

statements do not imply that he took any part in the actual building operations, but that he was merely the promoter of the scheme,
and as such found the necessary funds and was concerned with
'ways and means'. According to William of Malmesbury, Edred,
the grandson of Alfred the Great, 'with his own hands measured
the sites of the buildings of Abingdon and laid the foundations,
intending to erect there a monastery of famous renown'. This may
have been no more than directing in a general sort of way the lay-
out and dimensions of the abbey buildings. Prior Alan of Walsingham, who is spoken of as the builder of the Octagon at Ely, had
little to do with the construction of this amazing feature, but acted
as a clerk of the works. It is recorded that he searched far and wide
to find oak trees sufficiently large for the eight angle posts of the
timber lantern that crowns the Octagon; but the sacrist's Rolls of
Ely give the names of the masons and carpenters employed by the
prior for the building operations. The eight stone piers that carry
the Octagon were planned and erected by Peter Quadraterius,
assisted by other master-masons named John and Attagreene. The
master-carpenter who devised and built the timber lantern was
William Hurle, a craftsman of such repute that he was paid a
retaining fee of £8 a year. Working with him were other carpenters named Thomas and Galfrido. The central boss of the Octagon
was carved by John of Burwell, who in 1339 was paid 2s. and 'his
keep at the prior's table'.

The great nave of Canterbury cathedral has always been attributed to prior Chillenden, 1392–1411, who is described by Leland
as 'the greatest builder of a prior that ever was at Christ Church;
he was the great setter-forth of the new body of the church', which
means that he initiated the project and in consultation with the
master-mason decided upon the general character that the new
nave was to assume.

When the site for a monastery had been acquired the abbot
would make known his requirements to the master-mason, who
was responsible for the lay-out and the design. An abbot would
prescribe the form that a new choir or a long-desired Lady Chapel
should take, and would tie the master-mason to definite conditions
as to the plan, the size of the building, and the costs, but the actual
building operations were the work of lay masons of varying degrees
of skill. Likely enough some of the brethren of the house would
lend a hand in the carting, carrying, and fetching of the materials
such as timber, stone, and lime. During the building of Selby
abbey, c. 1100, it was not beneath the dignity of abbot Hugh to
assist in the donkey-work, for 'every day, putting on a workman's
smock he used to carry on his shoulders to the wall, stones, lime,

and anything else required for the work; and every Saturday he received his wages as one of the workmen and bestowed them on the poor.'

When the Angel Steeple at Canterbury was nearing completion, prior Selling, 1472–94, wrote to Archbishop Morton: 'Most reverend father in God, the master surveyor and I have communed with John Wastell, your mason, to preserve what form and shape he will keep in raising of the pinnacles of your new tower. He drew unto us two patterns of them.'

It is now definitely established that in general the heads of religious houses took no active part in the work with which their names are usually associated. When the malcontents of S. Mary's abbey, York, settled in the wild valley of Skelldale in 1132, they felled timber and built themselves an oratory and huts for their temporary habitation, but the permanent structures of stone, the church, the cloister, and conventual apartments of Fountains abbey, commenced in 1135, were the work of skilled masons employed by the convent. There can be little doubt that all the early Cistercian abbeys and churches in this country were planned and built under the direction of master-masons from Burgundy, men who were well acquainted with the almost rigid uniformity that was dictated by the parent houses of Citeaux and Clairvaux.

In the great wave of Benedictine building that followed the Conquest, masons were imported from Normandy and Burgundy, craftsmen who were steeped in the traditions of their own land. Comparatively little is known of the master-masons who reared the Norman abbeys. At S. Albans was a master Robert 'the most skilful mason in England', so skilful indeed that abbot Paul presented him with the manor of Sarret, a gift that the monks disapproved of, as the property belonged to the convent. Of the many masons who were employed at Durham for the building of that mighty church, the earliest whose names are known are Richard and William, who were working on Pudsey's Galilee Chapel c. 1175. They are described as *ingeniatores*, and Richard (Ricardus) became the owner of considerable lands in the county of Durham, the reward probably of his skill as Pudsey's architect.

The religious houses of the Gothic centuries were the work of native craftsmen, of men who had been reared in the tradition of masoncraft. When the news spread of the founding or the rebuilding of an abbey, masons, craftsmen, and labourers made their way from far and wide to the site in search of employment. After the fire that destroyed the church of Christ Church priory, Canterbury, in 1174, the convent summoned artificers, both French and English, to the city to consider how and by what means the

ruined church might be repaired. Amongst them was the Frenchman, William de Sens, 'a man active and ready, and a most
curious workman in wood and stone'. After hearing his proposals,
the brethren chose him for the undertaking 'on account of his
lively genius and good reputation . . . and he, residing for many
days with the monks, went on preparing all the things that were
needful'. He arranged for the importation of stone from Caen; he
devised machines for loading and unloading the stone from the
vessels, and for its transport to Canterbury; and he prepared
'molds' for the masons who cut the stones. After the work had been
in progress for four years, William de Sens fell from the scaffolding
in the choir, and sustained such severe injuries that he was compelled to abandon the work and return home to France. Thereupon the convent chose as his successor William the Englishman,
who was probably the right-hand man of the French master-mason
and was therefore well acquainted with his designs. He was spoken
of as 'a man of diminutive stature, but in many ways extremely
ingenious and honest'.[1]

The designation 'architect' was not used in the Middle Ages,
the man in control being known as the master-mason or *cementarius*. In the spandrels of the wall-arcading in the south aisle of the
retrochoir at Worcester cathedral formerly monastic are relief
carvings dating *c.* 1230, one of which shows a patroness of the
priory instructing a master-mason, who is indicated by the pair
of dividers he is carrying; and another represents a mason sub-
mitting a plan to an abbot or a monk acting as the clerk of the
works. A life of Edward the Confessor, written *c.* 1270, now preserved at Cambridge, describes how the King summoned masons
and other craftsmen for the building of Westminster abbey, and
an illustration in the manuscript portrays the Confessor issuing
instructions. The master-mason, clad in the dress of the thirteenth
century, holds a long levelling straight-edge, and kneeling by him
is the master-carpenter bearing an axe, and apparently passing on
instructions to other workmen beyond.

The master-mason was an experienced and well-travelled man,
and often a person of substance and repute. He engaged the masons,
craftsmen, and labourers, supervised their work and controlled the
whole of the building operations. The ordinary masons and other
'artificers' were journeymen in the literal sense of the term,
travelling in bands from place to place as employment offered.

---

[1] An account of the rebuilding of the choir-arm of Canterbury is detailed year by
year in a tract *De Combustione et Reparatione Cantuariensis Ecclesiae*, written by Gervase,
the monk-historian of Canterbury who was an eye-witness. The tract is invaluable as a
record of the procedure adopted when a building project was undertaken, and of the
time it occupied.

Second only to him was the master-carpenter, who had a number of assistants some of whom might be skilled wood carvers. Other workmen were of various grades. There were the diggers and labourers who cleared and levelled the site; the quarrymen, the hewers and rough masons who cut and prepared the blocks of stone before they were carted to the building site. After the blocks had been shaped and dressed, they were placed in position by the setters. Of the highest grade were the freemasons, who chiselled the mouldings, carved the capitals and corbels, and cut the window tracery. Stone was a costly material, and often the master-mason would require the masons who dressed and shaped the blocks to mark them with an initial letter or a sign-manual, particularly if the masons were not known to him. The incised banker-marks were a means of identifying any craftsman who was guilty of faulty or slipshod work. This practice obtained from Norman times. A considerable number of masons' marks are to be seen in the masonry of Ely cathedral, and in the choir transepts of Canterbury are many incised by the masons who worked under William de Sens and his successor. In addition to plasterers, plumbers, smiths, and tilers, there were countless labourers, tree-fellers, scaffolders, carters, men who burned the lime and mixed the mortar, and others who sharpened the tools.

Human nature being what it is, the masons and craftsmen of the Middle Ages had all the failings common to any group of men at all periods. Some were idle, others guilty of theft; they quarrelled amongst themselves and on occasion they downed tools. In the year 1245, during the reconstruction of Westminster abbey by Henry III, there seems to have been a strike amongst the workmen, for on 7th November the King ordered that 'money should be provided out of the Treasury . . . to recall the workmen who have left us, as the King is informed'.

The journeymen worked for a weekly wage, but were not bound by an agreement to remain at the job. They could and often did take themselves off to find more profitable work, particularly at harvest time. As a rule the master-mason and his skilled assistants remained for many years, until the work was completed. Sculptors and carvers were sometimes paid for task-work, i.e. piece-work. In the Fabric Rolls of Westminster abbey (*temp.* Henry III), a master Alberic amongst others is named as being paid for task-work in the cloister and at the entrance to the chapter-house. Two images which Professor Prior suggested represent the Virgin Mary and the angel Gabriel, were wrought by task-work, the sculptor being paid 53s. 4d. for his labour.

On a big undertaking the master-mason was given a furred robe and gloves as symbols of his office; hence the French idiom 'se donner des gants' (to take credit for a job).[1] In 1256 John of Gloucester, the King's mason, and Alexander, the King's carpenter at Westminster abbey were given furred robes twice a year. Master John owned a house and curtilage in Westminster as well as property in Southwark, and was rewarded by the King with gifts of houses for his services. The status of the master-mason was usually highly regarded by his monastic clients. In 1436 an agreement between the abbot of Bury S. Edmunds and John Wode of Colchester, a master-mason, provided that 'the seyd John Wode schall have hys bord in the couentys [convent's] halle for hym and hys man, for hymself as a gentilman and for hys servaunte as for a yoman'.[2]

Masonry being the chief building material, the master-mason would visit quarries to select suitable stone. The transport of stone from distant quarries often entailed the making or surfacing of roadways and the strengthening of bridges to stand the wear and tear of heavy carts and waggons. In preparation for the building of the Octagon at Ely in 1322, the tracks from Soham and Stuntney were mended with fresh rushes, and the bridges they crossed were repaired with timber and iron to facilitate the transport of materials. An open space at Ely called Seggewyk near the water-side was cleared and surfaced at a cost of $7\frac{1}{2}d$. to bear the weight of stone-laden waggons, and a crane or *frene* was constructed for unloading. In 1339 an old wooden bridge across the river on the road to Soham had been so weakened by the heavy loads of stone that it was almost swept away by a flood and, being rotten and not worth the mending, a new bridge of stone had to be constructed at the expense of the convent, towards which Bishop Hotham of Ely contributed £5 5s. 6d.

On his part the master-carpenter would survey the forests in the neighbourhood and arrange for the purchase and the felling of the timber. He and his assistants made the templates and centrings for the masons, and were responsible for the scaffoldings, the timber roofs, doors, screens, and finally the choir stalls. Where the site of a new abbey was in a remote spot, huts had to be erected for

---

[1] H. Daniel-Rops, *Cathedral and Crusade.*

[2] The contract dated 25th August was for the building of a tower of the abbey church, and is printed in *Archaeologia*, Vol. XXIII. Wode and his man were to work on the 'stepil' for seven years, and the master (clerk) of the works, appointed by the chapter, was to pay him the sum of £10 at Christmas, Easter, Midsummer, and Michelmas. Both masons were to be given a robe, or in lieu of such an allowance of 23s. 4d. When Wode was not 'ocupyd in hys werk', presumably when the operations were held up by wintry weather, he was to attend on the prior. He was not to go into the town more than two days in each quarter; if absent longer, 5d. a day was to be deducted from his pay, and 3d. a day from that of his man.

housing the workmen. In the Fabric Rolls of Vale Royal abbey occur entries relating to the building of dwelling houses and lodges for the craftsmen. Under the heading 'Wages of carpenters' is a payment of 45s. for erecting huts for this purpose. In addition the carpenters put up other huts or *loges* to be used as workshops by the masons and woodworkers. In 1279, 1,400 boards were purchased for building a lodge for the masons, and another 1,000 the following year. These huts and workshops were constructed of timber and roofed with straw or reeds. In 1394, when the nave of Westminster abbey was in course of erection, a house called 'the masons' logge' was built on the north side of the nave and remained in use for nearly a century and a half; and at Canterbury in 1429 thirty-two craftsmen, mostly masons and setters, are described as 'lathomi [masons] de la Loygge'. The treasurer's Roll at Ely for the year 1396 records the payment of 8s. to a carpenter for 'unum loge per cementariis', who were then building the western gate-house now known as the Ely Porta. One of the loges was usually a tracing-house (*tracynhous*), the office of the master-mason where he sketched his plans and designs on Eastland boards or on sheets of parchment. Rough and ready plans or *platts* were drawn with chalk, but there were no elaborate designs on paper, for the training of the mediaeval mason was not that of an architectural draughtsman. Details of pier-plans, mouldings, window tracery, and ribbed vaults were roughed out by the master-mason on stone flags, the freemasons under his supervision and guidance needing little else.

On the founding of an abbey the patron would appoint an official, probably the abbot-designate or one of the prospective monks, to administer the fabric funds; but where the work consisted of an enlargement or the remodelling of an existing church or apartment of the abbey buildings, it was usual for one of the obedientiaries, the sacrist or sub-sacrist, to act as clerk of the works or, as he was often called, the *custos operis*. As such he was responsible for the financial side of the building operations. Week by week he recorded in full the disbursements made for the purchase and transport of materials and equipment, the wages paid the various craftsmen, and all other expenses. Comparatively few of these records or Fabric Rolls are extant, for the majority that were preserved amongst the muniments of monastic houses were thrown into the flames at the Dissolution or otherwise disposed of.

The rebuilding of Westminster abbey by Henry III in 1245–69 is more documented than that of any other monastery. The Fabric Rolls, of which there are nearly a hundred, the Pipe Rolls, and the Close Rolls give in detail the sums paid for specified quantities of stone, Purbeck marble, and other materials, and the rates of pay discriminate between the craftsmen according to their trade. These records are preserved in the British Museum, in the abbey muniment chamber, and at the Record Office. The Roll of 1253[1] gives full accounts of the expenditure incurred for thirty-two successive weeks following Easter of that year. In the second week the entry is as follows: 'To wages of 49 cutters of white stone, 15 marblers, 26 stone layers, 32 carpenters with John and his partner at S. Albans, 2 painters with an assistant, 13 polishers [of Purbeck marble], 19 smiths, 14 glaziers, with 4 plumbers, £15 10s. 1d. [This gives an average of 1s. 10d. a week for these skilled men.] To wages of 176 inferior workmen with overseers and clerks, and 2 two-horse carts daily, £9 17s. 2d.' Amongst the payments for materials in the same period appears: 'Item. For 22 hundred and 3 quarterns of freestone, £6 16s. 6d. To Roger of Reigate for 8 hundred and a quartern of freestone, 53s. 7½d. To Richard the limeburner for 3 hundred of lime, 15s. To Agnes for 2 hundred and a half of lime, 12s. 6d. To Richard of Eastcheap for 2 dozen hurdles or crates with poles, 9s. 7d. To Richard Oggel for 5 dozen hurdles with poles, 12s. 6d. To Henry of the bridge for iron nails and whetstones, 19s. 8d. To Benedict for carriage, porterage, and weighing of 23 cartloads of lead, 9s. 4d. To Richard for litter [straw], 18d.' The sum total for this week amounted to £53 0s. 1½d., and may be regarded as a fair specimen of the whole. Certain Feast days of the Church, e.g. Ascension Day and the Birth of the Virgin Mary, were kept as holidays by the masons and craftsmen. The rebuilding being a royal undertaking, the keeper of the works was not one of the convent but a clerk appointed by the King. The first was Odo, a London goldsmith, and the last Adam de Stratton, a clerk of the Exchequer.

Similarly, the rebuilding of the nave of the abbey church, 1376–1528, is documented in a series of Computus Rolls that were prepared by the warden of the New Work (*custos novi operis*), although the accounts for many years are missing. As the nave was built at the expense of the convent, the office of warden was held by one of the obedientiaries and sometimes by the abbot, who was entirely responsible for the administration of the fabric funds.

Records of the building of the Cistercian abbey of Vale Royal, Cheshire, for the first three years after its foundation, 1278–80,[2] shed much light on the expenses incurred in the employment of masons, carpenters, quarrymen, and other 'artificers', and in the purchase of materials and tools. The master-mason was Walter of

---

[1] Gilbert Scott, *Gleanings from Westminster Abbey*, 1863.
[2] D. Knoop and G. P. Jones, *Ars Quatuor Coronatorum*.

Hereford, whose wages were 2s. a day, and his right-hand man was John de Bataille, who was paid 3s. a week. On the average 135 men were at work in this period; of that number fifteen were quarrymen and twice as many were employed in carting stone from the quarry at Edisbury, five miles distant from the abbey site. The cartage of 35,000 loads of masonry cost £347, a little less than a quarter of the total expenditure for the three years. The clerk of the works recorded the purchase of spades, forks, hammers, hatchets, and other tools for use in the quarry, where a smith and several assistants kept them in repair.

Within thirty years of the completion of the abbey, the whole of the eastern arm of the church was remodelled at the instance of Edward, the Black Prince, the contract for which, dated 1359, is extant. The master-mason William de Helpeston was engaged by the Prince and the convent 'to build twelve chapels round the east end of the choir of the abbey church. He is to have a free hand over details, and is to carry up the walls from the plinth to the level of the crest of the parapet of a chapel beside the choir already built by him. He shall choose such masons as he needs, the convent procuring them, and shall discharge them if unprofitable; and shall pay them their wages, and provide iron and steel for their tools. He shall construct a tracing-house [drawing office] in the north transept for 10 marks paid down. The convent shall provide lodging for the workmen. The Prince shall pay him [Helpeston] yearly 200 marks, to the total amount of £860. If these payments stop before a third of the work is finished, Master William may withdraw and work elsewhere, but shall also have a due proportion of the life pension or corrodie [worth £40 a year] which the convent have agreed to pay him when the work is completed. If the convent cause any delay, they shall pay him the whole pension'.[1]

Of exceptional interest in respect of the cost of materials and wages of a later period are the 'ij jurnalles' (Fabric Rolls) preserved in the Record Office, relating to the building of the wealthy Briggitine house, Syon abbey, founded in 1414. The total amount expended in building the church, the cloister, and dorter reached £4,833 6s. 10d. The purchase of ashlar freestone and ragstone, its transport, and the 'vantyng and ffurryng of the pilers' by the masons and labourers cost £2,549 11s. 1d. From October 1479 to October 1480 the wages of the freemasons amounted to £245 12s. 11d; of hard-hewers, £30 11s. 7d; of bricklayers, £16 16s. 2d; of chalk-hewers, 41s. 3d; of carpenters and joiners, 46s. 9d; of sawyers, £9 16s. 4d; of smiths, £44 19s. 10d; of labourers,

---

[1] *Exchequer Treasury of Receipt.* Misc. Books, Vol. 279.

£36 19s. 7d; and James Powle brickman was paid £76 8s. 4d. for 'makyng of breks'. The building of the roof of the church, including cartage of the timber, cost £965 18s. 3d; the casting of the roofing lead and jointing with solder, £535 10s. 10d.

When an abbey was first built, the actual operations began with the clearing and levelling of the site, work that was done by local diggers and labourers, after which the plan was pegged out and the foundations laid.[1] The irregularities that frequently occur in the planning and alignment of monastic churches is an indication of the rough-and-ready methods employed in the laying out. Building operations above ground always commenced at the east, so that the choir would be available for use by the convent as early as possible. Then followed the transepts and one or two bays of the nave, sufficient to provide abutment for the central tower and space for the ritual choir. The building of the nave proceeded westwards, often intermittently, its completion being dependent upon the funds available at any time. After the Norman and Transitional periods, it was rare that a large monastic church was built from end to end without interruption.[2]

When the choir-arm of a monastic church was to be lengthened the work began at the east beyond the existing choir, so that the divine offices could continue uninterrupted for as long as possible. Often a wider and longer eastern arm was built round the old choir which remained in use until it was demolished to permit the joining up of the new choir-arm to the rest of the church. Then the High Altar was removed from the sanctuary and was set up in

---

[1] There was a great diversity of practice in the matter of foundations, particularly in the Norman period. Often the builders dug to a great depth to find solid rock for their footings; those of the eastern apses at Durham were sunk some 14 feet, and at S. Mary's abbey, York, the foundations of the Norman choir were carried down to a depth of 26 feet. At S. Albans on the other hand the walls of the aisles of the nave were reared on foundations only 6 inches below the surface, although the Norman piers stand on singularly large and strong footings. In the late Norman Lady Chapel at Glastonbury the foundations consist of walls of rubble more than 12 feet in depth, so that when the crypt was dug in the sixteenth century, all that was necessary was to excavate the earth and roof the crypt with a vault. It often happened that the foundation stopped short of a solid stratum. At Crowland abbey, where a bed of gravel lay 11 feet below the surface, the peat above it was removed to a depth of only 6 feet for layers of rubble foundation. As a rule the builders of the Gothic centuries were more thorough especially in marshy districts. The Early English retrochoir of Winchester was reared on piles and layers of beech logs, which were laid in the peaty subsoil. In 1905, however, the raft had given way and the south wall was heeling over and threatened to collapse. New foundations had to be put in below water level, and divers were employed to stabilise the footings with sacks of concrete. It was sometimes the practice to build the piers of a nave or choir arcade on continuous foundations, as was the case at Beaulieu and Hayles. At Westminster abbey the outer walls of Henry III's choir stand on foundations of concreted rubble, 10 feet in depth and 30 feet wide at the bottom.

[2] Cistercian churches were generally completed throughout, the nave being required for the ritual choir of the conversi.

the nave, which was boarded up at the east to exclude noise and dust.

The remodelling of the choirs of monastic churches, particularly those of the greater Norman churches of the Benedictine Order, was fairly general in the thirteenth century, but the naves were far less subjected to reconstruction. Those of Ely, Peterborough, Tewkesbury, and Durham are substantially as the Norman masons left them. Any intention on the part of a convent to sweep away an outmoded nave and erect one more in harmony with a remodelled choir-arm had to be abandoned unless the necessary funds were forthcoming. At Gloucester, where the choir and transepts are Perpendicular Gothic in character, the nave is wholly Norman except for the two western bays, which bear witness to a scheme of transformation that had to be relinquished c. 1437.

Mediaeval masons, fired with a progressive spirit as regards both design and construction, showed little respect for the work of their predecessors; they would ruthlessly tear down a great Norman nave and erect in its place one in the Gothic mode of their own age. It mattered little that the new work would not harmonise with, say, the earlier Gothic of the choir. The naves of Winchester and Canterbury, splendid examples of Perpendicular Gothic, bear no relation in their architectural character with the eastern arms of those great churches.

In this respect the nave of Westminster abbey provides a unique exception. Henry III's masons had ceased work at the fourth bay of the nave in 1270 (Fig. 12), and for a full century and a half the old Norman nave remained at the west, an incongruous pendant to the Gothic building. Gifts and bequests of Cardinal Langham, formerly abbot of Westminster, enabled the convent to embark on the reconstruction of the old nave, seven new bays being added to those of the thirteenth century. The master-mason responsible for the design from 1376 to 1400 was Henry Yevele, a famous 'architect' of his time; and the chief interest of his work lies in its uniformity with the earlier building, as regards both proportion and design. In the words of Professor W. R. Lethaby the nave of Westminster is 'the most conscious piece of architectural imitation that Gothic affords in England'. The proportions of the bay design, the clustered piers of Purbeck marble, and the Geometric openings of the triforium stage differ little from those of the thirteenth-century work, and are in striking contrast to the Perpendicular work of the same period at Winchester and Canterbury. Throughout the fifteenth century Yevele's successors adhered to his design, although the building operations were constantly at a stand-still through lack of funds. The nave of the abbey was finally completed and the western towers raised to the level of the nave-roof during the rule of abbot Islip, 1500–32.

Necessarily the conventual buildings of a religious house, in particular the chapter house, the dorter, and frater, were erected simultaneously with the church, and were less subject to enlargement or remodelling through the centuries. In the main it was the cloister-walks and arcadings that were rebuilt, chiefly for the purpose of improving the lighting of the walks.

XVI. Dissolution of the Monasteries

THE ANTI-PAPAL LEGISLATION of 1532–3 marked the beginning of
the end of the monastic system in this country. For five years
the Papal Court had temporised in the matter of Henry VIII's
divorce from Katherine of Aragon; Wolsey, who had fallen from
royal favour for his mismanagement of the affair, had been dismissed from his office as Chancellor and survived his downfall only
a year, dying in 1530. The year 1534 was memorable for the Act
of Succession, which secured the Crown to the offspring of Queen
Anne Boleyn, and for legislation that forbade all payments such as
annates and Peter's pence to Rome. Further, the Pope was denied

the privilege of appointing bishops to vacant sees in England; in future the Crown alone possessed such authority. The oath of Succession was administered to English monks of all Orders, an oath that admitted the legality of Henry's union with Ann Boleyn and acknowledged the the King as Supreme Head of the English Church, the bishop of Rome thereby having no jurisdiction whatsoever. In general the oath was taken by most of the religious, but the Friars Observants and the Carthusians who declined were treated with the utmost severity and their property confiscated. These early suppressions were to be followed two years later by confiscations on a much larger scale, the conception of Thomas Cromwell, a shrewd lawyer and formerly Cardinal Wolsey's right-hand man. He was well experienced in the legal business connected with the transfer of monastic property, for to him had fallen the task of alienating the estates of the religious houses that had been suppressed for the endowment of Wolsey's colleges at Oxford and Ipswich.

There can be no doubt that the General Suppression was contemplated by the King and Cromwell directly the breach with Rome had taken place; for the existence of the monastic Orders, owing allegiance to the Pope, would have constituted a danger to royal supremacy. 'Their traditions, their vast power, the principles which guided their life and work, were all too closely bound up with Rome . . . for them ever to acquiesce in a separation from the Roman obedience.'[1] Of no less importance was the enormous wealth that would fall to the Crown from the wholesale confiscation of the properties and revenues possessed by the religious houses. In consequence of the Act of 1534, the first-fruits and tenths which had hitherto been paid to the Pope were seized by the Crown. It was, however, necessary to find out what wealth and property was possessed by the Church, in particular by the monasteries; and to this end Commissioners were appointed by the Crown in 1535 and their investigations, embodied in the *Valor Ecclesiasticus*, left no doubt in the minds of the King and his minister of the rich harvest to be reaped by the Suppression.

Under the title of Vicar-General in Spirituals the King's chief minister, Thomas Cromwell, was vested with almost absolute authority, although the Suppression was carried out under a thin veil of constitutional means. Acting in his new capacity Cromwell appointed two commissions to conduct visitations of all religious houses in the autumn of 1535, and to further the scheme he sent preachers throughout the land to prepare the general public for the contemplated seizure of monastic property. They were en-

[1] Dean Spence, *History of the English Church.*

joined to denounce the monks as 'hypocrites, sorcerers and idle drones', and to declare that 'if the abbeys went down, the King would never want for any taxes again'.

The Commissioners entrusted with the task of visitation were carefully chosen creatures of Cromwell, unprincipled knaves devoid of sympathy or scruple, self-sufficient and greedy, and many of them utterly depraved. The most notorious of these self-seekers were Doctors London, Layton, Legh, and ApRice, whose letters to Cromwell have been preserved. During the summer of 1535 the monasteries of the West Country were visited; in October and November, those of East Anglia and the eastern counties; in December the Midlands; and early in January 1536 the visitors reached the North. On their arrival at a monastery they interviewed the inmates singly, browbeat them and by means of threats coerced them into admitting abuses and incriminating their brethren. Where they found nothing amiss, they accused the monks of conspiring together to conceal the truth. From time to time they sent reports of their investigations, known as *comperta*, to Cromwell. To these findings no unprejudiced person can attach much importance. The charges of iniquity brought against the religious, monks and nuns, were grossly exaggerated, and in innumerable instances were utterly false.

Acting upon the Commissioners' reports, the Parliament that met in February 1536 passed an Act of Suppression that dissolved all the religious houses with a revenue of less than £200 a year. The preamble to the Act set forth that 'manifest sins and vicious and carnal living is daily used in such small abbeys and priories of monks, canons and nuns, where the congregation of such religious persons is under the number of twelve; and that in spite of many visitations, no reformation is had hitherto. Such small houses therefore [are to be] utterly suppressed and the religious therein are committed to the great and solemn monasteries wherein, thanks be to God, religion is right well kept and preserved.' These 'great and solemn monasteries' not possessing their full complement of religious, were to receive the dispossessed from the doomed houses. So unwilling were the Commons to pass the Bill that the King threatened 'I will have it pass or I will have some of your heads'. No further persuasion was needed. All the abbeys, priories, and nunneries whose income did not exceed £200 a year were swept into the net of confiscation. The same Parliament legalised a Court of Augmentations, whose function was to deal with the property that fell to the Crown. By the terms of the Act, the King's 'majesty is pleased and contented of his most excellent charity to provide to every chief and governor of every such religious house a yearly pension for life', and for the other members of the convent 'his majesty will ordain and provide that . . . they shall have their capacities[1] if they will; or else shall be committed to such honourable great monasteries of this realm where good religion is observed'.

On the passage of the Bill only a few months after the completion of the *comperta*, a commission was appointed under the Court of Augmentations to make a survey of the smaller houses and report on the number of professed inmates and their dependants, and 'the conversation of their lives', together with a statement as to their income, their debts, and the state of the conventual buildings. The commissioners, six in number for each district, were composed of three officials, viz., an auditor, a receiver, and a clerk, and 'three discreet persons of the neighbourhood'. The returns of these mixed commissions for several counties have been printed and prove that the country gentlemen who sat on the commissions arrived at very different conclusions from those of Doctors Layton and Legh.

Of the 370 or more monasteries that came within the provisions of the Act of 1536, a considerable number escaped suppression by purchasing a licence from the Crown to continue. The treasurer of the Court of Augmentations acknowledged the payment of sums of money or 'fines' from thirty-three houses, and twenty-one others are recorded in the Patent Rolls. More than half of those that gained a new lease of life by this means were nunneries, and this temporary respite enriched the Treasury by the large sum of £5,948 6s. 8d., the fines varying from £20 paid by the Carthusians of S. Anne, Coventry, to £400 by the Benedictine nunnery of Polslo in Devon. The nunneries in particular made bids for exemption from the Act by purchase, for only twelve of the eighty-four Benedictine nunneries of that time enjoyed a revenue of £200 a year or more.

Of the twenty-six Cistercian nunneries, only Tarrant and Stixwold were granted exemption. The nuns of Stixwold wrote to the King's commissioner: 'Right wirshipful Sir, as your poor and daily bedeswomen, we humbly commend us unto you, that by the goodness of my lord privy seal . . . our house doth stand, paying to his highness 900 marks fine, besides our first-fruits which is £150, and also a pension of £34 by the year for ever. . . . We be 18 nuns and a sister in our house, besides officers and servants to the num-

---

[1] A capacity was a licence to serve as a secular priest and take a living or other cure. The majority of the displaced canons of the Augustinian and Premonstratensian priories, experienced in parochial administration, accepted benefices in the rectories appropriated to their respective houses,

XXXVI. North arcade of the nave, Buildwas Abbey.

XXXVII. Arcading of the porch at the west end of Fountains Abbey church.

XXXVIII. The nave, Fountains Abbey.

XXXIX. The nave of Kirkstall Abbey church.

XL. The ambulatory and eastern chapels at Abbey Dore.

XLI. The ambulatory, S. Bartholomew's, Smithfield.

XLII. The choir and transepts, Rievaulx Abbey.

XLIII. The nave, Tintern Abbey.

XLIV. North transept and Norman stair-turret, Christ Church Priory, Hampshire.

XLV. Interior, Austin Friars church, London.

ber of 50 persons in all; and our stock and cattle being delivered up this year past, which was our chief hope and living. . . . And if by my lord privy seal's goodness and yours, we may obtain redemption of the same yearly pension [of £34], we shall take pains to live poorly and serve God, and pray daily for the King's majesty, my lord privy seal and you during our lives.' The petition bears the date 9th January 1537, and the patent for the continuance of the house 9th July of the same year (*Cal. Pat. Rolls.* 29 Henry VIII).

Many of the greater houses foresaw their ultimate fate and sought to stave off disaster by free-will offerings to Cromwell. The papers of the avaricious Vicar-General reveal that he enriched himself by accepting bribes from religious houses all over the country, and ample evidence exists that such payments were more in the nature of exactions than gifts. In 1534 he was paid an annuity of £20 by the abbot of Reading; from the same source he received 5 marks in February 1537, £10 in April and a further £10 in May of the same year, and these were repeated in 1538. Only a few months before he wrote 'The abbot of Reading to be sent down to be tried and executed at Reading', Cromwell had accepted another £10 from abbot Cook.[1] In 1533 the abbot of Westminster bestowed the office of seneschal or steward on Cromwell, an office that involved the holding of manorial courts on the estates owned by the convent, and proved a source of financial profit; and the following year the abbot paid further tribute by granting him long leases of the rectories of Battersea and Wandsworth. In an effort to secure exemption in 1536, prior Dyrham of Great Malvern enlisted the help of Bishop Latimer of Worcester, who wrote to Cromwell offering 500 marks to the King's highness and '200 marks to yourself for your goodwill'. But there as elsewhere the offer of a bribe was futile.

Under the Act of 1536 more than two-thirds of the Cistercian abbeys ceased to exist, the inmates being as a rule transferred to larger houses of the same Order. When Netley was dissolved in February the brethren went to the mother house of Beaulieu close by.

Undoubtedly there were many descendants of the founders of monasteries who did their utmost to preserve the houses of which they were patrons. In March 1535 Thomas West, 9th Lord de la Warr, wrote to Cromwell begging that Boxgrove priory should be spared. 'And so hyt ys that I have a power [poor] howse called Boxgrove very near to my power howse called Hanaker, whereof I am founder [patron]; and there lyeth many of auncytorys [my

---

[1] *V.C.H. Berkshire,* II.

ancestors], and also my wyffy's mother; and for cawse hyt ys of my foundacyon and that my paryshe churche ys under the roofe of the church of the said monastery, and have made a power chapell to be buryed yn; wherfor yf yt myght stande with the Kynge's gracy's pleasure for the power servyce that I have doyn his Highness to forebere the subpressunge of the same, or else to translate yt ynto a college of such nombre as the landes will bere.' Needless to say his appeal was unsuccessful.

A provision of the Statute of 1536 imposed upon the grantees of the monastic lands the obligation of keeping 'a continual house [for hospitality] on the same site or precinct', and as much of the demesnes in tillage as had the monks or the farmers under them. Nevertheless much of the arable land was converted into sheep-farms by the new owners; labourers were thrown out of work, wages were low, and as less corn was grown bread became dearer. The peasantry were not slow in realising what the Suppression meant, and the time was ripe for rebellion. The first general up-rising occurred in Lincolnshire in 1536 under the abbot of Bar-lings, a Premonstratensian house, but on the arrival of the King's troops under the Duke of Norfolk the rebels broke up; the ring-leaders were arrested, tried in London, and sentenced to be hanged, drawn, and quartered. A much more serious revolt that spread from the Humber to the Scottish border and threatened the throne itself was the Pilgrimage of Grace, led by a determined young lawyer, Robert Aske, whose demands were for the old order of things; the ejected monks were to be reinstated, no further suppressions were to take place, Cromwell was to be dismissed from office and Papal authority in England restored. In a short time the rebels numbered 40,000, and in their ranks were members of the nobility and gentry of the North country. Under their ban-ner of the Five Wounds of Christ they occupied York, Hull, and Pontefract, and in October 1536 they marched southwards to Don-caster. Acting upon instructions that had been affixed to the door of York cathedral by Aske, many of the monks and nuns returned to their houses. 'Work is done rapidly by willing hands', and within a week the 'King's tenants were universally expelled; the vacant dormitories were again peopled; the refectories filled with exultant faces. Though it was so late [in the day] when they returned, the monks sang matins the same night.' (*Cal. State Papers*. XI). The monasteries of Sawley, Newminster, Lanercost, and S. Agatha, Richmond were re-occupied by their former inmates. When Saw-ley abbey, which had been sold to Lord Darcy for £400, was re-gained by the abbot and his twenty-one monks, the men of the district bound themselves together to foil any attempt to expel the brethren a second time.[1] In October 1536 Henry VIII wrote to the Earl of Derby: 'If on your coming to Sawley you find the abbot and monks restored again . . . you shall at once cause the abbot and certain of the chief monks to be hanged on long pieces of timber or otherwise out of the steeple'. The rebels were still in possession of Sawley in February 1537, and the King wrote again, 'You shall without pity or circumstance cause the monks to be tied up without further delay or ceremony'. The unauthorised abbot intruded by the rebels was William Trafford, who was hanged at Lancaster in 1538.

The situation was fraught with extreme peril to the King and the Government. The Duke of Norfolk was sent to Doncaster with promises of conciliation and pardon, and Aske being assured that a Parliament at York would redress grievances, the rebel forces dispersed. Aske was 'invited' to London and after being received by the King returned north, only to find Sir Francis Bigod up in arms again. At the head of a strong force and with incredible speed Norfolk crushed the insurrection. Aske was seized and hanged in chains at York, other leaders were barbarously executed, and abbot Sedburgh of Rievaulx, and Thirsk, ex-abbot of Fountains, who was in some way implicated in the Pilgrimage of Grace, were hanged at Tyburn.

Strange to say, possibly on account of their poverty, the houses of the Mendicant Orders were not suppressed under the Act of 1536, but in 1538 after the Northern revolts all the English friaries, great and small, were dissolved and the inmates, numbering about 1,800 in all, were treated with scant consideration. In only a few instances were the dispossessed priors awarded pensions; more generally were they sent into the world with a small gratuity. Being more receptive of the New Learning and the Lutheran doctrines than the conservative monks, many of the friars were willing to forswear the mendicant life and garb, and to serve the Church as secular clergy, though a certain number of them clung to the past. The chief agent entrusted with the task of suppressing the friaries was Richard Ingworth, Bishop-suffragan of Dover, who encouraged the inmates of the houses he visited to surrender voluntarily, apparently without much difficulty.

It was inevitable that sooner or later 'the great and solemn monasteries wherein thanks be to God, religion is right well kept and preserved' should share the same fate as the lesser houses. Including those houses that had purchased exemption, there were

---

[1] Eleven years before, when the Premonstratensian abbey of Bayham in Sussex had been suppressed by Wolsey to provide for the building of Cardinal College at Oxford, the men of the locality 'disguised with painted faces and visors put back the canons', and held themselves in readiness to defend them in case of any attempt to expel them.

some 250 that remained after 1536, but no Act was passed that
legalised their suppression until most of them had already fallen.
After the Northern risings many of the greater monasteries, antici-
pating the general dissolution, surrendered voluntarily or under
coercion. Abbot Pyle of Furness, with the fate of the abbot of
Whalley fresh in mind, signed the deed of surrender in April 1537
and others followed suit. Again, 'dissolution by attainder' was the
process employed to expedite the fall of a number of the greater
houses, including Sawley, Jervaulx, and Whalley, the abbots of
which were charged with high treason. In 1539 when the majority
of the remaining houses and their possessions had been confiscated
a new and amazing Act of Parliament was passed, the purpose of
which was not to dissolve more monasteries, but to sanction all
that had been done and so secure to the Crown all the monastic
property that had fallen into the King's hands since February 1536.
Unlike the first Act it alleged no reasons for the measure, but
merely stated that 'sundry abbots, priors, abbesses, prioresses and
other ecclesiastical governors and governesses . . . of their own free
will and voluntary minds, good wills and assents, without con-
straint, coercion or compulsion [have] resigned themselves and
their properties into the King's hands. . . . Let the King and his
heirs possess these houses for ever.' But the Act went still further,
for it legalised all future suppressions, for 'other religious houses
may happen in the future to be suppressed or otherwise to come
into the King's hands. Let him enjoy them'. The properties and
revenues that were to fall to the Crown were defined as 'all the
sites, circuits, premises, manors, lordships, granges, meases [mes-
suages], lands, tenements, meadows, pastures, rents, reversions,
services, woods, tithes, pensions, portions, parsonages, appropriated vicarages, churches, chapels, advowsons, nominations, patron-
ages, annuities, rights, interests, entries, conditions, commons,
leets, courts, which appertained or belonged to the said late . . .
religious or ecclesiastical houses.'[1]

Shortly before the Dissolution the convents of many houses had
sought to capitalise their revenues by selling their lands and advowsons, or by granting long-term leases to their relatives and the
local gentry. When the Commissioners visited Lacock abbey, they
found that the properties of the nunnery had been leased out to
various relatives of abbess Temmes.[2] To have called in the leases
would have incurred the hostility of the lessees, but a clause in the
Act of 1539 annulled such transactions that had been concluded
within one year before the Suppression.

[1] H. Gee and W. J. Hardy (eds), *Documents illustrative of English History,* 1921.
[2] G. Baskerville, *English Monks and the Suppression of the Monasteries.*

Many of the Deeds of Surrender in the Court of Augmentations are preserved in the Record Office in London. That of the Augustinian priory of S. Bartholomew the Great, Smithfield, may be quoted as typical. Put into English from the Latin it runs: 'To all the faithful in Christ . . . know ye that we [Robert Fuller], the aforesaid abbot and the convent . . . by our unanimous agreement and consent and of our spontaneous will, have given, granted, and by this our present charter, confirmed to our most excellent prince and lord Henry VIII, by God's grace King of England and France, Defender of the Faith, lord of Ireland, supreme head on earth of the English Church, all our aforesaid monastery and priory of S. Bartholomew and the whole site of our late priory and all our demesnes, manors, churches, chapels, rectories, vicarages and chantries . . . as well spiritual as temporal, as well in the counties of Middlesex, Hertford, Essex and in the City of London as anywhere else in the kingdom which belong to the monastery . . . and also all and every kind of our church ornaments, jewels and goods which we have in right of the said monastery; to have, hold, and enjoy all the aforesaid demesnes and manors to our lord the King, his heirs and successors for ever. And we the said abbot and convent and our successors will warrant against all peoples for the lord the King and his successors, all the monastery and the demesnes and manors with their appurtenances. In testimony of which we have set our common seal to this our present charter. Dated at our chapter house the 25th day of October in the 31st year of our said lord the present King Henry the Eighth. Acknowledged before me William Petre, one of the clerks of the Chancellery . . . the day and place written above by me William Petre.'[1] The document, which was duly sealed, was not signed by any of the canons.

The year 1540 saw the end, the last house to be dissolved being the mitred abbey of Waltham, in March of that year. There was short shrift for any who resisted, such as abbot Whiting of Glastonbury, abbot Cook of Reading, and prior Houghton of the London Charterhouse, all of whom were sentenced to death.

The abbots, monks, and nuns of those houses that had voluntarily surrendered were given pensions. In this respect the abbots were treated generously, receiving pensions ranging from £60 to £100. Abbot Reeve of Bury S. Edmunds enjoyed an annuity of 500 marks worth £15,000 today. A number of the displaced abbots and priors were installed in bishoprics as they fell vacant, thus effecting an economy in the award of pensions. Abbot Wakeman of Tewkesbury became the first bishop of Gloucester; Henry Holbeach, formerly the prior of Worcester, was installed in the

---

[1] E. A. Webb, *Records of S. Bartholomew's Smithfield*, I.

see of Rochester, and later was translated to Lincoln; Robert Holgate, master of the Gilbertine Order and prior of Watton, was promoted to the bishopric of Llandaff, and in 1545 to the arch-see of York. The provincial of the Carmelite Order of Friars, John Bird, became Bishop of Bangor whence he was translated to Chester on its elevation to cathedral status; and Paul Bush, the superior of the Bonshommes of Edington, was the first Bishop of Bristol. The rank and file of the suppressed houses received pensions of £5 a year, worth £250 to-day, and many of them were given capacities by the Archbishop of Canterbury or the Lord Chancellor. The many thousands of labourers, servants, and menials attached to the monasteries were offered 'rewards', viz. sums of money equivalent to a year's wages, when they went out into the world to fend for themselves. Undoubtedly many who had been employed on the landed estates and farms by the monks continued to work in the same capacity for the new owners.[1]

After a monastery was dissolved, royal agents appointed by the Court of Augmentations and accompanied by a retinue of 'strangers' from London, made an inventory and valuation of the property both within and without the house, and effected the transfer to the Crown, incidentally enriching themselves in the process. By fraudulent practices they robbed the King of vast amounts. A great number of men who, when appointed to the office were possessed only of an inkhorn and pen, were after two years able to rank with the highest in the land. (*B.M. Arundel MS.* 151, f. 386.)

The methods employed by the agents are described in an account of the destruction of Roche abbey, Yorkshire, written by one who was a boy in the locality at the time. 'In the plucking down of these houses', he wrote, 'for the most part this order was taken; that the visitors should come suddenly unawares . . . to the end to take them napping as the proverb is, lest if they should have had as much as an inkling of their coming, they would have made conveyance of some portion of their own goods, to help themselves withal, when they were turned forth of their houses. For so soon as the visitors were entered within the gates, they called the abbot and other officers of the house and caused them to deliver all the keys, and took an inventory of all their goods, both within doors and without. For all such beasts, horses, sheep and such cattle as were abroad in pasture or grange places, the visitors caused to be brought into their presence. And when they had done so, they turned the abbot and all his convent and household forth of the doors. But such persons as afterwards bought their corn or

---

[1] G. Baskerville, *English Monks and the Suppression of the Monasteries.*

hay or such like, finding all the doors either open or the locks and shackles plucked down, went in and took what they found and filched it away. Some took the service books that lay in the church and put them upon their wain coppes to piece them; some took windows of the hay-loft and hid them in their hay, and likewise they did of many other things. Some pulled forth the iron hooks out of the walls that bought none, when the yeomen or gentlemen of the county had bought the timber of the church. The church was the first thing that was put to spoil, and then the abbot's lodging, dorter and frater, with the cloister and all the buildings thereabout within the abbey walls. Nothing was spared but the ex-houses and swine-cots, and such other houses of office that stood without the walls. . . . And when the lead was torn off and cast down in the church and the tombs in the church all broken (for in most abbeys were divers noble men and women, for to what end should they stand, when the church over them was spared for their sakes), all things of price either spoiled, carried away or defaced to the uttermost. . . . The persons who cast the lead into fodders plucked up all the seats in the choir, wherein the monks sat when they said service . . . and burned them and melted the lead therewith, although there was wood plenty within a flight-shot of them, for the abbey stood among woods and rocks of stone. In these rocks were found pewter vessels that were conveyed away and there hidden, so that it seemeth that every person bent himself to filch and spoil what he could.' (*B.M. Add. MS.* 5813.)

The first solicitude of the royal agents was the countless treasures of gold and silver in the monastic sacristies; the sacred vessels, crucifixes, plate, censers, chalices, rings, and jewelled gloves. An immense amount of booty was obtained in 1538 by Henry VIII's crusade against shrines and reliquaries, the sole purpose of which was to satisfy the royal cupidity. The jewels and precious metals torn from Becket's shrine at Canterbury were packed into two chests so large that it took two men to carry them away. The return of the Canterbury spoils included 4,994 oz. of gold, 4,425 oz. of silver-gilt, and 5,286 oz. of plain silver; and for the removal of the lesser treasures twenty-six carts were said to have been needed.

In general, objects of exceptional value were conveyed to the royal treasury in London, where they were broken up and the metals melted down; but many treasures disappeared in transit. Vestments, copes, and altar-frontals, richly embroidered with silver thread, were dispersed and scattered. Some were sold to pay the expenses of the commissioners and agents, others were shipped across the Channel for sale. 'Many private men's parlours were hung with altar-cloths, their tables and beds covered with copes, and many made carousing cups of sacred chalices. It was a sorry house not worth the naming which had not somewhat of this furniture in it; though it were only a fair-sized cushion made of a cope or altar-cloth to make their chairs to have somewhat in them of a chair of state.' (*Eccles. Restaurata.* Heylin.)

Hundreds of priceless manuscripts from the monastic libraries, many of them enriched with exquisite illuminations but held to be of little value by the commissioners, were sold for a mere song, and thousands of books were purchased by merchants and grocers who used the vellum for wrapping their commodities. Large numbers of books that found no ready sale were thrown into the fires that melted the roofing lead. In the Account of the Treasurer of the Court of Augmentations for the period April 1536 to Michelmas 1547, the amount realised from the sales of ornaments, vestments, bells, furniture, lead, and buildings is given as £26,502 1s. 0½d., a sum equal in modern value to perhaps one and a half million pounds. Then there was the sale of the livestock and of the grain and produce in the barns and storehouses. Some idea of the wealth of a prosperous monastery may be gained from the inventory of Fountains abbey, which possessed an estate of more than 60,000 acres, much of which was rich farming land. The wealth in flocks and herds included 1,976 head of cattle, 1,106 sheep, 86 horses and 79 swine, and the abbey granaries near and far yielded 247 quarters of wheat, 134 of oats, and 352 loads of hay.

The dismantling of the churches and the conventual buildings followed. Altars were wrecked, images torn from their niches; choir stalls, screens, lamps, hangings, pavements, glass, and all other vendible articles went to the highest bidder. By happy chance the canopied stalls of timber in Whalley abbey were bought by the parishioners of Whalley and set up in their church, where they may still be seen. The fourteen stalls in the chancel of Lancaster church came from Cockersand priory, and those now in Richmond church, Yorkshire, formerly seated the monks in the choir of Easby abbey. A timber parclose screen in Wensley church in the North Riding is also believed to have been removed from Easby. In Cirencester church a narrow little chapel dedicated to S. Katherine north of the chancel is roofed with a fan vault that is reputed to have come from the cloisters of the Augustinian abbey close by. It bears the date 1508 and the initials of the abbot, John Hakebourne.

All the conventual apartments of a suppressed monastery, the frater, dorter, cellarium, farmery, and the abbot's lodging, were stripped of their furniture and fittings and of everything that would add to the plunder, until at last the bare carcase of the monastery remained. The material of greatest value in the fabric was the lead of the roofs. Bands of workmen travelled about the land, stripped off the lead, and lighted fires in the church or the cloisters, feeding the flames with the woodwork of choir stalls and of screens that remained unsold. At Jervaulx abbey Richard Bellasis, who was responsible for the roofing lead in 1538, wrote to say that 'it was all melted down into 18 score of half fodders and 5 fodders, with 34 and a half fodders that were there before'. But 'the said lead cannot be conveyed or carried until the next summer, for the ways of that country are so foul and deep that no carriage can pass in winter.' The lead was carted away in waggons to storehouses such as the royal castles of Worcester and Tutbury, and large quantities were conveyed by barges to the coast and sold for export. The bell-metal, equally valuable, was mostly reserved to the King's use for the making of guns. In 1539 when the lead from the roof of Rievaulx choir had been cast into pigs stamped with the Tudor device, a rose surmounted by a crown, it was stacked at the west end of the nave to await removal; but before it could be taken away the high vault of the nave collapsed and buried it. There it remained until 1923, when during excavations undertaken by Sir Charles Peers the pigs were discovered leaning against the west wall.[1]

There were, however, many monastic churches that were not entirely dismantled and destroyed, owing to the prescriptive rights of worship long enjoyed by the laity, usually in the nave or one of its aisles. The Commissioners appointed by the Court of Augmentation were instructed to respect parochial rights in such churches, and this accounts for the many that survived the Suppression and are still in use. In the main they are churches that were served by Benedictine monks (p. 140), or Augustinian canons (p. 190); and in most cases the parish church is but a part of the original conventual church, as for instance Bridlington, Malmesbury, and Dunstable. The people of Bridlington begged that the priory church, 'which is the parish church for 1500 houseling people, and the shrine of S. John of Bridlington might be kept and not defaced', but Cromwell advised the Duke of Norfolk that 'the people of Bridlington should not be seduced in the offering of their money', and ordered that the shrine should be taken down and the jewels and plate be sent to him. The parishioners had to content themselves with the nave and aisles of the priory church.

Having no vested claim to the whole of a monastic church and

---

[1] The lead was sent to York, where is was used for re-leading the famous Five Sisters window in the north transept of the cathedral.

R

unwilling to purchase and keep in repair more of the fabric than they needed, the laity were powerless to stay the hand of the destroyer who in most cases swept away the choir and transepts, leaving the nave for parish worship. In a few instances the parishioners preferred the choir and transepts for their services and abandoned the nave, as at Boxgrove and S. Bartholomew's Smithfield. When Pershore abbey came under the hammer, the church was valued at £645, but the poor townsfolk were unable to raise so large a sum and elected to purchase the choir and transepts, and the rest of the building was taken down.

In some populous centres the townspeople made a bid for the whole of the monastic church. The nunnery church of Romsey was purchased for £100, and the deed of sale is now preserved in the vestry. Great Malvern priory was bought by the parishioners for £200. For the abbey church of Tewkesbury the townsmen paid the Crown the large sum of £453, the estimated value of the roofing lead at 5d. a foot and of the bells at 2½d. a pound. They had to pay £100 down, another £100 at the ensuing Easter and the balance at Christmas. The great abbey church of S. Albans was bought by the burgesses of the town in 1553 for the nominal sum of £400. Sherborne abbey with 'all the demesne lands of the monastery' was sold to Sir John Horsey for £1,250, and the parishioners of All Hallows bought the church of him for £230. In all probability the fine church of Christ Church, Hampshire, owes its survival intact to a letter written to Henry VIII by John Draper, the last prior, who appealed for the continuance of the house, which was not only a place for 'poor religious men' but was used for worship by 1,500 people of the town and the surrounding hamlets. 'The poor', he wrote, 'not only of the parish and town but also of the country, were daily relieved and sustained with bread and ale, purposely baked and brewed for them weekly to no small quantities, according to their foundation, and a house ordained purposely for them, and officers duly given attendance to serve them to their great comfort and relief.' The prior's appeal was fruitless for the house was suppressed in December 1539. Draper was awarded a pension of £133 6s. 8d., but by letters patent of October 1540 the church was granted to the parishioners.

The parishioners of Cartmel, who worshipped at an altar in the south choir-aisle of the priory church, had little cause for complaint against the Commissioner.

> 'It'm: for the church of Cartmell, being the priorie and also p'sh church, whether to stand unplucked down or not?
> Answer: Ord'd by Mr. Chancellor of the Duchie, to stand still.'

Under the Act of 1539 the ten monastic cathedrals were swept into the net of confiscation. With the exception of Bath, which became a parish church, and Coventry, which ceased to exist, the cathedral priories were refounded as collegiate establishments served by chapters of secular priests who were invariably designated prebendaries. Thus, Canterbury, Carlisle, Durham, Ely, Norwich, Rochester, Winchester, and Worcester were reconstituted as cathedrals of the New Foundation, in every one of which the displaced prior was made the dean of the secular chapter.

To supplement the newly constituted cathedrals, Henry VIII prepared a scheme for the creation of no less than twenty-one new sees from the proceeds of the Suppression. In the preamble of a document in the King's handwriting amongst the Cottonian MSS. it is stated that 'it is thought unto the King's highness most expedient and necessary that more bishoprics, collegiate and cathedral churches shall be established instead of these aforesaid religious houses', and another document headed 'Bishoprics to be made' names the new dioceses and the seats of the bishops. Of the abbey churches, including Fountains and Bury S. Edmunds, that were to be made cathedrals, only Oxford, Peterborough, and Westminster attained that honour, to which must be added Chester and Bristol which had not appeared in the King's list.

The monastic buildings of the old cathedral-priories were granted by letters patent to the new chapters, but in many cases the dorter, frater, farmery, and other apartments were deemed unsuitable as residences for the dean and the prebendaries, nor was there need for the cloisters. As a visible sign of the importance and dignity of the cathedral body, the gatehouses giving access to the precincts were in general retained, as were also the monastic chapter houses that served for the meetings of the secular chapters. Dwellings had to be provided for the dean, the prebendaries, and other officials. The housing shortage in the precincts at Canterbury resulted in the demolition of many of the cloistral buildings solely for the sake of building materials; but the granary, bakehouse, and laundry on the north side of the Green Court were used as dwellings. The cellarer's hall and lodging were retained for the King's use; and at Rochester all the conventual buildings were reserved to the Crown, alterations being made immediately after the Suppression to provide lodgings for the King and Queen, the accounts for which are preserved in the Bodleian Library. At Chester the chapter refrained from destroying monastic buildings that might or might not be needed. There the four cloister walks, the chapter house, the frater, calefactorium, and cellarium remain

in situ, and are invaluable as indicative of the general arrangement of the apartments of a mediaeval abbey.

The bulk of the real estate, the landed property that came to
the Crown, was sold or leased, but the master-mind Cromwell,
the Chancellor of the Court of Augmentations, Sir Richard Rich,
and a few of the temporal peers such as the Dukes of Norfolk,
Suffolk, and Northumberland who had rendered valuable service to the Crown were granted lands by gift of the King. Sir
Richard Rich was described by Fuller as 'a little hammer under
Cromwell, to knock down abbeys; most of the grants of which
lands going through his hands, no wonder if some stuck to his
fingers'.

One of the properties granted to Cromwell was the Cluniac
priory of Lewes, suppressed in 1537, the demolition of which was
entrusted to a John Portinari, who dutifully wrote to his master
in March of that year to report the progress of his destructive
operations. In modern spelling the letter runs: 'The last I wrote
unto your lordship was the 20th day of this present month . . . by
the which I advertised your lordship of the length and greatness
of this church and how we had begun to pull the whole down to
the ground, and what manner and fashion they used in pulling it
down. I told your lordship of a vault on the right side of the high
altar, that was borne up with four great pillars, having about it
five chapels, which be compassed in with the walls, 70 steps of
length, that is 120 feet. All this is down on Thursday and Friday
last. Now we are plucking down an higher vault, borne up by four
thick and gross pillars, 13 feet from side to side, about in circum-
ference 45 feet. This shall [be] done for our second work. As it
goes forward I will advise your lordship from time to time, and
that your lordship may know with how many men we have done
this, we brought from London 17 persons, 3 carpenters, 2 smiths,
2 plumbers, and one that keepeth the furnace, every one of these
attending to his own office. Ten of them hewed the walls about,
among which were 3 carpenters. These made props [struts] to
underset where the others cut away, the other brake and cut the
walls. These men are exercised much better than the men we find
in the country. Wherefore we must both have more men and other
things also that we have need of; of all the which I will within this
two or three days show your lordship by mouth. On Tuesday they
began to cast the lead, and it shall be done with such diligence and
saving as may be, so that our trust is in your lordship shall be
much satisfied with that we do, unto whom I most humbly commend myself, much desiring God to maintain your health, your

honour, your heart's ease. . . . Underneath here your lordship shall see a just measure of the whole abbey.'[1] Then follow details of the size of the church, the thickness of the walls and piers, the height of the vaulting, and 'there be in the church 32 pillars standing equally from the walls'.

Excepting those abbey churches that were reconstituted as cathedrals and those that were preserved wholly or in part for parochial worship, the buildings were sold either in one lot or, more often, were disposed of piecemeal. At Bath abbey all the iron and glass was sold to one Anthony Bale for £40; the dorter was purchased for £10; a Walter Dennys paid £6 for the frater, and the cloisters fetched £8. At Dover priory the timber roof of the Lady Chapel was bought by Thomas Portway for 13s. 4d. and the altar stones and several gravestones for 12s. The people in the vicinity of a monastery that was being broken up had few scruples about pilfering anything that could be put to use. Petty theft was inseparable from such an orgy of destruction. At Northampton a tinker was caught in the act of stealing lead and was hanged: Sir William Parr, the seneschal of Pipewell abbey, helped himself to fish out of the monastic fishpond. Curiously the nursery rhyme 'Little Jack Horner', dating from the sixteenth century, relates to an incident in the Suppression. The 'plum' proved to be a share of monastic property secured by John Horner, formerly the steward of Glastonbury abbey. To him were entrusted the title deeds of certain monastic lands, hidden in a patsy which he was charged to deliver to the Commissioners in London. Curiosity got the better of him, and lifting the crust of the pie he took out a plum that happened to be the title deeds of Mells manor, which he accordingly appropriated. On occasion Henry VIII himself disposed of his gains as fancy took him. Fuller speaks of 'not only cooks but the meanest turn-broach in the king's kitchen [who] did lick his fingers; and I could add how he gave a religious house of some value to mistress ——, for furnishing him with a dish of puddings which pleased his palate'.

The new proprietors of the monastic estates often incorporated parts of the conventual buildings in the mansions they built on the site, though the church was invariably demolished, the masonry being used for purposes of road-making. When the Augustinian priory of Stavordale in Somerset came into the possession of John, Lord Zouche, he pulled down the cloistral buildings and converted the church into a residence, which eventually became a farm-

---

[1] W. St. John Hope, *Archaeological Journal*, Vol. XLI.

stead. The choir and an adjoining chapel were used as a dwelling house and the nave as a barn.[1]

A great number of monastic churches, derelict and roofless, served as stone quarries, from which quantities of masonry were carted away to be used for building purposes. In 1555–6 nearly three thousand loads of stone were removed from Grey Friars Cambridge for the erection of the chapel of Trinity College, to whom the suppressed friary had been granted by the Crown. The same College also purchased stone from the remains of Ramsey abbey. In 1541 masonry from suppressed monasteries at Canterbury and Faversham was shipped across the Channel for the fortification of Calais.[2]

Many abbey churches and their conventual buildings, such as Fountains and Tintern, were allowed to fall into decay and ruin, a prey to the wind and weather.

Of the 650 houses suppressed between 1536 and 1540, about one third have disappeared without leaving a vestige of their existence, and of less than a third are there substantial remains.[3]

According to the Accounts of the Treasurer of the Court of Augmentations the total receipts derived from the Suppression up to Michelmas 1547 amounted to £1,338,422, a sum that included the sale of landed property, the revenues from the monastic estates, fines paid by tenants for the renewal of leases, payments made by convents for royal licence to continue, and deductions from the pensions of the religious, as forced loans. The spoils have been computed as being equal to about 100 million pounds (present value), exclusive of the enormous waste and leakage. Of this money a considerable sum was set aside for the pensions of the dispossessed, large amounts were spent on the royal palaces of Westminster, Hampton Court, and S. James's, and about one half for coastal defence. In 1539, a significant date, the King started to erect twenty or more forts or castles to protect the southern shores from invasion by the French; many of them were built of masonry from destroyed monasteries, as for instance Hurst castle from the stones of Beaulieu, and East and West Cowes with material from Quarr abbey.

On the accession of Queen Mary in 1553, a determined opponent of the Reformation, Pope Paul III sent the exiled Cardinal Pole as his legate to effect the submission of the English Church to the yoke of Rome, and before long it became evident that the

---

[1] Some sixty years ago it was carefully restored; the nave was divided into two floors, the upper of which retains the original chestnut roof.

[2] D. Knoop and G. P. Jones, *The Mediaeval Mason*.

[3] A. H. Thompson, *English Monasteries*.

Queen intended to refound a number of religious houses. The dispersal of the monastic properties and endowments made restoration a far from simple or politic matter. Although the Queen was ready to renounce the properties held by the Crown, an enforced and general restitution of such possessions would have obstructed the union with Rome, and the owners were therefore to receive a dispensation to retain them. Nevertheless a few religious houses were refounded in Mary's short reign. The first religious to be re-instated were the Friars Observants of Greenwich in 1555, and in December of the same year Sir Richard Rich made a grant of what remained of S. Bartholomew's priory, Smithfield, to the Queen for another friary. 'This yeare', wrote Wriothesley, 'at Easter, the churche of St. Bartlemewes in Smythefielde was sett up with black friers; Fryer Perwyn beinge head thereof'. The convent was composed of English, Spanish and Belgian Dominicans. In 1556 an abbot, Feckenham by name, and sixteen Benedictine monks were installed at Westminster, manors and rents being conferred upon the house as endowments by Queen Mary. The charter re-establishing the abbey, dated 10th November 1556, is preserved in the muniments of Westminster and bears illuminated portraits of Mary and King Philip of Spain. Then followed the founding of King's Langley and Dartford, both served by Dominican nuns, a Carthusian house at Sheen, and Syon, a Briggitine nunnery.

The church historian Fuller wrote of one Thacker, who had acquired Repton abbey at the Dissolution, and hearing that Queen Mary had set some of the monasteries up again, 'upon a Sunday (belike the better day the better deed) called together the carpenters and masons of that county [Derbyshire] and plucked down in one day . . . a most beautiful church'.

Queen Mary died in 1558 and in the first year of Elizabeth I's reign was passed 'an Act to annexe to the Crown certaine Religious Houses and Monasteries, and to refourme certayne abuses in Chantries'. Within a year all the resuscitated monasteries had come to an end.

In its conception and execution the Suppression is an unhappy chapter in the story of the Reformation. For nearly a thousand years the religious houses of mediaeval England, apart from their spiritual purposes, were the main force in civilisation and in the spread of learning and culture; and they furthered the prosperity of this country by their achievements in farming, in agriculture, and in the wool industry. The monastic churches and buildings that have survived, and others in their ruined state afford some indication of the wealth of mediaeval architecture that was lost to posterity in the orgy of destruction that marked the Dissolution.

ORIGINS OF CHRISTIAN MONACHISM

Before Constantine gave Imperial sanction to the Church in the year 313, there were Christian ascetics who sought to attain a higher spiritual life by abandoning the world and retiring to some remote spot where as hermits they subjected themselves to a rigorous self-discipline and to a life of unceasing prayer. A great number of Christian solitaries or anchorites dwelt in the deserts of Egypt in the third century A.D., leaving behind them nothing but a memory of sanctity.

By banding together a number of such hermits into a community with himself as their superior in the year 305, S. Anthony, who had spent twenty years in the desert as a solitary, inaugurated what were virtually monastic houses in Egypt, although the inmates lived apart in their own cells 'out of earshot of one another', and met together for Divine service only on certain days of the week. A few years later a further advance was made in the organisation of monachism by S. Pachomius, who founded monasteries in Tabennisi in the south of Egypt. Each house was ruled by a president, or *praepositus*, but they were all subject to a superior or a centralised authority. Real community life in which the brethren lived together and according to a Rule was not a feature of the monachism of S. Anthony or S. Pachomius. It was S. Basil who *c.* 360 introduced a broader version of Egyptian monachism to his monks in Cappadocia. His Rule established a common life for the inmates of a religious house, so that they lived and took their meals in common, and worshipped together as a corporate body, subjecting themselves to the will of their superior.

In one form or another Eastern monachism found its way to Rome early in the fourth century, where undoubtedly it was embraced by ascetics of the Early Church who had been members of the Christian community living in the catacombs. Drawing inspiration from the Egyptian systems, it took root in Italy, whence it spread to France: in the year 360 a monastery was founded at Ligugé near Poitiers by S. Martin, and when he became Bishop of Tours ten years later he established another monastery outside the city. In the fifth century religious houses were founded at Marseilles, Marmoutier, and other places, many of them of royal patronage.

The one man who was responsible for establishing the monastic system in Western Christendom and for composing a Rule based on the principle of a common life was the great S. Benedict, a native of Nursia near Spoleto. In the year 515 he drew up his *Regula Monachorum* (Rule of Monks) that ultimately became the standard code of western monachism; it was not a hard and fast code for any particular monastery, but a general guide for the religious. S. Benedict expressly referred his adherents to the Rules of S. Basil and other Fathers. Individual monks might pass from one house to another in which the religious life was followed. As a code of discipline, the Rule was entirely subordinated to the end, and the way of life in every house was largely dependent upon the will of the abbot. It was not the intention of S. Benedict to found an Order, i.e. a corporation of monasteries under a centralised form of government. The independence of each house and the latitude of the code enabled the abbot or superior to adapt the Rule to local conditions and circumstances which varied greatly in different lands.

APPENDIX B

CELTIC MONASTERIES

AMONGST the many injunctions in the Rule prepared by the monk of S. Columba's community, the brethren were advised:

'Be always naked [destitute of worldly goods] in imitation of Christ and the Evangelists.
Whatever little or much thou possessest of anything, whether clothing or food or drink, let it be at the command of the superior and at his disposal, for it is not befitting a religious to have any distinction of property with his own free brother.
Yield submission to every rule that is of devotion.
Pray constantly for those who trouble thee.
Let thy vigils be constant, from eve to eve, under the direction of another person.
Practice three labours in the day, viz. prayers, work, and reading.
The work is to be divided into three parts; thine own work and the work of thy place as regards its real wants; secondly, thy share of the brethren's; lastly help thy neighbours by instruction, or writing, or sewing garments, etc.
Follow almsgiving before all things.
Take not of food till thou art hungry; sleep not till thou feelest desire.
Every increase which comes to thee in lawful meals or in wearing apparel, give it for pity to the brethren that want it, or to the poor in like manner.'

The earliest monasteries in Ireland were virtually anchorite settlements, for the monks had so little to do with their brethren that it is doubtful whether they ever took their meals in common. Each brother passed his days and nights in his own little beehive-shaped cell or *claghann*, constructed of slabs of stone fitted together without mortar, the entrance to which was so low that the inmate crawled in on his hands and knees. In no case was there a single large church for their worship, but a number of small oratories. The cells and oratories of the English establishments of the Celtic Church were of the simplest character, the walls being constructed mainly of oak trees split in two and thatched with reeds. The small oratories, of which there were often two or three in each settlement, were used separately by the monks and nuns, and stood

within an artificial enclosure. Surrounding them were a number
of independent cells, and one or two larger buildings that served
as a guest-house and refectory. Excavations undertaken in 1924–5
at Whitby abbey revealed the foundations of several cells in the
area lying north of the present ruined church. It is believed that
they may have been occupied by the nuns of the early Saxon abbey.

More is known of the arts that were practised by the monks of
the Celtic Church than of their habitations. They produced copies
of the Scriptures and of works of the Fathers that are of world-
wide fame for their superb illuminations, in themselves as noble
as anything in the sphere of art ever produced in these islands. A
distinctive style of illumination, emanating from the Irish monasteries, was spread far and wide by the monk-missionaries. The
seventh-century Book of Kells in Trinity College, Dublin, and the
Lindisfarne Gospels of the eighth century made by the monks of
Holy Isle and now in the British Museum, are works of incomparable loveliness both for the palaeography and the illuminations.

APPENDIX C

CONFEDERATED ABBEYS

FROM the earliest days it was the custom for monasteries to enter into the spiritual fraternity with other convents, by virtue of which each offered up prayers on behalf of the souls of departed brethren of the confederated houses. Once a year a messenger or *rotularius* was despatched from each house bearing a roll inscribed with the names of the deceased brethren for whom prayers were desired. The earliest obit roll extant, dating *c.* 1230, records the death of the foundress and prioress of Hedingham nunnery, and this was sent to no fewer than 120 houses, each of which acknowledged it in the following terms: 'May the soul of Lady Lucy, prioress of Hedingham, and the souls of all the faithful departed by the mercy of God rest in peace. We concede to her the benefits of our church. We pray for you; pray for us.'

In the chartulary of the cathedral-priory of Winchester, the abbeys of Abingdon, Chertsey, Romsey, Tewkesbury, and Wherwell are named amongst others as being in spiritual confraternity with S. Swithun's. Lay benefactors also sought 'to be joined' with the family of the abbeys in this respect, and are frequently alluded to in monastic records as *confraters* or *familiares*. From Saxon times kings, queens, nobles, and people of all classes associated themselves in this way with the religious houses. A roll of confraters was kept in every monastery, the brethren of which offered up prayers for their well-being during their lifetime and for their souls after death.

The familiares are referred to in the *Gesta Abbatum* by a monk-scribe of S. Albans: 'Moreover of benefactors, who from the goods God hath given them, living or dead, to the fabric of our church or of any of the abbey buildings, or for the sustenance of the monks . . . become participants with us in the masses which are daily celebrated by a hundred monks or more in their night services and fasts and almsgivings and vigils, processions, scourgings, prayers with public and private and all other benefits in this abbey and in the cells thereunto appertaining.'

BIBLIOGRAPHY

THERE IS a wealth of literature dealing with English monachism and religious houses, though much of it is buried in the journals of the Archaeological and Architectural Societies. Several volumes of the *Victoria County Histories* contain historical and architectural accounts of the monasteries in their respective counties; and numerous plans and descriptions occur in the volumes of the Royal Commission on Historical Monuments. Brief but authoritative Guides to many of the ruined abbeys and priories now in the care of the Ministry of Works have been published by H.M. Stationery Office; and some twenty-eight plans, drawn to a large scale, of the principal monastic churches in this country are to be found in issues of *The Builder* between 1894 and 1901.

Calendar of Letters and Papers, Foreign and Domestic of the Reign of Henry VIII. Edited by J. Brewer, J. Gairdner, and R. Brodie.

Documents Illustrative of English Church History. Edited by H. Gee and W. J. Hardy, 1921.

Gesta Abbatum Monasterii S. Albani. Rolls series.

Valor Ecclesiasticus. Records Commissioners, 6 vols, 1810–34.

Aungier, G. J., *History and Antiquities of Syon,* 1840.

Baskerville, G., *English Monks and the Suppression of the Monasteries,* Cape, 1937.

Bilson, J., 'The Architecture of the Cistercians', *Archaeological Journal,* LXVI.

Bond, F. *Westminster Abbey,* 1909.

Bowles, W. L., and Nicholas, J. C., *Annals of Lacock Abbey,* 1835.

Burnet, G., *History of the Reformation of the Church of England,* 6 vols, (ed. N. Pocock), 1865.

Butler, C., *Benedictine Monachism,* 1919.

Clapham, A. W., 'The Architecture of the Premonstratensians', *Archaeologia,* LXXIII.

'The Friars as Builders', *Some Famous Buildings and their Story* (with W. H. Godfrey), n.d.

Lesnes Abbey, 1915.

Cranage, D. H. S., *The Home of the Monk,* 1926.

Dugdale, Sir William, *Monasticon Anglicanum* (ed. Caley), 1817–30.

Fosbroke, T. D., *British Monachism,* 1802.

Gasquet, F. A., *English Monastic Life,* 1904.

Henry VIII and the Monasteries, 1889.

The Rule of S. Benedict, 1909.

Giles, J. A., *Chronicles of Matthew Paris,* 1889.

Gilyard-Beer, R., *Abbeys: an Introduction to the Religious Houses of England and Wales*, H.M.S.O., 1958.

Godfrey, W. H., *The Priory of S. Pancras at Lewes*.

Graham, Rose, *An Essay on English Monasteries*, 1939.

S. Gilbert of Sempringham and the Gilbertines, 1906.

Hodgson, J. F., 'Difference of Plan of Churches of Austin Canons and Monks', *Archaeological Journal*, XLI, XLII, XLIII.

Hope, W. St. John, *The London Charterhouse*, 1925.

'Fountains Abbey, Yorkshire', *Archaeological Journal*, XV.

'Architectural History of Mount Grace Priory, Yorkshire', *Archaeological Journal*, XVIII.

Hutton, E., *The Franciscans in England*, 1926.

Knoop, D., and Jones, G. P., *The Mediaeval Mason*, Manchester University Press, 1933.

'The First Three Years of the Building of Vale Royal Abbey', *Transactions of the Quatuor Coronati Lodge*.

Knowles, D. M., *The Religious Orders in England*, Cambridge University Press, 1955.

and Hadcock, R. N., *The Mediaeval Religious Houses of England and Wales*, Longmans, Green & Co., 1953.

Lethaby, W. R., *Westminster Abbey and the King's Craftsmen*, 1906.

Micklethwaite, J. T., 'The Cistercian Order', *Yorkshire Archaeological Journal*, XV.

Power, Eileen, *English Nunneries*, 1922.

Raine, J., *Rites and Customs within the Monastical Church of Durham*, Surtees Society, 1842.

Roberts, H. E., *Mediaeval Monasteries and Minsters of England and Wales*, S.P.C.K., 1949.

Savine, A., *English Monasteries on the Eve of the Dissolution*, Oxford Studies in Social and Legal History, vol. I, 1909.

Snape, R. H., *English Monastic Finance*, 1926.

Thompson, A. H., *English Monasteries*, 1913.

'The Monastic Orders', *Cambridge Mediaeval History*, vol. V.

Thompson, E. M., *The Carthusian Order in England*, S.P.C.K.

Webb, E. A., *Records of S. Bartholomew's, Smithfield*, 1925.

Westlake, H. F., *Westminster Abbey*, 1923.

Wigram, S. R., *Chronicles of Elstow Abbey*, 1909.

Willis, J. W. C., *The Observances in Use at the Augustinian Priory of Barnwell, Cambs.*, 1897.

Willis, R., *Canterbury Cathedral*, 1845.

Architectural History of the Conventual Buildings of Christ Church Priory, Canterbury, 1869.

Wright, T., *Letters relating to the Suppression of the Monasteries*, Camden Society, 1843.

Index

Roman numerals refer to plates

S